Dr. Khalsa's Natural Dog

2nd Edition

Dr. Khalsa's Natural Dog (2nd Edition)

CompanionHouse Books™ is an imprint of Fox Chapel Publishing, Inc.

Project Team
Director of Product Development and Editorial Operations: Christopher Reggio
Editor: Amy Deputato
Copy Editor: Joann Woy
Design: Mary Ann Kahn
Index: Elizabeth Walker

Library of Congress Cataloging-in-Publication Data for this book has been applied for.
ISBN: 978-1-62008-142-6

Library of Congress Cataloging-in-Publication Data for the first edition of this book;
Khalsa, Deva.
  Dr. Khalsa's natural dog : a holistic guide for healthier dogs / by Deva Khalsa.
    p. cm.
  Includes bibliographical references and index.
  ISBN 978-1-59378-647-2
  1. Dogs—Health. 2. Dogs—Diseases. 3. Holistic veterinary medicine. I. Title.
  SF991.K48 2009
  636.7'0893—dc22
                    2008051862

This book has been published with the intent to provide accurate and authoritative information in regard to the subject matter within. While every precaution has been taken in the preparation of this book, the author and publisher expressly disclaim any responsibility for any errors, omissions, or adverse effects arising from the use or application of the information contained herein. The techniques and suggestions are used at the reader's discretion and are not to be considered a substitute for veterinary care. If you suspect a medical problem, consult your veterinarian.

CompanionHouse Books
1970 Broad Street
East Petersburg, PA 17520
www.facebook.com/companionhousebooks

Printed and bound in China
17 18 19 20   3 5 7 9 8 6 4 2

Contents

Dedication

For my mother and father, and for Sam and Lucy, who shared their love and chocolate with me.
To thank and help all of our dogs and cats, I created Deserving Pets Everyday Essentials.
The 21st century is all about disease prevention.

Praise for the first edition of *Dr. Khalsa's Natural Dog*

"Dr. Khalsa's approach to canine nutrition by encouraging the feeding of fresh wholesome foods is a winning formula shared by a handful of other colleagues, like myself, and a select group of commercial pet food manufacturers. The Canine Café recipes are scrumptious! This book is a lively, informative read for all those devoted to their canine companions!"

— W. Jean Dodds, DVM
President, Hemopet

"Dr. Khalsa has provided an invaluable book to help keep dogs well and to enable them to recover from a variety of health problems. Her holistically integrative approach to health maintenance and treatment is a welcome contribution to the advancement of veterinary medicine and the good of dogs around the world."

— Dr. Michael W. Fox,
Veterinarian, syndicated columnist and author of *Dog Body, Dog Mind*

"*Natural Dog* is the most comprehensive book on holistic dog care for the twenty-first century. Dr. Deva Khalsa is a pioneer in the field of holistic veterinary medicine in America and a dynamic international lecturer. Her years of experience with holistic therapies and energetic nutritional diets have given her invaluable information necessary to teach everything owners want to know to maintain optimum health, quality of life, and longevity for their pets."

— Joanne Stefanos, DVM,
Author of *Animals and Man: A State of Blessedness*

foreword

Deva Khalsa and I were founding doctoral spirits as the movement of holistic veterinary medicine was being born in the United States back in the 1970s. We are now referred to as "The Elders"—a term of which I am still proud. To me, Deva was not just "one of us" but someone I respected, consulted with, learned from, and truly admired as she was one of the few, even back then, who "got it." There are two types of medical training: that in which medicine is learned and spit back in rote when treating a patient, or that in which medicine is learned, understood, incorporated within oneself, and ultimately applied within that same context for the betterment of the patient. Deva is an embodiment of the latter. She knows, feels, and practices healing, patient by patient. Importantly, she also has always been one of her own patients. You've heard it countless times: "practice what you preach" or "if you want to talk the talk, you better know how to walk the walk." Well, she damn well did, and she still does. In the decades I've known Deva, she has barely aged. She beams. That's called health. And, when you have it, you don't have to heal—but you sure can when needed for others.

This book that she has written is nothing more than a mirror of the incredible spiritual energy of a true healer. If you want to call it holistic, then use the term to its fullest capacity—not just the whole patient but the entire picture—mind, body, spirit, environment, human/animal bond, and most of all, good old common sense. Learn from this book not to simply practice its methods but to really understand its contents, make them your own, and apply them. It's not that much more complicated. It is pure and simple. Well done, Deva, and you'll always have my love and admiration.

—Dr. Marty Goldstein
Author of *The Nature of Animal Healing:*
The Definitive Holistic Medicine Guide
to Caring for Your Dog and Cat

Preface

The Scottie Who Watched TV

Once upon a time there was a Scottish Terrier who lived with a bunch of other Scotties. He didn't like his canine brothers and sisters very much, but he loved to watch television. His people had a super-big-screen TV that happened to have a very large and easy-to-use button for changing the channel.

His basic routine was to lie on the couch and watch television all day long. He liked only animal shows. When an animal show ended and something else came on, such as a game show, he would leave the sofa, go over to the television, and change the channel until he found another show with animals.

His people brought him to me so that I could give him acupuncture for his stiff joints. When they returned two weeks later, I asked, "How's he doing?" and they said, "Well, we can't really tell. All he does is lie around all day and watch television, and he still seems stiff when he stands up and stiff when he moves around."

I gave him a couple more acupuncture treatments, asking "How's he doing?" before each one. And we'd have the same conversation. On his fourth visit, his people said, "He doesn't seem to be getting any better at all." I thought some more and told his owners, "I think his problem is television. Pull the plug out for an hour or two each day (he knew how to turn it on), put a leash on him, and take him for a good brisk walk." I also changed his diet to 70 percent vegetables with only 30 percent of his regular healthful kibble.

A month later, his people reported that he was like a new dog, moving around just fine. He liked his new diet and looked forward to his walks, and he still had a lot of time for television.

This book presents the readers with a genuine path to better health for their dogs, which can be as simple as finding the right diet and getting them some exercise. Of course, designing the right diet takes some thought and a bit of familiarity with some real data about nutrition. But it will all add up to better health for your dogs and fewer reasons to run to the veterinarian. Not that I have anything against veterinarians—I happen to be one. But I became one to assist my patients to be healthier, and this book serves that purpose well.

Learning the truth about what really keeps your dog in good health will free you from any confusion and make it possible for you to have a healthier dog, one who will give you many extra years of companionship.

Enjoy the journey!

Looking out upon a majestic mountain or a tranquil lake, we see the splendor of nature. As we play with our dogs, we marvel at their joy in living. The beauty and complexity of life surrounds us. Every living thing on this earth has a system that sustains that life, a complex machine bustling with activity and full of energy. How well this machine is maintained will define how healthy your dog remains and how long his life will be.

There's no getting around the fact that the amount of attention you can lavish on your dog depends on how many other demands are being made on your time. But if you're fortunate enough to find time to devote to your canine companion, you may find that it enhances the quality of your life as well. And if you're among the growing number of people who have largely given up nutritionally deficient and additive-laden processed foods in favor of natural options, you're probably inclined to include your pets (who, after all, are members of your family) in this way of life.

Cooking is one of the ways that some people express their love for each other. While I find that our two-legged friends appreciate a great snack or meal, our four-legged friends are ecstatic over the same. Cooking for your dog, if that is what you want to do, can be an act of love, contributing in yet another way to your bond as a family.

Part I

Eating for Life

1. That Special Connection

For as long as I can remember, I have felt good and somehow safe in the presence of dogs. I've always intrinsically trusted them. Dogs seem so dependable, sincere, and genuine. They have all of the good qualities we hope to find in people and very few of the bad qualities that we sometimes do find in our human kind.

I marveled, like many kids, at the frogs, butterflies, and squirrels that wandered through my little world. I tried to feed abandoned baby birds, and I rescued "stray" cats who just happened to belong to the neighbors; however, my attraction to animals went beyond a child's natural curiosity. Even before I could put thoughts into words, I somehow realized that, in my world, animals were special. I would sit and watch the cooperation among the ants in the colony in my backyard. On the morning of my second birthday, rather than dreaming of presents and cake, I was painstakingly loading ants onto a shoebox lid and moving them to a "safe" location so that my mother wouldn't kill them with boiling water before the party guests arrived.

Yet it was with dogs that I felt a special connection. When my parents took me out strolling in a carriage along the city sidewalks, I would call out a cheerful "Hello, how are you?" as strangers walked by with their dogs. Only the dogs understood that I was greeting them, not the people on the other end of the leads. Actually, I was returning the dogs' greetings to me, which no one else seemed to hear.

I didn't know then that I was entering into the ancient bond between humans and dogs, one so solid and so old as to seem primordial. In their exploration of this special bond, scientists have speculated about the domestication of the wolflike ancestors of the modern dog. Although they disagree about how and when it came about, they agree that this special connection between humans and canines exists. I like the perspective told in the following Native American legend:

Once we communicated with all animals as our equals, and we had great respect for all forms of life. But one day, the Great Spirit opened a chasm between the humans and the animals. This chasm was narrow at first. The dog looked at the human and was uncertain whether to stay or go with the animals. So he jumped over to his animal friends. As the chasm widened, he jumped back and forth, undecided, between the human and the animal worlds. Finally, at the last moment before the chasm was too wide, he took a great leap and forever joined with the humans. It remains this way to this day.

Evolving Together

The relationship with our "best friends" has continued to evolve in step with changing times and the changing needs for both species over the course of many millennia. Although humans no longer need dogs to ward off saber-toothed tigers, we have come to rely on their willingness to use their innate talents on our behalf in many other ways. Therapy and assistance dogs help people with various disabilities. Rescue dogs work alongside first responders at earthquakes and floods. Police dogs sniff out explosives and track missing children. The burly Saint Bernard bounding through alpine snowdrifts and the diligent Border Collie rounding up a flock of sheep are quintessential images of the canine service and work ethic.

Dogs don't need special training or a purpose-bred body to fulfill a role among humans. The Westie who alerts the household that the mail has arrived, the Golden Retriever who waits with tail thumping for his young friend to come home from school, and the Beagle who curls up at bedside when Mom has the flu are all doing important jobs that improve the welfare of their chosen pack. "Work" of any type keeps dogs healthy and whole. It tones their bodies, engages their minds, and strengthens their relationship with the human species. How else can we explain why dogs risk, and sometimes lose, their lives helping humans if not for the bond with their extended families? We have the chance to experience the moment and to connect with our ancient past in a direct, elemental way when we make room in our hearts for a dog. Our brain fog clears, our senses are heightened, our emotions are accessible, and our spirits are elevated and refreshed as we relax with our four-legged friends. If you want to feel what I mean, it's as simple as taking a walk with your dog. Suddenly, you will be able to smell the fresh air, see the beauty of your surroundings, and share the dog's thrill of adventure, even if you take the same route every day. You can let a wave of love wash over you that comes just from being with a trusted and trusting companion.

I feel sorry for someone who has never known the unconditional love of a canine companion. Too many people I meet are so busy going about their lives that they forget what living is all about. Our dogs provide an immediate and penetrating perspective into our real lives in a world where the value of joy of the spirit is too often forgotten.

The deep connection we have with our dogs is derived from a spiritual source. Dogs are a link to a spiritual—if you will, divine—dimension within all of us, a dimension in our lives from which we've become increasingly separated in our world of seemingly endless noise.

Both the story of the Garden of Eden and the aforementioned Native American legend remind us that we were once nurtured by the "family" of all living things, part of a harmonious whole. Today, our ears are filled with ringing cell phones instead of singing birds. We spend more time sitting in traffic than under the stars. No wonder we often feel empty and exhausted; we have lost touch with the pulse that beats through all life.

One way to become reconnected and recharged is through our relationship with dogs, reliable guides who can lead us along on a path toward oneness with ourselves, with others, with the world around us, and with whatever may lie beyond.

Best Friends

Our dog lends a sympathetic ear when we need someone to listen and a supportive shoulder when we need someone to lean on. If our emotional train is heading down a destructive track, our dog can throw a switch to divert it in a more positive direction. If we're happy, our dog knows it and celebrates with us. Always aware, even of minute shifts in the emotional breeze, dogs neither judge nor criticize nor advise; they just love and listen unconditionally.

The root of the word *emotion* is "move," and dogs can move emotional mountains. Big boys who don't cry shed tears at an old canine friend's passing, and Type A overachievers discover the joy of stopping to smell the roses (or the fire hydrant) by following a dog's lead. Over the years, I've been heartened to see caregivers who are usually quiet or controlled break out of their shells to express uncensored feelings about their dogs. Those who are typically unaccustomed to going the extra mile will drive for hours to bring their sick pups for treatment.

Setting that Special Example

Dogs not only motivate feelings but also model them. Honest and not self-conscious, dogs wear their hearts on their furry sleeves. They display their emotions clearly, without calculation or hidden agendas, and respond spontaneously to the situation at hand. Dogs don't hold grudges. What would our lives be like if we could welcome home family members with genuine enthusiasm, no matter how hard a day it's been, instantly forgive a clumsy step on the toe, or feel vulnerable enough to seek comfort in a scary storm?

Dogs live closer to nature than humans do, without such layers of insulation as houses, cars, and clothes. Their paws are on the earth, their noses in the air, their eyes and ears alert to the faintest rustle in the leaves. As we go exploring at their pace, treading lightly as they do, we have the chance to get acquainted with the natural world, which evokes a sense of tranquility and wonder.

While the "civilized" world makes constant demands on us, nature is constant only in sharing its abundant beauty, with no expectation of return, letting us know that we are all members of a peaceable kingdom. This is why witnessing a rainbow, watching a hummingbird hover, or wading in the ocean waves simply feels so good: the spirit is being showered with the gifts it needs to flourish.

Besides increasing our awareness of the world around us and our own selves, dogs help us tune in to others. Precisely because they are not human, dogs show us how to value diversity and cultivate tolerance of others, regardless how different they may be.

Spiritual Support

While humans often have trouble deciding who they are and tend to define themselves by their jobs and their possessions, dogs act from an unwavering spiritual core without being distracted by the irrelevant. Dogs see our essence, accepting and appreciating each of us for the unique beings we truly are. They make us feel loved, and we in turn become the loving beings reflected in our dogs' eyes. When we spend an extra five minutes playing ball with our dog even if we're exhausted, we are exercising our soul along with our body. And the stronger our spiritual muscles become, the easier it is to flex them in all of our relationships.

There is an old joke about the neurotic dyslexic agnostic insomniac who lies awake at night, worrying if there is a Dog. Of course, dogs are not the ultimate divinity (that would be cats—or so they think!). But dogs have a singular capacity to reawaken our slumbering spirits by reminding us that we two-leggeds, with our opposable thumbs and vastly inferior sense of smell, are also integral parts of the natural world.

Poetry of Canine Communication

Dogs expose us to new forms of communication, improving our ability to interpret subtle cues such as body language or facial expressions. This develops our empathy, which expands when we not only recognize another's needs but also put them ahead of our own—which, not coincidentally, is how dogs behave toward humans.

Several of my canine patients have learned to smile, and they also, of course, know within what social contexts to smile. They usually "grin" when saying hello or to show pleasure. Their owners often need to explain to the uninitiated that their dogs are not growling or snarling, just smiling.

T. S. Eliot once said, "Genuine poetry can communicate before it is understood." And so it is with dogs. You don't have to understand them in the same sense that you might understand the meaning of a spoken word to know their feelings, desires, or needs—and vice versa.

Clever Canines

We can forever put to rest the term "dumb animal." Although dogs, like humans, have different categories of intelligence that vary somewhat by breed and individual, dogs in general are quick studies in a range of complex cognitive functions such as processing new information, analyzing, drawing conclusions, and planning for the future (such as when a dog brings his owner the leash in anticipation of a walk)—all of which get a workout in the human-dog relationship. Dogs have even learned a "foreign" language. Some researchers believe that dogs can comprehend several hundred spoken words—not tones, but specific words—and even distinguish nuances in pronunciation.

Social Workers

Dogs come already equipped with a natural courtesy and deference to social order because of their evolutionary history. In their connection with humans, they have simply transferred their social graces to a different pack. Just as they detect friend or foe in the wild, dogs can evaluate, for example, which human is fun to be with or which one needs cheering up. Likewise, they sense whether it's appropriate to greet a stranger with a sloppy kiss, a polite wag of the tail, or bared teeth. This type of skill makes them effective "social workers."

They are also social icebreakers. Dogs relieve loneliness and lend a sense of belonging to those isolated from larger society, such as nursing-home patients, shut-ins, and prison inmates. When children play "tea party" with dogs as guests, they are rehearsing for social exchanges later in life. The self-esteem, discipline, and commitment they develop in caring for a dog are fundamental to a range of abilities necessary for becoming responsible members of society.

Together through Time

Dogs are at heel and matching us stride for stride as we progress on our journey through life. They thrive when they help us thrive; they experience the dignity and nobility of their spirits by giving us the opportunity to experience ours. Most of all, in their connection with humans, they get to be their truest selves: they get to be dogs. In acting toward them out of love, we convey that we honor who they are, just as they are. When they fetch a stick, they get to indulge their senses with activity and togetherness. When they become eyes for the blind, they make contact with their dependability and selflessness. Snuggling with us on the sofa gives them a rush of devotion, barking at the delivery truck summons their sense of responsibility, and not stealing a juicy lamb chop off the table puts them in touch with their trustworthiness.

Whatever power you believe fuels the spiritual universe, dogs plug us right into it. They relay a divine spark of energy that transforms our burned-out spirits and propels our passage through life. Through our connection with dogs, we tap into a limitless source of meaning and purpose, a vital current of wisdom and values from which we draw such qualities as compassion, sacrifice, integrity, hope, and loyalty.

Dogs set an example in both the ways they lead their own lives and the opportunities they present to us in conducting ours. There are many accounts of dogs who endanger their own lives to save others and who in many other ways demonstrate character traits that we admire in humans. Dogs, more keenly than humans, understand the unity of all life and know that the good of the whole depends on the contribution of each part.

Admiration for a Forgotten World

We find ourselves noticing many of the sights and sounds of nature as we walk with our dogs. Unconsciously, we tune into a world we have largely forgotten, one meant to sustain and fulfill us with its life and beauty. This world is one discussed by contemporary author Thom Hartmann in his book *The Last Hours of Ancient Sunlight*:

"Is there conscious life in you," I said softly, looking at the maple and spruce... I wondered if the entire forest might answer me with "We are alive," but instead I got a powerful sense of individual aliveness from each life-form I looked at. Each tree, the bird and the chipmunk, the soil under my feet teeming with microorganisms, each seemed to assert its own individual aliveness. Like the individual musicians in a symphony orchestra, they played together to create a beautiful sound. When you learn to communicate with other living things, you are, in fact, helping to rehabilitate a lost art of mankind—an intuitive skill known to more ancient cultures, but which the development of civilization, technology, and science have managed to obscure.

I raised my hands, palms out, imagined my life comingling with that of the forest around me, and was filled with a thrill at touching the life of the earth.

Dogs enable us to once again appreciate the aesthetics of this universe, loving and living fully within the moment. By extending ourselves to each other, we evolve toward wholeness, toward a more complete version of ourselves, just as a tree grows fuller when it extends its branches to the light. Once you experience such a profound connection with your dog, the seed is nurtured by your relationship and blossoms into a love that forever changes the landscape of your lives. It has certainly changed, and immeasurably enriched, mine.

I no longer remember the presents I got for my second birthday; however, I carry the gift of the ants to this day. It is the foundation for the choices I've made in taking a different approach to healing, one that is shaped by reverence for life. That gift is the same one that is offered to each of us, each day, in our special bond with dogs—that when we open ourselves to another, we can reach beyond our limitations and touch the spirit that sustains, and connects, us all.

Underestimating Dogs

A study published in May 2007 in the *Journal of Current Biology* proved to researchers that canines had surprising mental abilities. Dogs were able to do something that previously only humans were thought to be capable of: understand the concept within a situation and decide if and when to imitate that behavior.

Guinness, a female Border Collie, was trained to push a wooden rod with her paw to get a treat. Three groups of dogs were involved in this study. The control group had no contact with Guinness. When they were shown the device, they smelled the treat and used their mouths to push around the wooden rod to try to get the treat. A mouth is the handiest thing a dog has to get a job done, so it would naturally be what the dogs used.

Another group of dogs watched Guinness retrieve the treat with her paw, but she had a ball in her mouth every time she did it. When this group went to retrieve the treat, 80 percent of them used their mouths. The last group watched Guinness get the treat using her paw with her mouth free (no ball). A significant 83 percent used their paws to get the treat. The group that had watched Guinness get the treat while she had a ball in her mouth figured that the ball was preventing her from using her mouth, so that is why she had to use her paw. They did not have balls in their mouths, so they went for the far easier method—using their mouths!

The experiment stunned many researchers, for it showed that the dogs took in all of the nuances of Guinness's retrieving her treats and decided accordingly which method would be best to use. In other words, the dogs assessed the situation. But as the researchers stand with dropped jaws, I am busy spelling out words like "walk" and "out" and adjusting my body language so my dogs cannot figure out some of the things I am up to.

2. A History of Dog Food

The very beginning of the human-canine relationship was probably a mutually beneficial hunting arrangement in which both parties shared the food. Fresh meat was necessary for the survival of a hunter society. As the ages progressed, the dog's role expanded. Dogs were used for a multitude of purposes, ranging from killing vermin and rodents to fighting in battle, wearing armor. Some dogs herded sheep while others fought bulls. The lap dogs who entertained the French and English nobility were the fellows with the cushy jobs.

As the roles of dogs changed as time passed, so did their diets. When we moved forward from raw meat to cooked and prepared meals, our canine friends marched on beside us. As written language was developed, the word *leftovers* must have had a special place in the doggy dictionary.

The Tables Turn

Up until the nineteenth century, our dogs ate what we ate. The more affluent the owner, the better the dog fared. The diet of a typical working-class dog living a couple of centuries ago may have consisted of bread, potatoes, and boiled cabbage, while the elite and privileged would lavish their dogs with roast duck and consommé. *Table scraps* had not yet become a bad word.

In the mid-1800s, an enterprising fellow named James Spratt noticed stray dogs eagerly consuming moldy biscuits (called hardtack) tossed onto the piers by sailors. That observation inspired Spratt to develop the first commercial dog biscuit, Spratt's Patent Meat Fibrine Dog Cakes, in 1860. Before long, similar products emerged. The sellers of dog biscuits claimed that they prevented all manner of canine ills, ranging from worms to distemper, and that everything necessary for a dog's health could be found in their products. Even the best table scraps, warned Spratt, "will break down his digestive powers," making him "prematurely old and fat." "Fresh beef," Spratt claimed, could "overheat the dog's blood." Rival products, such as veterinarian A. C. Daniels's Medicated Dog Bread, were advertised as being free of the inferior ingredients contained in other biscuits that caused "constipation, indigestion, and skin ills" (see Mary Elizabeth Thurston's 1996 book *The Lost History of the Canine Race*).

Enterprising individuals found that they could take table scraps to a new low, economizing by mixing moldy and rancid groceries into a dog chow. The real expenses were the processing, the bag itself, and the advertising. Food considered unfit for man was sold as the only healthy fare for a dog! Daniels had reason to advertise that his food did not cause skin ills and indigestion because his competitors' food did. Dogs were not nearly as healthy as they had been before this processed garbage was purchased and fed by misled owners.

Dog owners did not have much time to think about their dogs' diet because the Industrial Revolution was in full swing. Historically, the Industrial Revolution transformed agricultural economies into industrial ones. Goods, including food for families and pets, which had been traditionally made at home, began to be manufactured in factories. Cities grew quickly as people moved from rural areas into urban communities in search of work. The time that was once allotted to household duties was now spent working for an hourly wage. The rural way of life, with mothers cooking for their families, using products from their own farms, was quickly being replaced by a more frantically paced modern lifestyle.

Time for the Commercials

Cities now contained more concentrated populations, and the new working urban masses now needed to purchase their wares from stores. New businesses were formed, each competing with the others for sales.

Advertising first became a formal profession in the United States when Volney B. Palmer set up shop as an advertising agent in Philadelphia in 1841. Over the years, ads became more sophisticated and more cunning. Millions of dollars were spent on studies to discover what would persuade consumers to purchase a product. The phrase "truth in advertising" may make us think that what we see in an ad is indeed true, but truth, especially in presenting the results of research, can be ambiguous.

For example, I have always been amused by the Milk Bone advertisement claiming that these snacks help clean a dog's teeth. In fact, what the research showed was that dogs who ate only dry food had

cleaner teeth than dogs who ate only canned food. While the previous sentence is true, it does not mean that dog biscuits work to actually clean teeth. People can become confused when they learn that their dog will need to have his teeth cleaned—he got his Milk Bone every day! When people express skepticism and disbelief after I tell them what I just explained to you, I suggest that they stop brushing their own teeth for two weeks and eat two Milk Bones a day instead. So far, no one has complied.

Today, millions of dollars are spent every year to influence our choices and our thinking about dog food. Market researchers know when changes in public perception are starting to take place, and they are always scrambling to create the impression that they're helping lead the way. Often, after average dog owners become more aware of the unhealthy ingredients in many of the well-known brands of dog food, things suddenly become "new and improved."

Supposedly healthier products begin to appear on the same shelves as the food that we were previously, and falsely, told had all the "balanced nutrition" your dog needed. Commercials tell you that now there is real chicken in the bag. As before, however, manufacturers do not tell you that chicken by-products, composed of feet, feathers, beaks, and eyeballs, make up the bulk of the "real chicken" in the bag. Pictures of vegetables now decorate dog-food packages, and some boast of added vitamins. Supermarket brands usually heat and compress these vitamins, so any remaining vitamin content is negligible.

Media Myths

To dispel the myths perpetrated by the big advertisers, we first have to realize the extent to which we've been misled. Most dog owners have come to accept what these mega-companies have perpetrated—that our dogs cannot eat the same foods that we eat (disparagingly referred to as "table scraps"). Nothing could be further from the truth or better illustrate the manner in which advertising can corrupt our reasoning powers and plain common sense. A good starting point is to examine some widely held beliefs to see whether they make sense or, more than likely, are nonsense.

One such belief is that every single meal your dog eats must be nutritionally balanced. In nature, a wild dog achieves a balance over a period of time, rather than each time he eats. In any case, most prepared dog food is not balanced anyway, being abysmally lacking in some ingredients, such as greens, which provide necessary enzymes and chlorophyll. Dogs may be trying to make up for this by eating grass.

Another nonsensical decree is that changing your dog's routine diet in any way will upset his digestive system. This media conditioning has gained a real foothold in the public mind, but it simply is not so. Feeding your dog different foods and offering a variety of wholesome, healthful ingredients is just about the healthiest way to feed your dog. It is true that dogs who eat the same poor-quality dog food for years and are then suddenly switched to another poor-quality dog food may get diarrhea. And there are dogs with unhealthy digestive systems who get diarrhea at the drop of a hat. Generally, however, a healthy dog's digestive system will adapt to new foods. In fact, many chronically ill dogs recover from their illnesses once they stop eating dog food and are fed a variety of home-cooked foods.

Yet another myth is that dogs are strictly carnivorous and that animal protein must be their chief or only source of nutrition. Like a person, a dog can be a vegetarian, subsisting on veggies, grains, legumes, oils, and spices, or, for that matter, a lacto-vegetarian, living on a diet of eggs and dairy along with greens and grains.

Dr. T. Colin Campbell wrote *The China Study,* a book recounting the most extensive study ever done on cancer. Dr. Campbell participated in a groundbreaking study in which 2,400 Chinese counties were surveyed for death rates from cancer. Researchers then correlated cancer death rates with local dietary habits. Laboratory research confirmed the data amassed from the field. High animal-source protein levels in food predisposed people to cancer. Although the carcinogens in the environment do alter our cellular DNA and give cells the potential to change into cancer cells, it is a high level of animal protein in the diet that tips the balance and kicks off the actual transition into cancer cells.

Because much of this research was done on a cellular level, the findings would also apply to dogs. In 2006, I watched a documentary in which the commentator stated that one in two dogs is now getting cancer. This statistic does not reflect dogs who die of unknown causes at home or dogs who die with undiagnosed problems. Changing to a diet lower in protein can reduce the incidence of cancer in our dogs.

No Dogs Named E.T. Here

The fact is that dogs are not alien creatures from a strange planet who can eat only "special food" from a bag or can. They need vegetables, whole grains, and high-quality proteins, just as you do. Good nutrition is vital to your dog's health, well-being, and longevity and could well make the difference in his ability to resist or recover from disease.

Back in the pre-dog-food days, the family dog would partake of the family's bounty, as mentioned before. If it worked for people and their dogs back then, there's no reason why it can't work for you now. That doesn't mean that a dog should be allowed to eat just anything that goes on the table; certain types of "people food," such as chocolate, grapes, raisins, and onions, should be avoided. In addition, a lot of the chemical-imbued processed products intended for human consumption are fit for neither man nor beast. Excluding these items, there's no reason why your dog can't enjoy the same wholesome and nutritious foods that you eat.

The Dog Food Recalls

In March 2007, a massive recall of 60 million units of contaminated dog and cat food alarmed owners all over the United States. Dog food recalls are nothing new. Recalls had previously occurred in 1995, 1998, 2003, and 2005. The March 2007 recall was disconcertingly different, though, because many dogs who had partaken of the tainted food were rapidly dying.

Menu Foods of Canada is a very large corporation that produces pet foods for many major brand-name companies. They produce pet foods that I heartily do not recommend, and they also produce foods that are advertised as and that have the deserved reputation as some of the top holistic brands. Menu Foods simply cooks up, bags, and labels the pet food for many companies. The March 2007

Menu Foods recall spanned more than one hundred brands and labels that owners trusted.

The poisons found in the contaminated foods were thought to come from a single wheat shipment from China that had been delivered to Menu Foods in the United States. Thousands of concerned pet owners called their pet food companies only to find it an exercise in frustration. Many companies, to their credit, recalled foods that may have had contained wheat gluten from China even though no illnesses and deaths from their foods had been reported.

The Environmental Protection Agency (EPA) had the job of figuring out which ingredient in the food was causing dogs to become ill. At first, a rat poison, aminopterin, was blamed. A few weeks later, the EPA identified the contaminant melamine in wheat gluten purchased by Menu Foods from China. Melamine is a by-product of several pesticides, including cryomazine, a widely used insect-growth regulator. Made from melamine, cryomazine breaks back down into melamine after an animal ingests it. Cryomazine is also absorbed by plants and converted into melamine. The level of melamine in the wheat gluten was very high, at an astounding 6.6 percent.

In April 2007, the *New York Times* reported that the Xuzhou Anying Biologic Technology Development Company, one of the companies that shipped the poisonous wheat gluten, had run an advertisement looking for sources of melamine. It seems that just a little bit of this stuff added to wheat gluten falsely increases the protein content on testing, thus increasing the value of the sale. If the wheat gluten is higher in protein, the bag of dog food can boast of more protein without the expense of adding animal protein.

More and more pet foods were being recalled—more canned pet food, dry pet food, treats, and biscuits—all found to contain the Chinese wheat gluten. Investigators tried to locate every place this ingredient wound up, and the recall expanded as more and more products made with the contaminated wheat gluten were found.

Some early articles stated that a large number of dogs and cats died from the tainted food and that many more had become critically ill, suffering irreparable kidney damage. Although many animals may not have died immediately, their lives could have been shortened, with their kidneys eventually causing their demise. In the July 23, 2007, issue of *USA Today*, FDA spokeswoman Julie Zawisza was quoted as follows: "The sad truth is that we will probably never know with any confidence the number of animals that fell victim." The FDA had received 18,000 calls by this time.

Melamine was not the only contaminated ingredient; cyanuric acid was also found. Both of these ingredients combine to form crystals in those who eat products that contain them. The crystals accumulate in the kidneys, causing kidney disease and, in a number of unfortunate cases, death from kidney failure. The life span of many animals whose kidneys were damaged will also be significantly shorter.

One month after the initial recall in March 2007, contaminated rice protein, in addition to wheat gluten, from China was also identified as being associated with kidney failure in pets in the United States. Rice protein is more expensive than wheat protein, and even some very well-regarded manufacturers of premium holistic pet food were shocked to find that they would need to recall their foods. At the same time, exported Chinese corn gluten was associated with kidney failure in South African pets.

A federal judge, US District Judge Noel Hillman, approved a $24 million settlement hammered out a week before the *USA Today* article, aimed at compensating owners of thousands of pets who were sickened or killed by this recall. This settlement was not on the basis of emotional damage or pain and suffering, but was intended to reimburse pet owners for the expenses connected with the illnesses and deaths of their pets. The chief defendant in the suit, Menu Foods, Inc., and some other manufacturers had already paid about $8 million to settle claims filed earlier.

Menu Foods, to their credit, did set up a short-term test program. Over a period of less than a month, roughly seven out of forty animals died of kidney failure from eating the contaminated food.

Shockingly, another scandal connected to contaminated milk powder arose in September 2008. Thousands of Chinese infants became ill with kidney problems after drinking milk made from powder laced with melamine, the same poison found in the pet foods. Dairy farmers were suspected of lacing the milk used in Sanlu brand formula to, once again, boost its protein content. The Chinese health ministry knew the food to be contaminated but did not release the information until reports of sick babies began to emerge. More than 60,000 Chinese babies were sickened, more than 6,000 were hospitalized, and 4 died as a result of melamine in their baby formula.

Genetically Modified Foods

Renowned veterinarian and author Michael Fox states that many varieties of genetically modified (designated as GM or GMO [genetically modified organism]) rice have been planted in Asia and wonders whether other GM rice, corn, and wheat from China, as well as GM corn and soy from the United States, may have been involved in the tragic poisoning. He feels that the fact that the pet foods were found to contain the rat poison aminopterin, also used as a genetic marker for genetically modified crops, notably wheat, was strong evidence that GM wheat, imported from China and not approved (yet) for human consumption, had been put into pet foods by American manufacturers. The manufacturers believed that what they had purchased was wheat gluten or rice protein, but it turned out to be wheat flour. This flour had been spiked by Chinese processors with melamine and cyanuric acid to make the flour test high in protein. When these two chemicals combined in dogs' and cats' kidneys, they formed crystals that resulted in kidney failure and death.

DNA provides the sheet music that instructs the body parts how to sing the song of life. Each cell plays the tune given to it with dedication. Each cell also plays the specific melody of the bodily organ it composes. Cells and bodies are in harmony with the DNA encoded inside of them. This is also reflected on the planet, as all living things intermingle and coexist. Over millions of years, countless combinations have been played out, arriving at the ones that worked best.

Transnational life science corporations are in the process of disrupting the genetic music, or blueprints, of living organisms (plants, animals, and microorganisms) and patenting them for profit. An increasing number of scientists warn that the current gene-splicing technology is crude. In genetic manipulation, the genes of nonrelated species are randomly combined with each other. The results are not predictable and therefore are dangerous.

The biggest experiment in human history has begun, with planet Earth as the test site and us as the guinea pigs. The architects of life, in contemporary times, are a few gigantic international biotechnology conglomerates. The Native Americans made important decisions based on the effect they would have seven generations later. Corporations make decisions based on how they can profit now.

Hidden Changes

About 70 percent of all processed foods in the supermarket contain unlabeled GM products. Many vegetables and fruits contain spliced genes to maintain freshness longer, to keep away insects, or to improve their color. GM soy formula for babies is commonplace. Genetically modified ingredients are also, of course, in your dog's prepared foods.

Genetically engineered soybeans, canola, corn, and potatoes are found in packaged foods on the shelves of our supermarkets. There is a hidden menu, including GM squash, papaya, tomatoes, and dairy products, within the ingredient lists of prepared foods. Allergies skyrocketed after the stealthy introduction of GM foods to our food supplies.

It is more likely than not that soy is GM because about 70 percent of the soy grown in this country is modified for herbicide resistance. There is little or no regulation and no labeling requirements, so the best you can do is look for is "non-GMO soy" or "organic" on product packaging to protect your health. In North America, all soy that is labeled as "organic soy" is guaranteed not to have been genetically manipulated or treated with herbicides.

A Chilling Bedtime Story

The horror stories involving GM foods are too numerous to mention, but the story of L-tryptophan, a supplement once taken by people for sleeplessness or anxiety, offers a double insight into the mechanics of corporate greed and the suppression of the truth about genetic manipulation.

L-tryptophan is an amino acid derived from foods high in protein, such as meat and dairy products. Turkey is particularly high in tryptophan, which is why so many folks get sleepy after holiday feasts. Tryptophan is transported to the brain, where it is broken down by enzymes and turned into serotonin. Serotonin is used in the process of neurotransmission.

It's important to note that the supplements that you and your dog take can come from natural sources or synthetic sources. Natural sources are better. In 1989, thirty-seven Americans died after taking a particular brand of L-tryptophan supplement; 5,000 people were permanently disabled. The culpable brand came from a company that used genetically engineered bacteria to generate the L-tryptophan.

When all of the lawsuits were tallied, the damages paid out to the victims came to more than $2 billion. But the PR spin on this event never exposed the real reason that these innocent people's lives were destroyed. Instead, supplements were touted as dangerous and unreliable. The press never informed the public that the true cause was the use of GM bacteria to produce this particular brand. So every single brand of L-tryptophan was removed from the shelves, and the supplement was no longer available to the people it had helped.

There are two powerful lessons to be learned from this event. First, take any news that would affect a prominent corporation's sales with a grain of salt and do more research to find the truth. Second, corporations without morals are creating "Frankenfoods" and taking no responsibility for the effect they have on the balance in nature. There appears to be little use of foresight regarding GM foods although there are many analogous parallels about the dangers of introducing new species of animals and plants from one country to another.

What's Really in the Bag?

Back to pet foods. In the 2007 recall, one brand announced that it was recalling four foods containing rice protein concentrate that had been found to contain melamine, yet the package labels did not list rice. Dog food companies are legally required to represent on the labels what is in their foods. In addition, most pet food companies change the percentage of some ingredients from batch to batch. If

they reformulate a food, they are required to note these changes on an updated label.

Several other companies were in the same fix. They recalled foods because of melamine-contaminated ingredients contained in their foods, but these ingredients were never listed on the labels. In short, it seems that the ingredients in dog foods have not been represented accurately.

In an earlier pet food recall in 2004, dry food manufactured for Pedigree Pet Foods in Thailand resulted in reports of kidney failure in hundreds of puppies in Asian countries, but no toxic compound was actually found. A pet food recall in 2003 was caused by an unidentified toxin and also involved food from a contract manufacturer whose labels misrepresented the contents in the packages. In 1998, pets were sickened by food contaminated by an aflatoxin; aflatoxins are about the most potent carcinogens on the planet.

Early Warning

The Reportable Food Registry has been set up by the FDA as a means of providing earlier warning of possibly tainted human or animal food products. The FDA Amendments Act of 2007 was enacted during the investigation of the massive pet food recall and required the agency to set up a web-based portal that food producers should use within twenty-four hours to report cases of adulterated products that have left their control.

Who's the Watchdog?

What's going on here? Isn't anyone overseeing the production of pet food? The Association of American Feed Control Officials (AAFCO), a nongovernmental advisory body with no legal clout, administers tests on dog food. To pass these tests, a dog food must keep a small population of test dogs alive and seemingly well for the specified trial period, which is twenty-six weeks for adult dogs and less than twelve weeks for puppies.

As previously noted, federal law requires that commercial dog food contain no harmful ingredients and be truthfully labeled. Although the Food and Drug Administration (FDA) supposedly has responsibility for regulating pet food and food additives, as well as drugs for animals, the actual job falls to the individual states; therefore, the food is subject to regulatory codes that vary by state. Typical regulations consist mainly of testing for minimum percentages of crude protein, fat, fiber, and moisture. That is all—simply minimum percentages. There are no state or federal controls on additives, toxins, carcinogens, and the like.

Measurements of minimum percentages are duly reflected on the labels—but let's face it, the protein content cited is a far cry from the quality, nutritional value, and usefulness to the body provided by, say, a steak, a chicken breast, or eggs. In addition, once such products are packaged for sale, there is no way to determine whether they actually contain the ingredients listed on the labels. You or I could cook up a great soup with vegetables and old leather shoes and then proudly announce the protein content to our guests. Like the protein in our soup, the protein in many dog foods is of negligible value, being of poor quality and almost impossible to digest or assimilate.

4-D Ingredients

The average bag of dog food is filled with a mélange of ingredients that would turn your stomach, and, more importantly, adversely affect your dog's health. The protein in such dog food typically comes from what are called 4-D animals, meaning dead, dying, diseased, or disabled. Many have received potent drugs, including euthanasia cocktails, which have been shown to survive the rendering process. In fact, at least half of the dry dog foods tested several years ago by the FDA's Center for Veterinary Medicine were found to contain residue of sodium pentobarbital, a drug used chiefly to euthanize dogs and cats, and occasionally horses and cattle, even though the Code of Federal Regulations forbids the use of such drugs in animals intended for food. (See FDA Center for Veterinary Medicine, *Survey #1, qualitative analyses for pentobarbital residue*, "Dry dog food samples purchased in Laurel, Maryland," March–June 1998.) Although the FDA concluded after an eight-week study that the levels detected were "highly unlikely" to have an adverse effect on dogs, the effects resulting from long-term dietary exposure aren't really known.

The names used to describe the beef and poultry by-products you find listed on the labels of nearly all commercial dog foods are euphemisms used to conceal the noxious ingredients they really contain. A better description of these by-products would be "slaughterhouse waste products." These normally include such items as chicken eyeballs, feet, and beaks as well as cow hide and tendons that have been hydrolyzed into an unrecognizable mash. This recycled garbage can harm an older animal suffering from impaired kidney or liver function.

A practice similar to that of rendering horses, dogs, and cats from the pound and roadkill into a protein by-product brought about the scourge commonly known as "mad cow disease" in Britain and elsewhere. This brain-wasting condition, apparently caused by the replication of a misfolded protein known as a prion, is believed to have proliferated in the cattle population as the result of animal by-products' being used as animal feed. Basically, cows were fed the by-products of dead cows. The disease then crossed the species barrier, infecting humans unfortunate enough to have consumed beef from "mad cows."

The Consumer Makes a Difference

Consumer outrage and the work of courageous holistic veterinarians have brought about significant changes in the way dog foods are manufactured today. When consumers realized that a commonly used preservative, ethoxyquin, could promote cancer and contribute to reproductive problems, they wrote letters of complaint to dog food companies and government representatives. Consequently, most pet food manufacturers removed ethoxyquin from dog and cat foods in the early 1990s. One veterinary prescription food manufacturer added ethoxyquin back to its dry food formulas but announced in fall 2008 that it was to be removed again due to the requests from consumers and veterinarians.

Many new healthier pet food companies were created in response to the consumer demand for healthy dog and cat food. In fact, the pet food industry began to self-regulate when companies began to check the ethoxyquin content of their competitors' pet foods while claiming their own foods were free of the preservative. In fact, this self-regulating procedure found several companies to be untruthful in their claims, and the rival companies used this in their advertising claims.

Although BHT and BHA are still used today as chemical preservatives in dog foods, most of the preservatives in today's pet food are chosen with a healthier philosophy. Vitamins C and E and rosemary are commonly used to preserve many brands of dog food.

Pet food companies are in the business of creating loyal and lasting customers. It's simply the way to do good business. The ethoxyquin story shows the strong influence that pet owners can have when they are informed and active in their responses to these companies.

Don't Be Misled

In summary, the labels on cans and bags of dog food do not provide a realistic indicator of what's actually inside. In both the wording and graphic presentation, labels are designed to remove all references to the true nature of the contents. Words such as "rendered," which would truthfully define the ingredients, are replaced with appealing images and language that make the food seem healthful and appetizing. The appearances of the foods themselves are designed to be deceiving as well. Semi-dry dog foods, formulated to resemble real foods such as chunks of beef or cheese, are some of the worst offenders. These foods usually consist of poor-quality protein jazzed up with the likes of propylene glycol and corn syrup along with a number of harmful preservatives and dyes.

By-Products

By-products are defined by Webster's Dictionary as *"derivative(s) made from other products."* This includes such waste products as feet, beaks, tongues, eyeballs, connective tissues, peanut shells, and newspaper. For example, poultry by-products often consist of beaks and eyeballs, while typical beef by-products consist of hide and sinew.

Misleading descriptions are employed by supermarket brands that have been making garbage for years. My favorite is "real meat," because pet food producers give themselves away with that one! Products may be labeled as "natural" or as containing supplements to benefit the older or arthritic dog. In actuality, the amounts of vitamins or joint supplements they feature are often so tiny that they are of no benefit whatsoever to the dog. Beware of major name brands that try to give the impression of being healthy or perhaps even holistic.

When a company spends millions to advertise a product, that cost goes into the retail price, at the expense of quality. You, in essence, are paying largely for the advertising used to entice you to buy the product rather than for the actual ingredients. By contrast, one reason that smaller, holistic, and healthy brands are likely to give you a lot more for your money is that they invest in quality ingredients rather than in costly advertising campaigns.

Separating the Good from the Bad

After reading this, you may want to learn how to prepare wholesome meals for your best friend. Yet you may still need to depend on store-bought dog food on occasion. The good news is that there are many pet food brands known for their wholesome methods of preparation and that take special care to exclude most of the noxious ingredients previously discussed. In fact, since the 2007 dog food recall, many such companies have gone to even greater lengths to make sure that they know where they get their products, what goes into their brands, and what the final product comprises. Dog food producers know that their reputations and their future sales depend on their integrity.

With dog food, you get what you pay for. The smaller companies whose aim is to provide healthful prepared foods are typically advertised by word of mouth and are sold in smaller specialty pet-supply stores. Their money goes into their foods rather than into advertising, but those foods are still significantly more expensive than the cheapest supermarket brand. Take my advice and look for these quality brands, for they are well worth the money. Better food means fewer health problems in the long run.

Look for words that indicate that whole foods are in the bag. The better foods will have **chicken** listed rather than *chicken by-products* or *chicken meal* and **beef** rather than *beef by-products*. You also do not want *poultry by-products* or *poultry meal*. The same goes for *meat* and *meat by-products*. *Meat* is defined as "the flesh of an animal that is edible." If only *meat* is listed, then what animal(s) are we speaking of? It is better to purchase a bag of dog food that lists **wheat** rather than *wheat bran*, *wheat gluten*, or *wheat mill run*. **Tomato pomace** and **beet pulp** are acceptable ingredients. *Peanut hulls* are a definite no-no. *Cereal fines* are also unacceptable, as is *corn gluten*. You want **rice** on label, but not *rice flour*, *rice bran*, or *brewer's rice*.

Understand that the more generic and the more general the term, the more likely it is that the ingredient is undesirable. *Animal fat* is too general a term and can refer to restaurant grease. *Animal digest* is the enzymatic decomposition of animal tissue.

It is not in your dog's best interest to feed him foods containing artificial colors, artificial flavors, or toxic preservatives such as ethoxyquin, BHA, and BHT. Watch out for the imitation-meat moist dog-food packs because they often contain propylene glycol to make them look moist and meaty along with sugars to make them tastier.

Don't let the pictures and advertising on the bag sway your selection. Beware of those vegetables dancing on the bags of supermarket foods along with words like *natural*. As we've discussed, the healthy additives in such brands are most likely present in only tiny amounts, and the processing has destroyed just about any active ingredient in the food.

Purchase foods from companies that have open communication channels with pet owners, and don't hesitate to ask them your questions. You can shop at the superstores geared toward pets, but look for their superior natural and holistic products. You can also shop at boutique dog food stores that sell brands whose mission statement is to provide healthful foods for pets.

Compare the first five ingredients on the bag and look for whole foods to be listed, foods such as chicken, beef, salmon, venison, wheat, and rice. Look for products that use whole vegetables and grains. Organic ingredients are even more beneficial.

You should expect to have to look harder and to pay more for the better products. Once you have found foods that your dog does well on, it will be well worth it. Your dog is the ultimate indicator of what food is best for him.

3. Nutrition for the Novice

Nature's wondrous and diverse rhythms weave through all living creatures. Each and every living thing on this earth has a system that sustains the life within it. Although each being is unique, dogs and humans alike have physical bodies that follow nature's designs. Lungs oxygenate our bodies as we breathe; our hearts pump blood through our vessels and into our organs. Our kidneys concentrate and excrete toxins, while our livers and digestive systems work to feed our bodies. To be better able to understand the intimate relationship between what your dog eats and his health, it helps to know more about how this machine—the body—works. The dog's body is a complex machine that is bustling with activity and full of energy. How well this machine is maintained will define your dog's health.

Food is the fuel that runs the machine; nutrition is the science that deals with foods and their effect on health. Let's look at what the words we hear so often actually mean. A synonym for *nutrition* is *sustenance*, meaning something that supports life. Good nutrition sustains life; a synonym for *sustain* is *prolong*.

Nourishing food sustains your dog, improves his health, and prolongs his life. Healthful food equals good fuel, and fewer toxins in the food mean less cleanup for the system. How well the body parts function will decide how long your dog lives and how disease-free his life will be. A healthy dog will fight off diseases, infections, and cancer more "doggedly" than a compromised dog will.

Your dog needs food for energy and raw materials to build and preserve his body. Before his cells can use the food, it has to be broken down into small enough molecules for the cells to accept. Food goes on quite a journey before the cells consider it acceptable.

Spot's Digestive Tract

The story starts in your dog's mouth. The journey begins when he chews his food with his teeth. The teeth grind up the food and mix it with the dog's saliva, which comes from the salivary glands. The saliva contains a bacteria-fighting enzyme called *lysozyme* (from this comes the old adage that a dog's saliva helps fight bacteria). Most of the time, dogs do not bother to chew their food long—but they seem to enjoy it a great deal.

From the mouth, the food slides down the esophagus into the stomach, which has many folds and ridges that help the stomach do its job. The digestive juices mix with the food, breaking it down further into smaller parcels. The stomach can absorb water but not food, so the food then travels on to the small intestine.

The Small Intestine: The Long and Winding Road

The small intestine works at absorbing the food. It has a great opportunity to do so because it is about 20 feet long in a medium-sized dog. This intestinal road is so long that its name changes along the way—first, the duodenum, then the jejunum, and finally the ileum. The small intestine ends at the large intestine, which becomes the colon.

The small intestine has friends—the liver and the pancreas—to help with its work. Located just outside of the small intestine, they help by releasing digestive juices that mix with the food. They give the small intestine these juices early on because just about all of the food is absorbed from the small intestine. The large intestine reabsorbs leftover water.

Friendly Bacteria: The Little Guys in the White Hats

The small intestine has other special helpers, called *friendly bacteria*, who reside within it and help it stay healthy. They fight the bad bacteria, keeping them at bay. Many of the good bacteria die in the process of helping the dog digest food and stay clean and healthy. The bulk of feces is composed of dead bacteria along with some undigested food residue.

Much of our experience with bacteria involves disease. Although some bacteria do cause disease, many kinds live on or in the body and prevent disease. Bacteria associated with your dog's body outnumber body cells ten to one. In your dog's intestine, a balanced community of bacteria is extremely important for health. In addition to protecting your dog from disease-causing bacteria, intestinal bacteria also provide your dog with needed nutrients, such as vitamin K, which the body cannot make itself, as well as B vitamins.

The communities of bacteria and other organisms that inhabit the intestine are sometimes called the normal *microflora* or *microbiota*. Friendly bacteria are often called *intestinal flora*, *beneficial bacteria*, and *probiotics*. Consider these bacteria as the "good guys in the white hats," for they are essential to good digestion. The B vitamins they manufacture help prevent digestive inflammation and upset. These bacteria also aid in the maintenance of a healthy pH in the body and fight off the dangerous pathogenic bacteria that wind up in the intestine. Additionally, they help break down the food the dog eats.

There are tens of millions of bacteria in your dog's intestine. Their Latin names, which you may see on bottles in the health food store, include *Lactobacillus acidophilus*, *Lactobacillus bulgaris*, *Lactobacillus bifidus*, *Streptococcus faecium*, *Bifidobacterium bifidum*, *Lactobacillus casei*, and *Lactobacillus salivarius*. These bacteria can help with bad breath, gas, diarrhea, indigestion, colitis, and even constipation. Often, bad breath is due to poor digestion rather than rotten teeth, and these bacteria assist digestion in the gut. When beneficial bacteria supplements are given on a routine basis, they help maintain and protect your dog's health and build his immune system. It is very important to give your dog some beneficial bacteria when he is on antibiotics and after he finishes them. Antibiotics don't differentiate between the guys in the black hats and the guys in the white hats. Oral administration of supplements in the food will counter the adverse effects of the antibiotics on your dog's intestinal flora.

Available from health food stores, these supplements come in liquid, powder, and capsule forms. The same dose you take can be administered to your dog, whether a small dog or a large one. Plain yogurt made from a natural culture, usually found in health food stores as well, also contains these beneficial bacteria. Be aware that many of the yogurt brands available at the supermarket do not contain beneficial bacteria. In the supermarket, you can often find a product called *kefir*, which contains an adequate number of these good guys. You can give your dog a tablespoon or more by itself, or you can easily add some kefir to any meal. Any of these oral probiotic mixes will help reseed the intestine with friendly bacteria.

The Liver: The Big Guy on the Block

About forty years ago, *Reader's Digest* ran a series of articles titled "I Am Joe's (insert name of body part here)." The articles featured "talking" body parts who would discuss with the reader who they were and what they did. Prepare yourself for a similar introduction to your dog's liver.

I am Spot's liver; I'm the largest internal organ in his body. The kingdom I rule over is extensive because I perform more than 500 functions. I won't bore you by listing all of them, but I will tell you about my role in digestion.

I am the warden of digested food. After the food is broken down and absorbed in the intestine, it leaves the digestive tract and heads out to the blood to be carried to each organ to feed the cells— but not before seeing me. Everything has to go through me so that I can remove any poisons or wastes from the digested nutrients. This is essential. I have special cells that pick up and hold the toxic material so that it does not make Spot sick. The nutrients are carried at a superfast pace by the blood and blood cells to all of the other cells in the body once my job is done. Also, when Spot takes medications, I have to clean up most of them with my filtering system.

Within me, I have smaller ducts (called bile ducts) through which my bile flows into the gall bladder; together, these ducts resemble a branchlike plumbing system. The gall bladder uses that bile to help me digest and emulsify fats. Some mammals, such as horses, do not have a gall bladder, but Spot does.

I also function as a storage system for many proteins and chemicals in the body and amass reserves, such as fat-soluble vitamins (A, E, and D), keeping them until Spot needs them. I can make a variety of proteins using the foods that I store, including some that work in the immune system.

In today's toxic world, I can get extremely overloaded and tired. What helps me function better is good food and vitamins, especially the green foods that contain chlorophyll. With them, I can grow back cells that have been destroyed by short-term insult or injury. This makes me special because I can actually repair and regenerate myself.

I have several sections, called *lobes*. We all work together to share the load because we have a tough job. If I keep getting assaulted by toxins and man-made poisons, I can become very damaged. If I get fibrosis, then I cannot grow back. This is why healthy food and healthy living make my job a lot easier.

The Cells: Building Your Dream Home

Your dog's body comprises trillions of cells. These cells are organized into specialized tissues making up specific organs, such as the liver, kidneys, heart, muscles, nerves, and skin. Each cell is like a miniature city, bustling with traffic. The molecules in cell town are shuttled from place to place in a perpetual rush.

The mitochondria supply the power for the cell's machinery to work, converting sugar and other nutrients into something called ATP (adenosine triphosphate). ATP acts as an energy source for nearly every cellular process. In fact, the energy from sugars that are converted by the cell into ATP is used to move the proteins, fats, minerals, and vitamins.

To construct a house, you need more than just an energy source such as electricity. You also need materials such as nails, steel, wood, and cement and tools such as a hammer, a saw, a ladder, and a screwdriver. A cell can be compared to a microscopic house that is always under construction. The cell continuously recreates itself, and, when it can no longer do this, it fashions another cell and bestows on this new cell the same ability.

Sugars are used in the cell to make the energy source. Proteins provide the wood for construction. Vitamins and minerals are the nails, cement, and paint; the enzymes and catalysts are the hammer, saw, and screwdriver. Other nutrients, the antioxidants, act as the cleanup crew. They remove cellular rust, garbage, and toxins. The food your dog eats is not used only for energy. While sugars in the food are used for energy, almost everything else in nutritious food is used to facilitate enzymatic processes and build and maintain the body. The food your dog eats should be supplying all the nutrients he needs to meet the cells' needs. By now you know that most of the processed, packaged, big-corporation dog foods simply do not provide the essential nutrients for health.

Although each cell is a model of independence, it is also a member of the family of cells composing each organ. The organs interrelate like some superbly organized business, with everything running off nutrition. Every cell and every organ and every tissue is in the business of living, and they need all kinds of building blocks to stay alive. The more nourishing their environment, the better they do. Your dog's cellular environment is largely created from what he eats.

All of the processes that cells complete—the errands they run, the items they deliver, the communication cycles they complete, the products they create, and even the cleanup after the party—could not be done without the help of nutrients.

Extracellular Fluid

Each cell is surrounded by a liquid bath called the *extracellular fluid*. It is from this fluid that the cell absorbs the nutrients needed for survival. Additionally, this fluid bath receives the wastes discarded by the cell. Cells have pumps to remove their waste products and send the rubbish into the extracellular fluid.

During the Middle Ages, human waste was commonly thrown out the windows. It eventually made its way into the rivers in the towns. When the first settlers from England came to America, they would not drink the water from the then pristine rivers and lakes because in England, disease and ill health came from drinking river water. Instead they brewed the water into tea or fermented it into beer. Unfortunately, what the early settlers mistakenly assumed about American water is now true. Today, we must carefully filter our water before we drink it.

A similar scenario exists within the cell's world. Pesticides, drugs, chemicals, toxins, and poisons all pollute the body, right down to the cells. Each little cell dutifully marches on, working incessantly to clean up its own mini-environment. Plenty of antioxidants in the diet help a lot, as does keeping the cell's bath of fluid at the healthiest pH possible.

Explaining pH

The letters pH stand for "parts of hydrogen." When you measure the pH, you find out if something is acidic or alkaline. In science class, you may have used litmus paper to measure the pH of a solution. Vinegar and lemon juice are acids, so they taste sour. Baking soda is alkaline and therefore tastes bitter.

What the Heck Is pH?

The pH is a measure of the relative acidity or alkalinity of a material or fluid and is one of the most important factors affecting health and organ function. The pH of the fluid around the cells in your dog's body will depend on the food he has eaten. The body functions best at a slightly alkaline pH.

The biological and chemical reactions in the body are controlled by enzymes, which function best at an optimal pH. Different systems within the body work and interact to keep the pH at the healthiest range for the body. The functions of the liver, pancreas, gallbladder, hormones, and other organs and systems depend on an alkaline situation. The more alkaline their environment, the better they perform.

Why Is the pH Important?

Predisposition to disease is directly related to the acid-alkaline imbalance around our industrious cells. Meats, poultry, and similar protein sources make the body more acidic. When meat digests, molecules of sulfur and phosphorus are formed, and the intestinal tract becomes acidic. Meat also contains nitrogen, which, when digested, transforms into ammonia. Ammonia is toxic to cells and thus needs to be neutralized and excreted.

pH Changes in Food

The pH of the food that you and your dog eat changes after being ingested. For example, a lemon is acidic outside the body but will, when eaten and digested, make the body fluid more alkaline. Milk, an alkaline outside the body, will make the body itself more acidic.

To manage these excess acids and toxins, the body stores away bicarbonate. These bicarbonate stores are pulled into the intestine to neutralize the acidic environment there. When these stores are released and lost into the bowels, the cells' fluid then becomes acidic.

Three organs are responsible for eliminating the extra acids and toxic molecules that build up in the body: the kidneys, lungs, and liver. The liver is the most important of these three; it can process forty times more of these toxins than the kidneys can. Too much protein, particularly poor-quality protein, puts great stress on all of these organs.

Diet is one of the most important things that influences the body's pH. When the diet is too high in foods that acidify the body, the liver and kidneys cannot handle the load. The body becomes acidic and open to many diseases. Virtually all degenerative diseases, including arthritis, kidney problems, bladder stones, and heart disease, are associated with excess acidity. An acidic environment is also ripe for the establishment of cancer.

When cells are hampered by an acidic environment, they cannot perform their tasks of maintenance, cleaning, and generating cellular ATP. Their batteries run low, and toxins, including carcinogens, build up. DNA becomes altered, and cancer and other diseases set in.

All-Meat Diets

Although I do not disagree with using raw meat and poultry as part of a complete diet for dogs, I am heartily opposed to a diet composed predominantly of raw meat and bones. This type of diet is high in acid-forming foods and thus has the potential to predispose a dog to disease and stress on all of the organs. Of course, it has been established that most dogs do much better on any kind of homemade diet that replaces a poor-quality commercial-grade dog food. That's fairly easy to understand based on what we know about commercial dog food in general. But a dog's diet must contain a balance of foods to promote health. This should include grains, greens, and other vegetables.

We know that the wild dog and his wolf cousins eat raw meat as a large part of their diet. However, this is only a part of their diet. The stomach and intestines of an herbivore (such as a downed deer or antelope), when eaten by a carnivore (such as a wolf or coyote), provide a delightful array of greens and grains that are digested just right for the carnivore's assimilation. Your dog chews on grass because this is pretty much all that is available to him, whereas his wild cousins dine on a variety of greens and botanicals whenever they fancy a bit of chlorophyll.

We all know that our dogs' ancestors were wild dogs and wolves. Because of this, we assume that they evolved primarily as carnivores, living mainly on flesh from their prey. We forget that early man did the same thing when he was a hunter and gatherer. Long winters would provide only high-protein food from the hunt. Just as you are genetically far removed from, say, Neanderthal man, our dogs have far more genetic distance from their early ancestors; because their individual life spans are shorter, their collective generations are greater than ours. There are more generations between your Westie and a wolf than there are between you and a Neanderthal human. You not only enjoy vegetables and cooked grains but also need them to avoid many modern-day diseases. So does your dog.

Protein: Once Thought the Perfect Food

The word *protein* is derived from the Greek word *proteios*, which means "primary." In its infancy, the science of nutrition equated protein with livestock products. This belief has been the status quo for more than a hundred years. The rich ate meat, and the lower classes ate grains. More animal protein must therefore be good, right? The answer to this is *no*.

Dangers of High-Protein Diets

Large-breed puppy owners are warned to be careful of their pups' taking in too much protein. Owners mistakenly believe that this is because big puppies grow too fast on a high-protein dog food and, as a result of this speedy growth, tend to get bone disorders. In fact, the disorders are caused not only by accelerated growth but also by the acidic systems that result from too much meat protein. The acidity in the body fluids leaches the calcium out of the bones, weakening them.

You can help restore alkalinity to your dog's diet by feeding green and yellow vegetables. Well-cooked beans and dairy can be mixed in with grains and vegetables as a protein source to decrease the protein made available from meat and poultry. Cranberry powder (available at health food stores or online) also makes the body alkaline; cranberry makes the urine (which is excreted from the body) acidic. Adding probiotics to the food can also help maintain a more alkaline pH.

The fact is that too much protein has been proved to increase the incidence of cancer, diabetes, high cholesterol, and high blood pressure, all of which are linked to high animal protein intake. Be aware that protein doesn't come from only beef, chicken, fish, eggs, and dairy. The next time you are in the supermarket, pick up some food items that contain only vegetables or grains. Read the label and note the protein content listed. Grains, vegetables, nuts, and seeds all contain significant amounts of protein.

The animal-source protein content of your dog's food does not have to be as high as you have been conditioned to believe. I am not saying that your dog should become a vegetarian, although I have found that dogs can do just fine as vegetarians. I'm simply saying that you have many choices, and most of us have been conditioned to lean toward too much animal protein in our dogs' diet.

Plant-based proteins supply all of the building blocks your dog needs to produce the required amino acids. Preparing meals for dogs from grains, vegetables, legumes, nuts, and fruit is relatively simple. Additionally, vegetarian dog kibble is readily available at many boutique pet-food stores. You may be surprised to learn that 1 cup of cooked spinach contains about 5 grams of protein, whereas 1 cup of sunflower seeds contains about 32 grams of protein. A medium-sized baked potato has roughly 5 grams of protein. One egg has 6 grams of protein, whereas 3 ounces of ground beef has 20 grams. Suffice it to say, there are many diverse protein food sources available. You should also be aware that the protein in many dog foods is from animal sources that are contaminated with hormones, drugs, and toxins.

In recent years, we have all been told that if we eat a better diet, we will improve our health, resist illness, and avoid cancer. Once again, while at the supermarket, take a look at the magazines that sit next to the checkout counters. One of the more popular magazine topics involves how consuming increased servings of vegetables, fruits, and grains is the key to people's enjoying better health. Headlines that advertise diets to help eliminate cancer will consistently talk about yellow, red, orange, and green vegetables and fruits.

Disease Starts and Ends with the Cell

It is important to recognize that the present-day dog does not live in the pristine environment that his ancestors and cousins did. Today, humans and dogs alike are constantly assaulted by toxins, in both our food and the environment, which daily threaten our health. One in two dogs gets cancer. Allergies are prevalent. Chronic diarrhea is a regular occurrence. Organs fail too early. The modern dog needs a correctly balanced diet and extra nutrients to promote the correct pH and to support his cells in their quest for health.

An essential fact about disease is that it does not happen in an instant. If a dog is diagnosed with cancer, for example, this condition did not develop in a day, a month, or even a year. It developed slowly, over a long period. Dogs (and people) can appear perfectly healthy for months or even years before a disease process reaches a critical state. In many instances, by the time the disease is detected, the body is in serious crisis.

What a Grazing Dog Tells You

To get a better idea of a dog's nutritional needs, take a look at how his first cousin, the coyote, eats. While some have said that meat is all that's necessary for a carnivore's diet, in the wild, the entire kill is consumed—this includes the prey's intestines and stomach, which are filled with predigested vegetables and grains. Consuming the liver, kidneys, and heart is important to the predator because these organs are filled with high-quality, easy-to-assimilate nutrients. Wild dogs and coyotes also chew on plant matter in the wild. They naturally know which plants are healthy and digestible. Although you will not see them grazing, they will occasionally munch on healthy greens, adding to the plant content they consume when they devour a herbivore. The wolf is really an omnivore, eating grains, vegetation, and protein.

Dogs need—even crave—chlorophyll, a potent detoxifier, purifier, and deodorizer. Your dog may try to fill that craving by eating grass, which, if it's sprayed with pesticides, is dangerous to consume. Dogs commonly throw up grass, which they cannot digest, in a yellowish fluid, or you might see it come out the other end looking much as it did when it went in. That's because the green grass on our lawns is decorative and was never designed to be eaten by a dog. Broccoli, sprouts, string beans, peas, kale, and other green vegetables, when lightly steamed or finely grated, are healthy and can be digested by your dog.

Why don't we detect disease earlier? It's because the disease begins on a cellular, microscopic level. With the advent of molecular and DNA studies, scientists are now absolutely certain that what happens on a cellular level is reflected, eventually, in the entire organism. One cell becomes diseased, and another takes over for it. This happens over and over again in healthy bodies. But when the insults to the cells begin to pile up, and they do not have the necessary nutrients to repair themselves, they either die or change, no longer functioning as they once did.

Cells were designed in nature long before lawn chemicals, toxic cleaning products, poisonous preservatives, and man-made carcinogens found their place on this planet. We now often purchase "spring water" in containers, but the plastic containers themselves leach their chemicals into the once-pure water. With each decade that passes, it requires more knowledge and work to stay healthy. Fortunately, advances in vitamins and antioxidants are attempting to keep pace and balance the scales.

Our canine friends are fortunate that the cells in their bodies work tirelessly to survive. In payment for this work, they should have a high salary of pristine nutrients and a support staff of vitamins, minerals, and herbs. Instead, they get preservatives, highly processed foods, ineffectual vitamins that cannot be absorbed and utilized, and many toxins to excrete. A healthier diet will most certainly be of benefit.

Our relationship with our canine friends has grown and evolved over the centuries. They provide irreplaceable emotional support for us with their kindness and unconditional love. It's time to give a gift to our furry friends to thank them for their good deeds. We can show our love in a way that they will so easily understand—food. Provide simple, easy, nourishing diets that, I hope, will be fun for you to prepare. It's time for a change, and a good one at that!

4. Cooking Up Canine Health

My grandmother loved to cook for her family. Of course, holidays served as the ultimate excuse. As a child, I used to pause next to the large stained-glass window in her foyer to experience the delicious aromas that wafted out from her kitchen. As my relatives poured into the house, I would stand quietly, my senses awash with the most delicious smells of freshly baked bread, pastries, homemade noodles, and cinnamon. My grandmother's kitchen was alive with love for her family, and I have always savored that memory.

Today, we have instant meals, take-out food, and microwave ovens. We also have grandmothers who are likely to be out working or volunteering. As Bob Dylan said, "The times, they are a-changin'." Nonetheless, the appreciation of home-cooked meals has not been lost.

When I did have the time to cook my young twin sons' favorite foods, I thoroughly enjoyed watching their eyes light up with anticipation and appreciation. We moved into our new house when the children were young, and thoughtful neighbors arrived with a basket of fresh home-baked goods. This kind act transformed a stressful moving time into one in which we felt welcome and excited about our new life. My husband is still delighted when my sons get excited about the latest pie he baked for them.

Cooking is one of the ways that some people use to express their love for each other. While I find that our two-legged friends appreciate a great snack or meal, our four-legged friends are ecstatic over the same. Cooking for your dog, if that is what you want to do, can be an act of love and a special way of bonding. You all become, in yet another way, a family.

Love and Togetherness

Mealtime can be a celebration of family life as the table transforms into a place where the events of the day are shared. We relax and let the stresses slip away as we converse and banter. The aroma of the food and the sounds of our laughter open us up as we enjoy each other's company.

We can learn a great deal about our dog and about the relationship we have with him if we take note of our behavior when dining. Our dog will, just like us, be lured by the aromas of the food; he will also be drawn to the joy and fellowship of the group. Our dogs are quick to settle into the "pack," reacting to our laughter and reading our happy, relaxed body language. Our dogs want to enjoy our company and be part of the moment because they see us as pack members.

Morse Code

We humans don't realize how many signals and messages we continually give to our dogs as we interact. Nor do we realize how astute dogs are at reading our nonverbal cues. When some of my canine patients arrive at my clinic for the first time, they are, understandably, nervous and worried. I yawn and then yawn some more. I explain to their owners that I am doing this because dogs yawn to calm themselves, and my yawning signals them to calm down. (If your dog is afraid of thunder and lightning, try yawning when the next storm hits and watch what happens!) Sometimes I forget to explain, and the poor clients think they are boring me to death. When I explain myself, we all laugh together, and the dogs relax even more.

Dogs seem quite capable of laughing at themselves, like true wise men. Who can forget a dog who quizzically looks toward his tail, comically amazed after a loud flatulent sound erupts from his back end, and then wags his tail and happily looks up as his family breaks into peals of laughter? Rather than hide in embarrassment, he wags his tail even harder, delighted to be part of the fun and amusement. No wonder our relationship with our dog can relieve stress. Indeed, laughter is the best medicine!

The Right Choice

When applied to our dogs, an old familiar saying has been altered slightly and carved in stone, or, better yet, bone: the way to a dog's heart is surely through his stomach. If you want to find your way to your dog's heart and are ready to improve his fare, this book will help you make the transition to healthier diets in a stress-free way. You may not have much free time. Maybe you don't even like cooking. Dry kibble, canned food, frozen meat meals (with or without grains and vegetables), quick-mix meals, and more are readily available from scores of companies that make good-quality products. Many of these are made with human-quality or organic ingredients. Perhaps you have three young children, one small dog, and lots of leftovers. It's easier than you think and takes just minutes to combine the leftovers into healthful meals for your dog.

You're going to decide which meal plan is best for you. Many of us are busy during the week but have some free time on weekends. Whatever your schedule, there is a path you can follow and many options to choose from; you will surely find something that suits both you and your dog just fine. Whatever path you choose, the information I provide will support you in making a dietary transition for your dog and choosing the best way to do so. This does not have to be a gargantuan task. If you wish to prepare your dog's meals, I will make it easy for you with all kinds of recipes that are at your fingertips in this book.

When we make the decision to lead our canine companion down the path of natural foods, we add a pound more of love, a cupful of fun, and a teaspoon of excitement to their lives and our own. When you reach your destination, your prize will be a happier and healthier dog.

Although some of us might bemoan the loss of sweet desserts and French fries when we decide on more healthful fare for ourselves, our dog will delight in the delicious meals he is served. Some of the good food he has smelled for so long will finally be his. Mealtime for your dog will be an even more special event!

Dogs have had to eat whatever they have been doled out, and most of the time it wasn't nearly as scrumptious or diverse as the meals we ate. Consider also that dogs have more than 500 times more sensory cells in their noses than humans do. Dogs can pick up a scent from a mile away. If those barbecued ribs smell good to you, imagine how they must smell to your dog!

The Wisdom to Know What You Can and Cannot Do

What does all this mean in practical terms? Do we have to do much advance planning or cook up specially prepared organic meats, grains, and veggies? Some dedicated dog owners are doing just that. However, many of us have lifestyles that leave little room to cater to our own dietary needs, let alone those of our dog. Before I moved to New Zealand, my busy schedule seldom allowed me any real time to cook for my dogs, as much as I love them. Now that I have more time, I thoroughly enjoy cooking for them, and they enjoy it, too.

It's possible to rustle up good meals for your dog no matter how much or how little free time you have. First, you need to evaluate your own personal "hassle factor," the limits of your capability when it comes to canine cooking. If you don't consider this honestly, you risk turning what should

Hassle-Factor Questionnaire

1. How much spare time do you have?

   A) None.   **B)** Limited amount.   **C)** Plenty!

2. How much spare refrigerator space do you have?

   A) None.   **B)** Limited amount.   **C)** Plenty!

3. How much spare freezer space do you have?

   A) None.   **B)** Limited amount.   **C)** Plenty!

4. Do you like to cook?

   A) No!   **B)** When I'm in the mood.   **C)** I do!

5. How much can you afford to spend to feed your dog(s)?

   A) As little as possible.   **B)** I'm on a bit of a budget.   **C)** Whatever it takes.

6. How much do you usually have in the way of leftovers?

   A) None.   **B)** Enough for the next day.   **C)** Plenty!

7. Do you eat a healthy, balanced diet yourself?

   A) I sometimes think about it.   **B)** I make an effort.   **C)** Religiously.

8. How many dogs do you have?

   A) More than three.   **B)** Two or three.   **C)** One.

9. How large is/are your dog(s)?

   A) 50 pounds or more.   **B)** 25 to 49 pounds.   **C)** Under 25 pounds.

be a loving effort into a major imposition on your time when you barely have enough to do everything else on your agenda. If you want to avoid feeling that those trips to the grocer or butcher on behalf of your canine companion are burdensome, you should use the questionnaire on page 46 as a guide in determining just how far you can comfortably go in changing your dog's diet.

A multitude of factors come into consideration when making the choice that fits your lifestyle best. These include time, your finances, your kitchen and refrigerator space, the number of dogs in the home, the size(s) of the dog(s), whether you have children, the area you live in (city or country), the resources available in your area, and your interest in cooking, preparing, and storing meals.

Plan A

If most of your answers are in the A column, you'll want to follow Plan A. Essentially, this plan involves using a healthy kibble as a base and augmenting it with a good vitamin-mineral supplement, nutritious leftovers, and perhaps some cooked fresh or frozen veggies. Healthy leftovers could consist of a variety of vegetables; potatoes; macaroni and cheese; spaghetti with plain or meat sauce; pieces of meat, fish, or poultry without the cooked bones; soup; or perhaps a slice of bread. They do not include leftover chicken and steak bones, sugary sweets, meat fat or gristle, bacon grease, or spoiled or moldy foods. Remember that the protein in good kibble is adequate, so toppers made of grains and vegetables would be more healthful for your dog than those made of meat.

An easy step up from Plan A: add cooked frozen veggies. There are many different vegetable combinations that are precut and frozen in bags. For example, add a cauliflower, broccoli, and carrot mix to your dog's meal each day. Cook the whole bag (do not microwave!), perhaps toss in some olive oil, and dole out the following amounts each day: ½ cup for a small dog, 1 cup for a medium dog, and 1–1½ cups for a large dog. Take another step and use frozen organic vegetables—better yet, fresh vegetables or fresh organic vegetables. Fresh veggies can be finely grated and sprinkled over your dog's dry dog food. No matter what type of veggies you use, avoid onions.

Plan B

If most of your answers are in the B column, Plan B is for you. Plan B centers more on home cooking for your dog, perhaps using some of the recipes we suggest later in the book, with the option of using a healthy kibble when that's more convenient. You can vary your approach by mixing a healthy kibble with veggies and leftovers on busy days, occasionally throw together a fun topper, and dedicate some spare time to preparing enough food to last a few days, such as a stew (portions of which can also be frozen). The Canine Café recipe section of this book offers many options for easy, healthy, and often inexpensive stews and casseroles. The recipes for quick-fix meals are easy to make, requiring only some basic supplies.

Plan C

If your answers are mostly in the C column, you will follow Plan C. Plan C means dedication to home cooking or raw-food diets. Your dog's diet can consist completely of food that you prepare for him, whether cooked or raw. This book provides you with many delicious and nutritious recipes for meals to prepare on the stove or in the oven. There is also a section on raw food in which you'll find a guide to special food that you can order, either packed and ready for preparation or raw and ready to defrost. (Many raw-food regimens are somewhat stringent about what and when dogs should be fed.) Remember, if you're in the C category and routinely cook for your dog, it would be totally fine to feed him a healthy kibble in case of an emergency until you get back to the cooked-food routine.

All Plans

All plans should be augmented with a vitamin supplement. The point to keep in mind is that allowing your dog to share your fare needn't involve an impossible commitment. A flexible "real-world" approach is always best, just as it's likely to be with your human family members. Ideally, you might prefer to prepare all of your family's meals yourself, utilizing only the purest and most healthful ingredients, but that doesn't necessarily mean that you can always take the time and trouble to do so. There may be days when you simply grab some ready-made dinners out of the freezer or order a pizza.

The same goes for the way you feed your dog. It needn't be an "all-or-nothing" situation. One night, you might simply fill his dish with one of the healthy brands of kibble; the next night, you might allow him to share some of what you've prepared for the family; and the night after that, you give him a combination of leftovers and dry food. A friend of mine had a dog who, whenever served something that the family was eating, no matter how much he liked it, never failed to cover the food with kibble from his dish before taking a bite. Perhaps he had been exposed to too much TV and was trying to cover up having strayed from what those dog-food commercials depicted.

You can put those dinner leftovers to good use without having to throw them away or store them in the fridge where, more likely than not, they'll get shoved in the back and have to be tossed three weeks later in petrified or putrefied condition. You'll find that your dog enjoys most of the same things you do—oatmeal and other cereals, yogurt, fruits, veggies, meat, poultry, and eggs—all of which can be either added to kibble or given to him in a separate dish.

Hassle-Factor Scenarios

Donna has two Labrador Retrievers and three small children. She does not have a job, but she seems to always be on the run. After reading about the healthy kibbles that are recommended here, she decides to try one with her dogs. Her children typically don't finish things like vegetables, yams, potatoes, and pasta, along with other foods. Rather than throw away such leftovers, she saves them in plastic containers and gives each of her dogs a cup of cooked frozen mixed vegetables along with adding leftover macaroni and cheese and other table scraps to their food. She also gives them a good-quality multivitamin and mineral supplement. She would be typical of someone in the Plan A column.

Vicky has three Pugs and a full-time job, but she still wants to cook for her dogs. She loves cooking and does not have the money to justify the expense of the already-prepared healthful foods. Therefore, twice a week, she cooks her dogs up a big batch of one of the dishes in the recipe section of this book. Many of the ingredients in her pantry, such as oatmeal and brown rice, are bought in bulk and store

A Woof to the Wise

Avoid feeding the dog from the table—or under the table, as kids have been known to do—unless you want to turn your pet into a pest at mealtimes. Whenever you share, do so at a place that's somewhat removed from the dining area, perhaps before or after everyone else has eaten. It's important to feed your dog out of his own bowl, not from the table. Additionally, do not let your dog see you placing food directly from the table into his bowl. Always take the food into the kitchen and wait a few minutes before putting it into his bowl and offering it to him.

well. Her grocer saves her chicken necks and ground meat at a good price. Vicky can change the menu as she pleases weekly, watching the sales. Each batch lasts her about three days for all three of her Pugs. If she is in a pinch or if a meal runs short, she whips up one of the items in the quick-fix meal section. She also gives her dogs a good multivitamin-mineral supplement. She fits the Plan B profile.

Martha, whose kids have entered college and are out of the house, has three Golden Retrievers. A dedicated mom, she is used to making good meals for her family and wants to do likewise for her dogs. She favors a raw-food diet but doesn't want to shop constantly for the dogs' food. She orders the raw food from a reliable supplier and feeds it to her dogs. She also prepares soaked or cooked grains and extra veggies to keep the protein percentage healthy. Martha purchases a special calcium supplement or makes one with egg shells to keep the minerals balanced, and she gives a good multivitamin-mineral supplement. Martha is more of a Plan C type.

Gillian is a wonderful cook and loves her time in the kitchen. She has plenty of freezer space and time to cook for her three Bulldogs. She has one teenage son. She chooses to follow the recipes in this book and cook for her dogs. Twice a week, she makes big batches, which she stores in freezer bags and defrosts as she needs. She also remembers her dogs' daily vitamin-mineral supplement. She finds Plan C easy to follow.

My husband, Monte, is a fabulous cook and loves being in the kitchen. He's also a busy guy. Before moving to New Zealand, we used good brands of kibble along with leftovers. Healthy dog kibble is extremely expensive in New Zealand, whereas healthy scraps of lamb and chicken, which are sold expressly for pets, are fresh and inexpensive. Monte found himself enjoying cooking up large pots of the "hearty dog" recipes while the dogs sat by the stove, wearing very happy expressions. We changed from Plan A to Plan C for financial reasons and found it to be rewarding and fun. When the protein content is adjusted to the ideal level and when oatmeal, rice, potatoes, and olive oil are purchased in bulk quantities, these healthy meals become very affordable. Add a bit of freezer space, and you've got it made.

Every one of these scenarios results in actual health benefits for the dogs. Shining coats and eyes, reduced shedding, and boundless energy provide indisputable evidence of the advantages of a good diet.

When Buying Dog Foods

Because of all of the dog food recalls, loving owners became distrustful and suspicious of many dog food brands. We all have doubts about the real ingredients in major commercial-brand dog foods, and there is good reason to expect more recalls in the future. Fortunately, there are convenient new solutions to this doggy dietary dilemma.

There are now pet foods available that contain far more beneficial ingredients and are made from much higher quality food sources than the conventional brands. The brands of dog food I do recommend are made by conscientious companies whose products are preserved with vitamins, offer various combinations of extra-healthy ingredients, and contain neither toxic or carcinogenic additives or preservatives nor disgusting by-products.

Some companies market only dry products, while others offer both canned and dry varieties as well as biscuits and snacks. You'll even find companies that produce foods you can cook for your dog. Others will send you raw, organically raised meat or even full doggy dinners, either cooked or raw. There are also a number of brands of natural kibble, containing vegetables such as carrots and peas, grains such as barley and oatmeal, fruits such as blueberries and apples, and vitamins. Several companies have actually made purely vegetarian kibbles available. All of these products offer a marked contrast to the noxious stew of chemicals and by-products from which standard preparations are made.

These foods are very palatable to dogs and more appealing to humans, too. For example, if you do opt for one of the healthy canned foods, you'll find them to be a pleasant change from the greasy and odoriferous products you buy in the supermarket. This makes it easier for the kids to feed the dog because they won't be repulsed by the smell.

You won't typically find these healthful prepared dog foods on your next trip to the supermarket. You're most likely to find them at health food stores, holistic veterinarians' offices, or independent boutique-type pet stores. The national pet supply stores also may have a selection of them. Many of these foods are also available by mail or can be ordered online.

These progressive brands of dog food represent an ideal solution for those of you who, like I, have hectic and busy schedules, or on days when your own dinner might consist of nothing more than a take-home pizza.

5. Designing Diet

Although it's true that what's good for you is, in most instances, likely to be good for your dog, there are also times when it's not particularly feasible to share your food. That's why you may want to make a little extra effort to prepare some cooked-to-order cuisine for your furry friend. If you do, I'd like to provide a few pointers.

You'll want to give your dog the benefit of a diet that contains as many nutrients and immune-boosting substances as possible while reducing or eliminating his consumption of toxic or disease-promoting ingredients. Your dog's well-being depends on what you put in his dish. The time to keep illness at bay, after all, is before it's had a chance to develop. This is what a healthy diet can do!

Vegetables, fruits, grains, and herbs are sources of nutrients that your dog simply cannot get from eating a diet of commercial dog food. Keep in mind that vegetables and fruits are "live" foods, filled with enzymes, vitamins, minerals, and other nutrients that disappear after heating and processing. Beyond their nutritional value, they possess the quality of freshness, the opposite of the "dead" products sold by the manufacturers of commercial dog food. Therefore, whenever you have the time to add, say, grated carrots to your dog's meal or give him a sliced broccoli stalk as a snack, do so. They will supply him with needed nutrients and help fill the void that a diet of processed or cooked food creates. The enzyme pathways of so many of a dog's organs need the vitamins and minerals that only fresh foods can provide. That's why I strongly recommend that a "real food" diet include a variety of these commodities, as well as a vitamin supplement.

It is also important to know what proportion of your dog's diet each category of "real food" should compose. Nowadays, there's a popular assertion that dogs should eat mostly, or only, raw meat. It's based on the premise that the wolf is the dog's closest relative and, therefore, dogs are virtually wolves. In fact, dogs were domesticated and began living lives that were quite different from their wild wolf cousins well over 100 centuries ago. A lot can change in the canine genetic makeup over 10,000 years, and it seems that it has. Our dogs have coevolved, along with us, to be able to eat what we eat. Early on, novel adaptations in their genes allowed the ancestors of modern dogs to digest and assimilate starches.

Eric Axelsson, an evolutionary geneticist at Uppsala University in Sweden, compared the DNA from dogs and wolves. Unlike wolves, dogs *had* developed genes for digesting starch. Dogs have up to thirty copies of the gene that makes *amylase*, a protein that starts the breakdown of starch in the intestine, whereas wolves have only two copies. The multiple genes for amylase are twenty-eight times more active in dogs, showing that our canine friends are many times better at digesting starches than are wolves.

There's also another gene that codes for an additional enzyme, *maltase*, important in the digestion of starch. It was found that dogs produce a longer version of the maltase digestive enzyme. In fact, it's the same type of elongated version seen in herbivores such as cows and rabbits, making it even more efficient in its ability to digest starch. Geneticists and evolutionary biologists became very excited about this discovery.

The bottom line is that dogs can eat starches and have adapted to a diet that's quite similar to a balanced human diet. In fact, in my thirty years of clinical practice, I've found that carbohydrates are good for dogs. It's my opinion that dogs, like humans, require a combination of meat, starches, and vegetables to meet their basic nutritional requirements. If dogs eat only protein, they'll lack important vitamins, which can lead to deficiencies. Vitamins and minerals are the tools that cells use to repair themselves and prevent disease. Vitamins are abundant in colored fruits and vegetables. Starches like sweet potatoes are also filled with many healthy vitamins and minerals. Grains like barley and brown rice provide healthy complex carbohydrates and fiber along with vitamins and minerals.

Oatmeal, rice, barley, sweet potato, and other starches are not only fine to feed but, importantly, very healthy for your dog. I must admit that when my twin boys were small, I had no time to cook for my dogs. Many people lead busy lives and cannot devote the time to cooking for their dogs, which is why, in this chapter, I give you numerous options and choices to design the diet that works for your schedule and your dog.

When you decide to create a meal from scratch, you'll need to know what your dog can eat and how to prepare it to make it appetizing. The following section will teach you how to make healthful food enticing to your dog. We all know the dog who loves his greasy, smelly can of dog food that is routinely mixed into his generic-brand kibble. Most of these fine fellows and gals will switch with absolute unequivocal joy to home cooking or just love the addition of nutritious toppers to a healthier kibble.

Believe me, if your dog seems to do fine on conventional dog food, you cannot and will not fail to make him healthier with some home cooking. And this is irrespective of whether you count calories or measure amounts precisely. You can't go wrong by taking this approach.

Portions and Proportions

The traditional formula used to figure out proportions is the "one-third" rule, which means feeding your dog one-third each of protein, vegetables, and grains on a daily basis. This formula has been around for a long time. More recent research has disposed me to recommend one-fifth protein, two-fifths vegetables, and two-fifths grains. The protein you will be feeding your dog will be a high-quality protein, and some will actually come from grains. Both the percentage and type of protein need to be considered in the quest for optimal health. For example, the recipe section has meal toppers that are purposely low in protein. When loving dog owners put more meat or poultry on top of a prepared commercial dog food, which has very adequate amounts of protein, they are doing a disservice to their pet's health.

Weight and Portions

Pounds	Amount of dry food a day (if you feed only dry food)	Amount of cooked food a day (if you feed only cooked food)
15	1½ cups	1½–2 cups
25	2 cups	1¾–2½ cups
40	3 cups	2½–3½ cups
60	4 cups	4–4½cups
100	6 cups	5–7 cups

Meals: How Big?

How big should a dog's meals be? You can refer to the above chart as a basic guideline for determining daily portions for your dog. If your dog is physically active, increase that amount. Just as with humans, each dog has his own metabolic rate. It's best to keep a watchful eye on your dog's weight and hunger level and alter the amounts if it's indicated by his condition.

Dogs are really a lot like we are in this respect. There are those who eat everything they want and maintain picture-perfect figures and those who stay heavy despite eating well. Dogs, like humans, also tend to gain weight more easily as they age. Some people and dogs exercise routinely, and some lie around all day. The combination of metabolism and lifestyle should strongly influence how much you feed your dog.

Weigh your dog first to get a reference point. If he is too heavy, he will lose some weight on this diet because of its roughage, fiber, and freshness. As his weight readjusts, you may find that you need to feed him less or more to maintain a desirable weight. The chart will provide you with guidelines for where to start.

Portion Points to Remember

A dog's daily portion does not need to be eaten in one meal. Dogs are pack animals, and they like to eat when their family does, which is usually in the morning and evening—breakfast and dinner. A 40-pound dog can have, for example, 1¼ cups of oatmeal and some yogurt or a "meal in a muffin" (see the recipe section) in the morning. Then, later on in the day, he can have 2¼ cups of one of the stews you'll find in the recipe section.

Most healthy holistic dog foods will have a chart on the bag with recommended feeding amounts. Each of these foods varies in the degree it is concentrated, how much fiber and roughage it contains, and the amount of oil and fat it contains, so suggested amounts can vary from brand to brand. However, such charts should help guide you as to the amount of dry food to feed your dog. Use such product charts when they are available rather than the one on the previous page, which cannot account for the variations in ingredients.

When cooking for your dog, remember that ingredients such as oil add calories, while vegetables serve as the "weight watchers." If your dog is eating loads of food and still seems to be thin, you may want to add more olive oil and other healthful high-calorie items in relation to the vegetables and fruits. For overweight dogs, the opposite is true. Use the portion chart as a guide as you keep tabs on your dog's weight, both with a scale and by watching his appearance. Ideas for specific menus for weight control can be found in the recipe section.

Fresh Vegetables

Vegetables can provide dogs with essential nutrients that they aren't likely to get from other sources. The chlorophyll found in greens, for instance, serves to flush and clean the liver, an organ essential to your dog's good health that can also benefit from some of the other substances and enzymes contained in vegetables. Vegetables and greens can also help in maintaining a good pH balance, which is thrown off by an excess of protein. Then, too, water-soluble calcium that is present in leafy greens can be readily utilized by the body, in contrast to the calcium in dried bone or oyster shells, which is poorly assimilated. Cooking or finely grating vegetables makes them easier for dogs to digest.

My dogs love raw broccoli stems and carry them away to devour with great joy. I eat mainly the florets, so we both win in the name of health. They will eat carrots only after they are cooked. In fact, raw carrots are hard for dogs to digest and come out pretty much the same way they went in, so I would rather cook the carrots anyway. Remember what your dog is used to eating. If you had eaten nothing but flavor-enhanced snacks like spicy corn chips every day of the year, steamed vegetables might seem bland and uninteresting. Come to think of it, plain steamed vegetables do seem uninteresting, no matter what you're used to. I like butter and salt on my vegetables, but dogs do not like salt, so please do not salt their food to suit your taste. Butter is another matter completely and is always welcome by the canine diner.

Benefits of Garlic

Despite fears about garlic being toxic to dogs, garlic has many benefits for our canine friends when given in moderate amounts. Garlic in a dog's food will help prevent fleas. Dogs don't perspire as we do. When we eat a lot of garlic, it quickly comes out in our perspiration. In a dog, however, the garlic comes out over time in the oil of the coat. The essence of garlic will take some time to build up and have its flea-repelling effect. The trick is to wash your dog with nondetergent castile soap when you bathe him to prevent the coat oil from washing off.

When you come right down to it, dogs can be a lot like little kids are with vegetables. And just like kids, some dogs need a little enticement to get out of the junk-food rut they're in. Many dogs truly enjoy certain vegetables, while others learn to enjoy them over time and need them doctored up a bit. Veggies that are lightly steamed until tender and tossed in butter or olive oil and then sprinkled generously with Parmesan cheese are rarely refused. You can also cook vegetables in liquid flavored with beef or chicken by either putting a bone from the butcher (which is later removed) in the water or adding a beef or chicken bouillon cube to the pot. This will impart a meaty overtone to the vegetables. A meaty flavoring can also be accomplished by opening a jar of chicken or beef baby food, diluting it a bit with water, and stirring the watered-down baby food in with the steamed vegetables.

Sometimes grating or dicing the vegetables, lightly steaming them, and mixing them in with the kibble works well. I often mix vegetables with cooked grains and olive oil and place it on the kibble.

Root vegetables such as carrots and parsnips can be sliced into rounds, sprinkled with olive oil and garlic powder, and baked in an oven at 250°F (121°C) for about forty-five minutes and then cooled. My dogs love these as snacks. Diced or grated raw veggies can be sautéed quickly in a bit of butter or olive oil. You can also sprinkle these lightly cooked veggies with some cheese. In general, though, vegetables work best when mixed in a prepared meal such as a casserole or stew.

Leftovers are an excellent way to add vegetables to your dog's meal. Dishes such as creamed spinach, baked yams or sweet potatoes, cooked squash with butter, and mixed-vegetable casseroles that the family did not finish can be refrigerated and then dished out at your dog's mealtimes. Most dogs love potatoes. Roasted potato wedges drizzled with olive oil and sprinkled with garlic are always welcome.

My dogs love Nori seaweed. These are flat sheets of seaweed that are used to roll sushi. Seaweed is an excellent source of kelp and minerals.

Vegetable Dos and Don'ts

Below are recommendations for what to feed and what not to feed regarding vegetables.

Recommended

- asparagus
- brussels sprouts
- beets (in small amounts)
- beans*
- broccoli
- carrots
- cauliflower
- celery
- collards
- cucumbers
- kale
- kelp
- lentils*
- garlic**
- green beans
- parsnips
- peas
- potatoes
- pumpkin
- seaweed
- sprouts
- squash (all kinds)
- string beans
- tomatoes
- turnips
- yams

*Soak beans or lentils overnight, then pour off the water, rinse, and cook until nice and soft
**In moderate amounts

Not recommended

- onions in any significant quantity (although a little can be used for flavoring)
- onion soup

Fruit Dos and Don'ts

Below are recommendations for what to feed and what not to feed regarding fruit.

Recommended

- apples
- avocados
- bananas
- berries
- figs
- melons (including watermelon)
- oranges
- peaches
- pears

Pieces of fruit can be eaten raw, and a quarter of an apple or a piece of watermelon can help maintain electrolyte balance in hot weather.

Not recommended

- grapes*
- raisins

*Studies have shown that eating grapes or grape skins can be toxic to dogs and can make them severely ill with resulting death.

Fresh Fruit

The younger a dog is when you introduce him to fruit, the easier it is for him to love it. Apples are reliable favorites. Just slice up the fruit and offer some slices to your dog. If he seems uncertain, peel off the skin and try again. You can also dice up apples and put the pieces in a little chicken or beef broth to get your dog to try them. Bananas have always been a big hit in my house. Mixing bananas and plain yogurt can make a yummy quick snack or a meal in itself.

Watermelon slices are terrific on a hot summer day. Papayas are great for digestion, and fresh papayas or mangoes can be added to cereal mixes. Many dogs also like a slice of avocado.

If your dog looks at you quizzically when you offer him fruit, don't give up. Offer the fruit a few times and, if needed, doctor it up to help him take the first step.

Organic Produce

Those toxic pesticides routinely sprayed on produce can be every bit as hazardous to canine health as they are to human health. That's why, whenever possible, you should make it a habit to buy organically grown products that are raised without poisonous chemicals. Otherwise, you should thoroughly wash and soak all fruit and vegetables. You can use products especially designed for cleaning fruit and veggies; these products are generally available in supermarkets and health food stores.

Organic crops are believed to contain far more vitamins and nutrients than produce grown through conventional farming methods. The farming methods employed by organic farmers work to rebuild the health of the soil and restore the nutrients lost by overuse of the land and heavy chemical fertilizers. By eliminating pesticides, organic agriculture does not contribute to the toxins in our water, soil, and air that threaten our health, our children's health, and our pets' health. The cultivation of genetically engineered crops, a source of great concern to environmentalists, is likewise banned in organic farming.

Grains

We know that a dog is not intended to be merely a carnivore; he also requires carbohydrates to remain in top physical shape. That's why grains in their various forms are such an important component of a well-rounded canine diet—as long as you don't try to feed them to your dog raw.

Healthy products made from prepared grains, such as whole-grain breads, cereals, and crackers, are fine for mixing with your dog's food as is. Thin slices or squares of whole wheat bread toasted in the oven at 200° Fahrenheit (about 93°C) for thirty minutes also make excellent treats that your dog will love to chew on. Leftover pasta, such as spaghetti and penne, will surely set tails a-waggin'.

Unprocessed grains are whole grains that have not been preprepared. Instant oatmeal is not an unprocessed grain, but steel-cut oats are. Whole grains are full of nutrition and are essentially intact. While unprocessed organic grains, such as oats, barley, brown rice, millet, amaranth, and quinoa,

Recommended Cooking Time for Grains for Dogs

Grain (1 cup)	Water (cups)	Cooking Time
Amaranth	3½	35 minutes
Barley	4	70 minutes
Basmati rice	2¼	20 minutes
Brown rice	3	75 minutes
Buckwheat	2½	30 minutes
Couscous	1½	7 minutes
Millet	3½	40 minutes
Oatmeal	2–3	15 minutes
Oats (steel cut)	3½	60 minutes
Quinoa*	3½	30 minutes
Wheat berries	4½	120 minutes
Wheat (cracked)	2½	30 minutes

Cooking tips: Sprinkle grains into boiling water slowly so that the water stays actively boiling. Stir only enough to moisten the grains. Reduce heat to a low boil in a covered pot, and don't overstir while cooking to avoid mushy grains.

*Make sure that quinoa seeds are rinsed in cold water thoroughly before cooking to remove their naturally occurring bitter coating.

certainly contain important nutrients, a dog cannot easily digest such grains in raw form because carnivores have shorter digestive tracts than do herbivores.

Grains, when fed to a dog, should typically be cooked even longer than they are for human consumption and with more water. Brown rice, for instance, would ordinarily be cooked for forty-five minutes on the stove, using 2 cups of water to 1 cup of rice. However, when preparing brown rice for a dog, you should cook it for one hour and fifteen minutes, using more water. Soaking grains overnight is a way to cut down on cooking time the next day. Oatmeal soaked for about twelve hours may require no cooking whatsoever. Generally speaking, oatmeal is easier than brown rice for dogs to digest. Although oatmeal is the one grain that can simply be soaked overnight, I believe cooking makes it more digestible.

Grains intended for your dog can, if you wish, be cooked with a meat, chicken, or fish stock to add flavor. Grains and vegetables can be cooked together and added to a quality commercial kibble. The commercial dog food already has adequate protein, so there's no need to add more animal protein. Better yet, a stew containing grains, vegetables, and meat or poultry can be portioned out on a daily basis. If that's your preference, it's best to cook the grains first and then stir in lightly steamed or grated vegetables.

You also have the option to use prepared grain mixes, which are now being offered by a number of companies and can be purchased at a specialty pet store or ordered online. While each has its own unique ingredients, the mixes typically consist of a combination of some of the following: oat flakes, rye flakes, wheat germ, bulgur, sesame seeds, kamut flakes, spelt flakes, and oat straw. They also normally include veggies such as potatoes, alfalfa, peas, carrots, beets, squash, and broccoli plus healthy stuff like garlic, dandelion root, ginger, rosemary, parsley, and peppermint. All you need to do is add water and perhaps some protein to the mix.

Wheat Bran

Wheat bran is a good home remedy for both constipation and diarrhea. Bran is not irritating to the bowels and is easy to add to food. Add a spoonful to one of your dog's stew or casserole servings at mealtime.

Note: If you're using wheat bran for constipation, make sure that your dog also drinks a lot of water. Constipation is not very common in dogs. If your dog is chronically constipated, please take him to the veterinarian for a thorough examination.

Eggs and Milk Products

If your dog is the sort who rolls over to show appreciation for a favorite treat, he'll do backflips over eggs and cheese. Canines can receive many nutritional benefits from having these products, along with other dairy products, included in their diet.

Egg yolks, for instance, contain health-promoting fatty acids such as omega-3, a nutrient that is important for protecting the heart and is also good for the coat and skin. In addition, eggs contain high-quality protein that is also highly digestible.

Eggs can be fed to your dog cooked or raw. Unlike people, dogs are relatively impervious to the salmonella that raw eggs might contain. I would advise, though, if you feed your dog three or more eggs a day, that you cook some of them because raw egg whites can impede the absorption of biotin, an important vitamin.

Since a taste for eggshells is something that also tends to set dogs apart from humans, here's another suggestion. Boil the egg in its shell for two to three minutes, then mash up the entire egg, including the shell, and feed it to your dog. I like to eat egg-white omelets for breakfast, and I find myself with a lot of leftover egg yolks and shells. A bit of butter goes into the pan, and I add all of the shells after I lightly crush them. After quickly beating the yolks, I pour them on top of the shells and flip when the first side is done. After the concoction cools, I break it apart and my dogs have their morning crunchy egg-yolk snacks.

An omelet filled with some chopped parsley and veggies and topped with cheese can be an ideal dish for your dog, particularly as a way of sneaking vegetables into his diet. Dogs like eggs done any style, whether scrambled, poached, or hard-boiled.

Because dogs do not suffer from thickening and hardening of the arteries (arteriosclerosis), as some people do, and are not subject to high cholesterol, there's no need to worry about these

problems resulting from their consumption of eggs and dairy products. So you can relax and let your dog indulge in some of the foods that offer him benefit and enjoyment.

Various types of cheeses will set your dog's tail a-thumpin'. Favorites include Swiss cheese, cottage cheese, farmer's cheese, and ricotta cheese. None of these relatively bland cheeses should cause any sort of digestive disturbance. Unlike meat, which contains nitrogenous waste, which is hard on the kidneys, dairy products such as cottage cheese are excellent sources of protein and calcium. I also strongly recommend yogurt and kefir. Sold near the yogurt at supermarkets, kefir is a more liquid form of yogurt and is very tasty. Both are easy to digest and can help prevent diarrhea.

The beneficial organisms used to produce these cultured milk products are very healthy for the digestive tract. Make sure you buy yogurt that has these beneficial bacteria because the yogurts made from mixed cultures often do not have enough of them.

Milk powder is a concentrated source of protein, calcium, riboflavin, and other nutrients. When mixed with a cereal-based meal, milk powder can give your dog an inexpensive boost of protein.

Remember, dairy products can be excellent sources of protein and calcium. The protein in dairy is gentler on the kidneys than is meat protein, which, again, contains nitrogenous waste. Many commercial foods designed for dogs with kidney problems have dairy as their main source of protein.

Meat

Now that we've reviewed the variety of canine-friendly foods that you might never have considered feeding your dog, it's time to discuss what many people still consider the main course: meat.

To Cook or Not to Cook

One source of controversy when it comes to meat is the question of whether the so-called raw diet is actually better for your dog than the cooked kind favored by humans. As in most debates, there are arguments for both sides, but it boils down to what type of diet is best for your dog's particular situation. Most of the opinions I've heard have been subjective—that is, based on each dog owner's individual experience.

Many owners report that their dogs are thriving on raw diets. There are a variety of raw-food diet plans to guide dog owners, as well as data based on solid research and analysis of the most popular raw diets. One study, for instance, shows the calcium/phosphorus ratio and zinc content of raw-food diets to be inadequate. This is why supplementation is absolutely necessary. (See "Evaluation of Raw Food Diets for Dogs," by Lisa M. Freeman, DVM, PhD, DACVN, and Kathryn E. Michel, DVM, MS, DACVN. *Journal of American Veterinary Medical Association*, vol. 218, no. 5, March 1, 2001.)

First of all, it should be emphasized that dogs are generally better equipped to handle raw meat than are people. That is, their digestive tracts have better defenses against bacteria and parasites, such as *E. coli* and *Salmonella*, that would make us sick.

However, that's not necessarily the case with all dogs, particularly older ones whose digestive systems have likely slowed down and secrete fewer juices. That's why I would not recommend placing a senior dog who is used to cooked and processed food on a raw diet. The same goes for a dog with a weakened immune system. I would also be careful about feeding raw meat or poultry to any dog prone to digestive problems. If you're not sure about your dog's ability to resist such microorganisms, there are compromise measures you can take, such as lightly steaming the meat or soaking it in grapefruit seed extract, which may help deter pathogens.

Doggy Breath

It's not just bad teeth that can cause doggy breath. A little bit of yogurt each day can help improve bad breath due to poor digestion. Your dog's teeth and mouth should be checked if the problem persists.

Avoid the Microwave

Preparing your dog's food in a microwave is not something I recommend because microwave cooking destroys many important nutrients. Just two seconds of microwaving, for instance, can destroy all of the enzymes in grains and vegetables. Using plastic dishes in a microwave can also cause plastic molecules to end up in food.

That being said, a dog can benefit from eating meat in its uncooked state. Raw meat provides nutrients, such as essential fatty acids, that cooking destroys. There are stories of dogs making miraculous recoveries from serious health problems once raw meat was introduced into their diet. By contrast, I have heard of many dogs who have done very poorly on raw-food diets. Some of these dogs become painfully thin, with no muscle mass and poor-quality coats. These particular dogs look and feel much better when fed a cooked diet with grains or even a healthy kibble. Each individual dog has his own metabolism.

Years of study have brought me to conclude that a diet consisting solely of raw meat is far from ideal. *The China Study* provided evidence that a high dietary percentage of animal and dairy protein points toward increased cancer incidence. It is well documented that an acidic cellular environment (of which one of the causes is high levels of animal protein) is more prone to disease and cancer than is an alkaline one. Carbohydrates are needed for the brain, thyroid, and liver to function optimally. Vegetables are a live food source, providing enzymes and phytonutrients that prevent cancer and other diseases.

If raw meat is your preference, you can leave the fat on any uncooked meat you feed to your dog (a fat content of 20 to 30 percent is fine). Dogs do not suffer from such human problems as clogged arteries, high blood pressure, and high cholesterol and can actually benefit from saturated fat. Since fat turns into unhealthy grease when heated, however, it should be trimmed from meat before you cook it.

It's a good idea to freeze raw meat for fourteen days before you feed it to your dog. This amount of time in the freezer should kill any parasites encysted in the muscles and organs. Should you opt for cooking, you can do so by baking, boiling, or broiling after trimming the fat and perhaps adding organic olive oil as a fat source as well as grains, vegetables, and herbs.

Meats such as beef and lamb are good sources of protein, vitamins, and minerals, whether cooked or raw. Pork and rabbit meat, however, should always be cooked because of the danger of diseases such as trichinosis (caused by the parasite *Trichinella spiralis*) that can infect your dog. In addition, pork should be fed to dogs only in small amounts and should not be used as a dietary staple.

It may also be best to avoid venison in those areas such as the Rocky Mountains and upper Midwest, where deer have been known to suffer from a condition similar to mad cow disease. No amount of cooking or freezing will destroy the prion "proteins" that cause this disease. The dictionary defines a *prion* as an infectious particle of protein that, unlike a virus, contains no nucleic acid and is not destroyed by extreme heat or cold.

Poultry

Fowl fills protein requirements quite nicely, although chicken is preferred for dogs. It's second only to eggs, in fact, in its ability to be easily assimilated. Be careful not to feed your dog cooked chicken bones, however, since these can splinter and perforate the intestine. Exceptions to this rule are the back and neck bones, which consist of cartilage and are thus safe for your dog to chew and swallow.

Turkey is very high in an amino acid called tryptophan, a natural tranquilizer that has a calming and sedating effect. This is the reason why we tend to feel so sluggish and sleepy after a big holiday feast. During the holidays, I do see my share of dogs who have been "turkeyed out." Turkey can be added to stews or other items, including kibble. If available, game birds such as pheasant, duck, and quail can also be fed to dogs.

Organ Meats

Whatever you do, don't confuse *organ meats* with *organic meats*. By organic meats, we mean the kind that come from animals whose feed and environment were free of pesticides, hormones, antibiotics, steroids, and other toxic substances, residues of which are usually present in conventionally raised meat. I highly recommend organic meat and poultry, both for dogs and their meat-eating masters.

Organ meats, however, are those made from animal organs, such as the liver, kidneys, heart, and gizzard. These are often readily available from the grocer at a very reasonable cost. As a rule, however, organ meat should not be fed to your dog more than once or twice a week, and it should not make up the bulk of your pet's diet.

The source of the liver you choose to feed your dog is important because the liver contains more toxic hormones and drugs than any other organ meat. Remember, the liver is the organ that pulls toxins out of the body. Commercial chickens, for instance, are fed hormones and antibiotics and live in quarters sprayed with pesticides. All of these compounds are cleaned by and are harbored

Beware of Hazardous Wastes

Since studies have shown that *E. coli* and *Salmonella* can pass through your dog's digestive tract and wind up in the end product, you should be especially careful about disposing of waste from a dog who is being fed raw meat. You should also be aware of the risk of exposure to children who might be playing in your yard and be sure to scoop the poop as soon as possible.

in their livers. When your dog eats chicken livers, he is also eating the hormones, antibiotics, and pesticides that the chickens were exposed to.

I'd recommend organic chicken livers or liver from calves rather than cows. Full-grown cows, simply because they lived longer, had more exposure to poisons. Organ meat from sheep might also be preferable since sheep tend to have less exposure to toxic substances than do other commercial livestock. The only real reason I can think of for feeding a dog liver every day is if he's anemic, in which case I'd again recommend organic liver.

Fish

As a protein source for your dog, you can't do much better than fish—especially white fish, such as flounder and tilapia, and cold water fish, such as salmon, mackerel, and trout. The latter are also rich in omega-3 fatty acids.

But there are a number of caveats you've got to keep in mind, the first being that fish should never be fed to your dog raw. Your dog could fall prey to the parasites that raw flesh sometimes harbors. Second, make sure that all bones are removed because they can cause damage to and even puncture the intestinal wall. Third, while canned salmon and mackerel are fine for dogs, canned tuna is not, as it can decrease your dog's ability to utilize some fat-soluble vitamins. Remember, too, that tuna and swordfish are both very high in mercury. For that reason, the US government recommends that tuna and swordfish not be eaten by pregnant women or eaten more than once a week by children. Although there are no such advisories in regard to dogs, they can also do without the effects of mercury. I often opt for fresh farm-raised tilapia, which is relatively inexpensive, and canned salmon, which stores well and is handy in a pinch to make up a quick meal.

Nutritional Yeast

Nutritional yeast, also known as brewer's yeast, provides an excellent source of protein, B vitamins, and iron. On an ounce-for-ounce basis, brewer's yeast contains almost three times the protein of beef, although we do not consume brewer's yeast in such large quantities. For the most part, dogs love the taste of nutritional yeast, which has a meaty flavor and odor. It is available flaked or finely ground and can be added to just about any meal your dog eats. However, if your dog has either skin or digestive allergies, be careful about adding nutritional yeast to the food because it is highly allergenic.

Keeping Your Dog Well Oiled

There are many kinds of oil you can use in feeding your dog. The supermarket shelves are filled with many different types of oil.

Some are better for certain purposes than others, and some are healthier than others—the latter being olive, walnut, hazelnut, and coconut oil. Healthy oils provide monounsaturated fat and other healing fats. Because olive oil is readily available and is the least expensive of these, I highly recommend it for general use.

Olive Oil

For cooking for your dogs, I particularly recommend olive oil—more specifically, cold-pressed virgin olive oil. Olive oil has a high content of fatty acids and oxidative substances. It is very well tolerated by the stomach and helps maintain a good level of vitamin E.

Oils should be refrigerated after opening to keep them fresh and to prevent them from being degraded by heat or light. You can buy olive oil in a cardboard box; a plastic bag of oil is inside, attached to a tap. As the oil is used, the bag collapses, keeping air away from the oil. Boxes of olive oil will stay fresher for longer outside of the refrigerator. This works well because olive oil firms up when left in the refrigerator, although it will liquefy when exposed to room temperature.

Depending on his size and his coat condition, a dog can be given anywhere from a teaspoon to a tablespoon of olive oil each day on top of his food. It is wonderful for the coat. You can also cook his food with it. Ordinarily, the breakdown of other common oils during cooking creates ingredients that are not well digested. Because this isn't true of olive oil, it is the only oil you should use when cooking for your dog. I use loads of olive oil and rosemary in my dog's meals, and their coats shine. Dogs love olive oil in their food.

Coconut Oil

At one time, coconut oil was a significant part of the American diet. The food industry considered coconut oil to be the superior dietary oil for use in baking and food preparations. However, during World War II, when the Japanese occupied most of the South Pacific and the Philippines, supplies of coconut oil were cut off. Americans had to turn to alternative sources for cooking oils, and this is when many of the polyunsaturated oils entered the market.

Coconuts and their oil are classified as "functional foods" because they provide many health benefits beyond their excellent nutritional content. Coconut oil possesses healing properties far beyond that of any other dietary oil and is extensively used in traditional medicine among Asian and Pacific populations. It is used around the world to treat a wide variety of health problems, including abscesses, asthma, baldness, bronchitis, bruises, burns, colds, constipation, cough, dysentery, earache, fever, flu, gingivitis, gonorrhea, jaundice, kidney stones, skin infections, toothaches, tuberculosis, tumors, and more. Coconut palm is so highly valued by Pacific Islanders as a source of both food and medicine that they call it "the Tree of Life."

Modern science is confirming that coconut oil, in one form or another, can be used to kill viruses, bacteria, and yeast; protect against osteoporosis; relieve the symptoms of Crohn's disease and stomach ulcers; prevent tooth decay; support thyroid function; dissolve kidney stones; and prevent obesity.

Only recently has modern medical science unlocked the secrets to the coconut's amazing healing powers. Researchers have known for quite some time that the secret to health and weight loss associated with coconut oil is related to the length of the fatty acid chains contained in coconut oil. Coconut oil contains what are called medium-chain fatty acids. These medium-chain fatty acids are different from the common longer-chain fatty acids found in other plant-based vegetable oils. Vegetable oils are typically stored in the body as fat, whereas coconut oil is quickly burned in the body for energy. This is akin to adding kindling, rather than a big damp log, to a fireplace.

Coconut oil is nature's richest source of medium-chain fatty acids. These acids not only raise the body's metabolism, which leads to weight loss, but they also have special health-giving properties. The most predominant fatty acid chain found in coconut oil, for example, is lauric acid. Recent research has discovered the value of these lauric oils. Excepting a human mother's breast milk, coconut oil is nature's most abundant source of lauric acid and medium-chain fatty acids. The medium-chain fats in coconut oil are similar to fats in mother's milk, and both have been shown to have miraculous healing power. When lauric acid is consumed in the diet, through either human breast milk or coconut oil, it forms a monoglyceride called monolaurin, which has been shown to destroy several types of bacteria and viruses, as well as protozoa such as *Giardia*. Monolaurin is sold in tablet form in the United States, and I commonly use it to prevent or nip in the bud any flu or cold. Once word got out about how effective it was, I could not keep it on the shelf in my practice. Dogs love coconut oil on their food as a condiment. Its daily use results in a glowing coat with less

dandruff and odor. It also supports your dog's thyroid function and hones his metabolism. Easily found in health food stores, coconut oil should be kept in the refrigerator. Half a teaspoon a day for a medium-size dog is the average portion. A jar of coconut oil will last a long time.

Bones: The Bonus with a Caveat

Yes, it's OK for your dog to enjoy a bone or two. In fact, it's even desirable, just as long as it's the right kind of bone. The kinds of bones I'm talking about are marrow bones, such as the large femur or leg bones and knuckle bones from a cow, which are practically impossible to swallow or chip. Even so, you should make sure such a bone is big enough for your dog. A bone may be served raw, parboiled, or cooked (meaning baked, boiled, or broiled). It should always follow a meal, since it is too rich to be given to your dog on an empty stomach. The marrow may be a bit rich for some dogs, so you can remove at least some, if not all, of it at first—then, as your dog gets more accustomed to it, you can leave more in.

Boiling is the best way to prepare marrow bones. Keep them in boiling water for eight to ten minutes and then scoop out the marrow. To bake knuckle bones, put them in the oven on a baking tray at 300°F (149°C) for thirty minutes or so.

Chicken necks, because they are made from cartilage and will not splinter, can also be used as treats for medium-sized dogs or as chews for small dogs. Chicken necks are easy to locate at butcher shops or in the meat section of most supermarkets. You can either feed them raw or prepare them by broiling or baking in a preheated oven at 350°F (177°C) for fifteen to twenty minutes. After they cool, cut them into 1-inch pieces for small dogs or let your medium-sized dog chew on the whole neck. Cook up several at a time and freeze the extra ones for a later date.

Because a whole chicken neck is small for larger breeds, watch that a large dog does not swallow it whole. Like chicken necks, chicken backbones are made of cartilage rather than bone, are easy to digest, and will not splinter. Although chicken necks and backbones are usually OK when raw, they should not be given to a dog who has no experience with bones because he could conceivably swallow a chunk too big to exit the stomach.

The good news is that gnawing on a bone helps stimulate the gums and remove tartar from the teeth, acting as a substitute toothbrush of sorts. It's certainly preferable to dental surgery for your dog. In addition, it can enable a dog to exercise his jaw muscles.

However, the wrong kind of bone can result in a variety of problems—some merely inconvenient, such as getting pieces stuck between the teeth, while others are more serious, such as pieces lodging in the stomach or piercing the intestinal wall. The most dangerous bones are those that can splinter or be swallowed, such as cooked chicken and turkey bones and bones from steaks, cuts of lamb, veal, beef, and pork.

You have to watch that a bone doesn't get too small; if it does, exchange it for a new one. In addition, a dog who gets overly enthusiastic about a bone can sometimes chip a tooth, which is why a dog who's savoring his very first bone requires supervision. When your dog is chewing on his bones safely, relax and enjoy the fact that his teeth and gums will be healthier for it.

6. The Cure Is in the Cupboard

xotic is the word I think of in relation to the history of herbs and other spices: perilous ocean voyages, colorful cultures, secret maps delineating spice routes, danger, and excitement. Commerce in spices began more than 3,000 years ago. Prior to this, the ancient Egyptians recorded and cataloged their knowledge of herbs, and a Chinese emperor published a book, *The Great Native Herbal*. Many plants mentioned in that book are still used today in Chinese herbal preparations.

At first, Arab merchants controlled the trade routes to India in the Middle East and, therefore, the spice trade. Once sea routes were discovered, Egypt became a major commercial center for trading spices. Later, Venice monopolized the spice trade between the Middle East and Europe. Countries became very wealthy from trading in spices.

As Venice was demanding exorbitant prices, Portugal and Spain looked eastward for new routes and then began to search westward. On his first voyage, in 1492, Christopher Columbus was looking not for a new land but for a shorter ocean route to India to gain access to its spices. His expedition received the majority of its financial backing from spice traders. In commerce, spices were considered more valuable than gold.

The great value that was placed on obtaining herbs and spices is recorded in history. Each region had plants and herbs that were specific to that particular area and climate. Countries were motivated to discover and control new routes for spice trade because these herbs were precious. Spices were big business.

A large part of their value lay not in their uses in food preparation but in their medicinal uses. The phrase "the spice of life" can be taken literally. With few exceptions, the spices known today were used very early in human history and played important—sometimes magical—roles in medicine. Before the advent of industrially prepared medicines, herbal remedies were commonly prescribed. In this chapter, we will rediscover some of this ancient herbal lore and learn how to use these natural materials to improve our dogs' health.

A World of Herbal Medicine

Herbal medicine is probably as old as humanity itself; the discovery of many spices predates the founding of the earliest civilizations. The first humans learned about herbs by trial and error and passed that knowledge from one generation to the next.

Herbs and Spices

The term "spice" includes herbs, which are the fragrant leaves of herbaceous plants, many of which are native to particular temperate regions.

The ancient Arabs, Babylonians, Chinese, Greeks, Romans, Hebrews, and Persians were all familiar with the practice of herbal medicine. The Chinese developed a systematic methodology of prescribing herbal medicines. In their view, the body is a reflection of nature, filled with a life energy called *Qi* (pronounced "chi"). Illness is a sign that a person's flow of the Qi is out of balance. Healers use herbs to rebalance the Qi and return the person to health. Combinations of Chinese herbs are formulated to have a deep and powerful healing effect. In these formulations, herbs that complement each other are combined, resulting in a synergistic effect and more potent healing. It's a magnified version of the synergistic effects of the whole leaf or the whole plant. Chinese herbal combinations have a powerful ability to heal illness and deserve a great deal of recognition and respect.

India, too, developed a sophisticated knowledge of botanical medicine. The Indian system of Ayurvedic medicine is one of the most ancient and complete systems of holistic healing. This form of medicine recognizes that there are different metabolic types. A practitioner observes whether his or her patient has an excess or deficiency in a specific area and uses diet and herbs to restore balance.

European proponents of a system known as the *doctrine of signatures* believed that the configuration and structure of a plant could help them understand what problem that plant could be used for. According to the doctrine, plants with a yellow signature, such as dandelions, can treat liver conditions like jaundice, a condition in which the whites of the eyes and the skin become yellow due to liver failure. The leafy greens of the beet top with red veins are considered good for cleansing the blood. Hawthorn berries (*Crataegus*) are bright red and shaped like hearts, and they prove to be very helpful in heart conditions. Ginseng root resembles the trunk, arms, and legs of a man and therefore has been used as a tonic for the entire body. The leaves and the cross-section of the fruit of the Ginkgo biloba resemble a brain; this herb is used for memory loss.

Western herbal use stems from the ancient uses of medicinal plants in Europe. The herbs used by the Native Americans are also incorporated into Western herb lore. The Western approach tends to view the body as a system of organs and cells that must be kept in balance.

Each culture had its particular sacred and common herbs. Over time, just about all have been shared throughout the world. We can now go into a health food store and buy herbs that were considered more precious than gold hundreds of years ago.

In all forms of herbal practice, the restoration of balance and harmony in the body is the primary goal, for this balance is the key to maintaining and restoring health. The World Health Organization estimates that about 80 percent of the world's people now rely on herbs for health care.

The Necessity of Herbs

For many centuries, in all ancient cultures, healing herbs were simply a part of the daily diet. Turmeric, the main ingredient in Indian curry, contains a natural antioxidant and anti-inflammatory called *curcumin*, which helps relieve the pain of arthritis. One of the most valuable spices traded from ancient India was cinnamon, another common ingredient in Indian food. Today, cinnamon has been shown to help regulate blood sugar in diabetics, while caraway and fennel seeds—Indian spices as well—promote digestion.

Mediterranean cultures also routinely used healing herbs as spices in their food. Wild oregano and rosemary act as antiseptics. Rosemary also supports endocrine balance and, in our dogs, promotes a healthy coat.

Animals have instincts that draw them to graze on particular plants to mend their ills. In the spring, horses and sheep will eat certain herbs from the fields that kill intestinal parasites. Wildlife documentaries often show animals deliberately choosing certain plants to eat.

Your dog's body has a built-in system to maintain good health. This system works in a powerful, almost miraculous, way to heal your dog of disease and illness. It is more efficient and effective than any computer could design. This multifaceted system needs certain enzymes, minerals, and vitamins to do its job well. Our domesticated dogs need supplements because dogs are not a part of the wild food chain that would supply them with fresh food all of the time. Many dogs suffer from the same diseases as humans do, and they can benefit from herbs in their diet. Every body, human and canine alike, must have the fuel it needs for its systems to make repairs.

Our First Medicines

Herbs are really concentrated food sources. Since herbs are foods, the body recognizes their nutrients and utilizes them in ways that naturally promote health. An herb provides a multitude of nutrients that are balanced and easily absorbed. Today, we need herbs even more because the majority of our food sources are grown on depleted topsoil. To sustain a good crop, farmers have resorted to mass-produced agriculture, which employs fungicides, pesticides, and tons of fertilizer. This results in an "empty harvest." The produce on the supermarket shelves lacks the nutrients that the cells need to thrive. Herbs in the diet help replace and balance this (as does organic produce).

An Ancient Payment Plan

In ancient China, a doctor was paid when the patient was healthy. When the patient became ill, the patient stopped paying the fee, but the doctor was expected to spend his time and use his knowledge to return the patient to health. Imagine how this payment plan would change the practice of medicine in modern times!

Herbs contain usable forms of vitamins and minerals from nature. Herbal medicines help replenish the building blocks that a body needs in order to heal.

Partners in Health

Personal philosophy about the body determines whether a user chooses herbs or prescription drugs for healing. Those who choose herbs trust the body's innate intelligence to heal and regenerate, and they believe that herbs help the body by providing the missing ingredients needed to heal. Herbs are part of nature, and our bodies have long known how to utilize their gifts.

Herbs can help stimulate the immune system and adjust the balance of the body for good health. This is vastly different from how an antibiotic works. The antibiotic, which enters the bloodstream, kills off the bacteria in the body and leaves toxic debris behind. The end result of this therapy is a weakened immune system. Herbal medicine increases the immune system's ability, and, most important, the body itself becomes stronger and smarter. Herbs nourish the body and entice tissues to heal.

You may be familiar with the widespread use of an herb called echinacea, commonly used for nipping a cold or flu in the bud by giving a big boost to the immune system. It's important to understand the difference between how antibiotics and herbal medicine works.

The therapeutic effect of herbal medicine stems from its inherent ability to support the functions of the body so the body can more effectively correct the problem. Herbs are often touted for their use as drug alternatives. This is good, because when they are used instead of drugs, they heighten your or your dog's ability to heal. Of course, this also improves general health in the long run because a wiser body system is a better body system.

It is important to understand that herbs act as assistants. The body will use the nutrients it needs from them. Herbs should not be thought of as miracle drugs.

The Whole Pie, Not Just a Piece

Once the pharmaceutical company extracts and purifies what is considered the "active ingredient," they then own that singular product and are able to charge extraordinary prices for it. Often, the "active ingredient" in the drug now comes with a plethora of side effects. Have you ever been alarmed while listening to the side effects listed at the end of pharmaceutical drug commercials on the television?

Each herb has a unique combination of ingredients that work synergistically to produce their effect. Once the healthy cocktail of the herb is disassembled, each isolated ingredient is imbalanced. Without the other ingredients present, and in its altered state, it now causes side effects. The synergistic quality of the whole herb has been lost. Of course, pharmaceutical companies would not have any interest in the whole herb because they are unable to patent it and own it, and thus they cannot profit from it. Noticeably, pharmaceutical drugs do not appear to cure, as plenty of folks who continually renew their prescriptions month after month after month well know.

How Safe Are Herbs?

Of course, some herbs are highly poisonous. Socrates was made to drink a preparation of poison hemlock to end his life. However, when used intelligently for beneficial purposes, herbal preparations are very safe. In fact, most herbal preparations are actually much safer than pharmaceutical drugs. (Adverse drug reactions are the fourth leading cause of death in hospitalized patients in the United States.)

While pharmaceutical companies search for the active ingredient in an herbal plant, herbalists use the entire leaf, the root, or the whole plant. Side effects are rarely seen with herbal preparations, although too many herbs used at once can cause diarrhea in dogs. The herbs you will learn how to use in this chapter, however, are very safe. Herbs definitely have a pharmacological power, and we will be portraying only those herbs that can safely and easily be incorporated into your dog's diet.

Many herbal preparations are available from health food stores. Liquid extracts of the herbs are usually easy to administer to your pet. Try to find extracts that have the alcohol solvent removed because most dogs do not like the taste of alcohol. Herbs and herbal combinations also come in tablets, which can be hidden in tasty cheese or butter if you wish.

Purifying and Preventing

Research has shown that dogs do not particularly like the taste of salt. Yet they do appreciate the taste of many of our culinary herbs when these herbs are added to their cooked food (simply sprinkling them on dry kibble has never been a hit with my dogs). My husband and I make stews, casseroles, and puddings for our dogs, and, as I've mentioned, we routinely add rosemary and lots of olive oil. I credit my dogs' shining coats to these two ingredients. The rosemary makes their food smell so good, and, when added to the mix, it only makes it taste better.

Many of the herbs that you can purchase at grocery stores can be added to your dog's cooked meals. These herbs add a wonderful fragrance to home-cooked food and impart a special touch. They can also help ease physical symptoms and problems.

Both caraway and fennel seeds are digestive aids. They help eliminate flatulence and intestinal cramping. Fennel stimulates lactation as well. (Tip: Guinness and other dark beers also stimulate milk production. This tip has never failed to get results and raise some eyebrows when I suggest it!) Asparagus and parsley are both good for the urinary tract. Parsley also acts as a diuretic and as an aid in kidney inflammation. Sage has been credited with soothing skin conditions and acting as an antibacterial with oral infections.

Basil works on the lungs and is a decongestant, along with having an antiviral and antibacterial effect. Dill acts as an expectorant and is antibacterial. Oregano helps with respiratory problems. Tarragon is indicated in use against colitis, sciatica, and parasites. In general, most of these herbs are simply healthy and tasty and well deserve to be added to your dog's meals.

While we are on the subject of cures in the cupboard, we can go over some common household foods that may be useful. Cucumbers can be peeled and sliced, with one slice held on each eyelid to reduce eye inflammation. Green cabbage leaves are good to wrap around itchy areas on the skin, sometimes called hot spots. To do this, beat the cabbage leaf with a wooden meat mallet and then, when the juices are freed, wrap the leaf around the inflamed area. The cabbage will get warm— you'll be amazed—and the inflamed area will cool down. Witch hazel is made from the witch hazel

plant and is also good to spray or dab onto inflamed skin or feet. Applying a paste of baking soda mixed with water will also help soothe an irritated area.

The Herbal Garden

In the Middle Ages, almost every monastery had a physic garden, which contained the herbs that the community needed for cooking and healing. At that time, *physic* was defined as medicine or healing as an art or a profession. Nowadays, it means something that lifts the spirits or energizes. A healing herb (physic) garden can do both for you and your dogs.

I love working in my herb garden. When I run my hands gently along the plants and rejoice in their fragrance, it's a healthy feeling. Just the smell of the garden puts me in a better state of mind.

How exciting your herb garden will be! Working in your herb garden is a good excuse to get back in touch with nature while getting some fresh air. Your dog will love the time outdoors, too. You may want to place some sort of relaxing seating arrangement near the garden so that you can enjoy the fragrance during the summer months as you sit and sip a cup of herbal tea.

Fresh herbs have a much higher concentration of *phytochemicals* (compounds found in plants that are used by our bodies for nourishment when we eat the plants) than do dried herbs sitting in a jar on a supermarket shelf. When freshly picked, herbs are a joy to use in cooking. I find it extremely enjoyable to go outside in the summer and snip bits of fresh herbs to use in cooking.

It is also fun to dry garden herbs at the end of the season. Gather the herbs when the growing season comes to a close, when the herbs are in their prime and before they begin to fade. Hang small bunches of each herb upside down until dry. You'll then have dried herbs to make into teas and to add to your and your dog's meals during the winter months. You can also make potpourri and rinses and enjoy your bounty in a variety of other ways.

Using plants as medicine brings us back to an understanding of how we fit into the cycle of nature. It may surprise you to learn that some of the plants you may typically purchase for your perennial garden are medicinal plants. The coneflower, also called purple coneflower or echinacea, for example, is a common garden plant. It gives a powerful boost to the immune system and is commonly taken when a person feels the onset of a cold or flu. Another example of a common healing plant is hypericum, or Saint John's wort, a pale green plant that produces delicate yellow flowers. This plant can help with depression and has an antiviral property.

In this next section, we make it easy for you to plant a garden that will provide you with healing herbs throughout the growing season in a 4-foot-by-4-foot space. The seeds and plants are easy to obtain; I usually go for the plants. It's a group effort to run this garden because you maintain it and your dogs eat the herbs. Of course, you and your human family members can join in and enjoy these herbs yourselves.

The herbs that we discuss here have been used for centuries as natural cures and to help maintain good health. They are safe and easy to use, and they were often used in the diet as spices. As well as making the food taste better, they have healing powers. Fresh herbs are always the best to use, but use them sparingly in the food because they do provide a strong presence.

Many herbs return year after year. In very cold climates, a covering of hay or burlap may protect the more fragile ones. Some, such as chamomile, spread quickly, but they can usually be easily controlled.

The Question of Garlic

Garlic, a member of the lily family, enjoys worldwide recognition and use. Among the oldest cultivated plants, garlic has long been renowned for its ability to ward off disease. Five-thousand-year-old Sanskrit and Chinese medical manuscripts describe the benefits of garlic. Garlic was a valued staple for many ancient peoples, including the Egyptians, Babylonians, Greeks, and Romans. In fact, 15 pounds (6.8 kg) of garlic was the going price for a healthy male slave in Egypt. Today, garlic is grown all over the world. Although it has been primarily used as a flavoring for food, garlic is making a strong comeback as a potent natural remedy. Modern research has shown that garlic has antifungal, antibiotic, antiviral, antiparasitic, and anticancer effects.

Did you know?

The price of a slave in ancient Egypt was 15 pounds (about 7 kg) of garlic.

For as long as people have been using garlic, they have been feeding it to their animal companions. However, the safety of garlic for dogs has come into question. Knowledge is a powerful thing, but astute pet owners should gather all of the data before shunning this celebrated bulb.

Garlic is approved as a flavoring, spice, or seasoning for use in pet food, yet the US Food and Drug Administration (FDA) has garlic listed in its poisonous plant database. Studies suggest that when garlic is fed in *excessive quantities* (5 grams of whole garlic per kilogram of the dog's body weight), it may cause damage to the red blood cells of dogs.

So what's healthy and what's excessive? Where's the line drawn on *how much* garlic is healthy, because we know that garlic is super healthy for your dog? Considering the data presented in the study on the FDA website, this means the average Golden Retriever at 75 pounds (34 kg) would need to eat five full *heads* of garlic, or about seventy-five *cloves*, in a meal before there would be any adverse effect on the red blood cells. Similarly, a dog weighing a mere 12 pounds (5.44 kg) would need to eat ⅔ pound (30 g) of garlic, which is a bit less than a entire head of garlic, or about eight to ten cloves, to experience any adverse effects.

The case is made for garlic safety: do you know anyone who feeds dogs *that much* garlic in one meal? Furthermore, reported adverse affects from garlic add up to a total *non-event* over the past twenty-two years. The National Animal Supplement Council responsibly records both adverse events and serious adverse events resulting from the use of natural products. A *serious adverse event* is defined as: "An adverse event with a transient incapacitating effect (i.e., rendering the animal unable to function normally for a short period of time, such as with a seizure) or non-transient (i.e., permanent) health effect." Nine hundred million doses of garlic over a twenty-two-year time span resulted in only two serious adverse events, and these episodes could very well have been due not to garlic but to another ingredient in the mix. This proves beyond the shadow of a doubt that the risk of using garlic is so low that it's simply statistically insignificant. That, in a nutshell, is the whole truth about garlic.

So, what's the moral of the story? Garlic is good for our dogs, and moderation is the key to good health.

What *is* significant is all the positive research delineating the medicinal powers of garlic. Of all of garlic's reputed benefits, perhaps the best known is its use as a natural antibiotic, with reports

going back through history. In fact, Louis Pasteur proved that garlic was able to kill fungi and bacteria in 1858. Modern researchers have compared the effectiveness of garlic with that of antibiotics and have found that garlic has a broad-spectrum antibacterial effect. Additionally, bacteria don't seem to build up a resistance to garlic as they do to many antibiotics. Garlic's antifungal, antiviral, and antibacterial effects are well appreciated today due to the great increase in antibiotic-resistance bacteria. Garlic also increases general immune activity along with the activity of *killer cells*, cells that seek out and kill invading bacteria and cancer cells.

There's a secret to releasing the healing powers of garlic. *Allicin* is the most powerful medicinal compound derived from garlic, the one that provides the most important health benefits. Garlic itself does not contain allicin. Rather, garlic first has to go through a chemical process so that the allicin can be released. When garlic is crushed, an amino acid contained within it reacts with an enzyme, creating allicin. You must finely chop or crush a garlic clove then wait a few minutes to allow the chemical reaction to occur. Additionally, allicin is unstable when exposed to air and heat, so don't wait more than twenty minutes before you top your dog's meal with some healthy raw garlic. I can't help but think of the old-fashioned homemade Caesar salad, where raw garlic is crushed and placed in the mix just before serving. It's healthier for me than I previously thought!

While cooking garlic destroys allicin, other components in the cooked or powdered garlic continue to provide some beneficial health effects. Compounds in garlic act as antioxidants and help flush toxins out. If you cook meals for your dog, it's totally safe to add garlic as a flavoring and for improved health (unless you add seventy-five cloves to one meal!). Additionally, garlic has been fed to dogs in order to help prevent flea infestation. There are many products on the market containing garlic for this very purpose. When using garlic as a flea preventive, it's important to use a castile soap or a detergent-free shampoo. Dogs don't sweat as humans do, and the garlic "aroma" (which comes from the sulfur-containing compounds that account for most of its medicinal properties) mixes in with the oil produced by your dog's oil glands and comes out in the coat's natural oil. It takes several weeks for the garlic compounds to build up in the oil; a detergent shampoo removes the oil, and you're back to square one.

A host of studies provides evidence that the allicin in garlic works to inhibit cancer formation. With cancer being the number-one cause of death in dogs in the United States, let's all get going with garlic! Buy a garlic press or simply chop some garlic very finely and let it sit for about fifteen minutes. You can then mix it in with a tablespoon of cooked, cooled chopped beef or chicken and place it on top of your dog's meal. Voila!—a meal fit for a king, or a pharaoh!

Daily usage of garlic supports the body in ways that no herb does. It supports the digestive tract, helping support and revive those good bacteria in the gut, and wards off worms. It can be useful as well for the treatment of ringworm. Garlic also helps regulate blood sugar levels.

Garlic is best used fresh, and your dog will enjoy fresh garlic in his food. Garlic is also available in health food stores in tablets or capsules. Supermarkets carry powdered garlic, but this form has lost most of its "oomph." If using fresh garlic, half a clove for a small dog and one clove for a medium or large dog is just enough each day. You can give garlic to your dog whole or you may chop it up and mix the pieces into his food. If you cook for your dog, add garlic to your recipes; it will still be of benefit to his health. Garlic can be used as a flavoring in many of the recipes listed in this book.

Other Benefits from the Garden
Aloe Vera

For centuries, many cultures have used the aloe vera plant to treat burns and heal wounds. Aloe originated in tropical Africa, where it was used as an antidote for poison-arrow wounds. Historically, it was used by the peoples of Greece, Rome, China, and India.

Each leaf contains a gel-like substance that works toward rapid regeneration of tissue on wounds and burns. This gel appears to increase the rate of healing in the cellular matrix and decrease inflammation. It also contains antibiotic and coagulating agents. It is useful for treating fungal infections of the skin and can stop the itch of insect bites. Additionally, taking 1 to 2 tablespoons orally three times a day acts as a tonic for the intestinal tract.

Aloe plants can be easily found at the local nursery or garden center and require little care to maintain at home. Place a terra-cotta pot with an aloe vera plant on your window ledge and watch it grow. The gel from the plant is much more effective than the gel available at stores. The active ingredients remain active for less than three days after cutting off a leaf.

Fresh gel can be obtained by removing a leaf and splitting it. Apply the green-tinged, clear, jellylike inside of the split leaf to burns, wounds, fungal infections, and insect bites. If you cut a leaf and use part of it, the remaining parts of the leaf need to be stored in the refrigerator.

Calendula

The vivid colors of its flowers are reason enough to plant calendula. This herb also earns a spot in the garden for its medicinal properties, which were recognized as far back as ancient Roman times. This herb is a favorite among herbalists, and for good reason. It has an almost magical effect in healing wounds. Calendula has a more powerful ability to hinder bacteria than many antibiotics do, and it has the benefit of having an anti-inflammatory effect while it promotes new healthy cell growth. It also works against fungal infections. It is ideal for first aid treatment and works well as an antiseptic lotion.

In Europe, calendula flowers are common ingredients in ointments and creams used to treat cuts, mild burns, inflammations, sores, and bee stings. Calendula is a long-blooming, easy-to-grow annual that reaches 2 feet (30 cm) in height. The flowers range from 1½ to 4 inches (4 to 10 cm) across and range in color from buttery yellow to deep orange.

To understand calendula's healing power, consider the following anecdote. A friend brought her dog in to see me many years ago. The dog's left front leg had been

Calendula—An Ancient Herb

The common pot marigold, or *Calendula officinalis*, has been around since ancient times. *Calendula* refers to the herb's blooming schedule, for it would flower on the *calends*, or new moon, of every month. *Officinalis* refers to its "official" medicinal value.

run over by a gravel truck. All of the skin, muscle, and tendon on the lower front part of the leg had been sheared off. To make matters worse, gravel had been ground into the wound. It looked like the best possible scenario would involve skin grafting. My friend did not have the financial wherewithal to do much at all. We decided that I would remove the gravel and clean it up the wound. Every day, under my direction, she placed fresh bandages, well moistened with calendula, on the wound. By the end of the month, the entire wound had healed and the leg appeared normal. No grafting was necessary, and all of the fur grew back.

I have to admit that calendula is my favorite herb, for it can do so much. In addition to acting as an antifungal and antibacterial agent, it is excellent to place on the skin of itching dogs and can sometimes stop a hot spot in a jiff. For hot spots, use a strong infusion made from the leaves and apply it frequently to the area.

Calendula is widely available in salve and ointment form in health food stores. A liquid tincture is also available. A pad soaked in the infusion or diluted tincture can be applied to speed up the healing of wounds.

Calendula Infusion

When making your own calendula infusion, it is best to use the petals alone for a more effective product. Harvest the petals from early summer through late fall. The petals can also be dried and used in a tea later in the season. The flowers can be mixed into handmade soap or mixed with olive oil.

To make a tea, pour 1 cup of boiling water onto 1–2 tablespoons of the petals and steep for fifteen minutes. The tea can be taken internally for gastritis or mouth ulcers and gum disease. Externally, as a compress, it acts as an antiseptic and has a healing effect on the skin. It also greatly helps stop itching.

Chamomile

German and French varieties of chamomile are often available at garden stores. Chamomile has a calming effect. Add this herb to your dog's diet when he is at that nervous adolescent stage. It also helps ease the pain of teething when prepared as a tea and can promote sleep in elderly animals who pace around at night. In the latter case, the animal should take it just before bedtime.

Chamomile supports the digestive functions and the liver. It will help ease flatulence, dyspepsia, and irritable bowel problems and will settle the stomach. It can also boost the appetite. This herb helps cleanse the blood and supports pancreatic function.

A strong tea of chamomile can help heal skin rashes and soothe irritated skin; this is very useful for allergic, itchy dogs. It also increases the speed of wound healing and acts to reduce inflammation and swelling. You can add it to the diet and use it on the skin. Fresh chamomile is also an excellent insect repellent.

Chamomile can be harvested throughout the summer. Pick the flowers and leaves when they are free of dew. Dry the herb quickly so the flowers retain their rich pungent scent, but do not dry them at too high a temperature. One home-dried flower can give more flavor than a commercial chamomile tea bag.

Chamomile Recipe

Chopped bits of chamomile—1 to 3 teaspoons is plenty—may be added to home-cooked meals. The flowers and leaves are the best parts of the plants to use. To make a tea, pour 2 cups of boiling water onto 2 teaspoons of the dried or fresh leaves and flowers and let steep for ten minutes. For digestive problems, this tea can be given with or after meals.

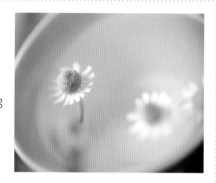

Your dog is not the only one who can benefit from chamomile tea. Enjoy a cup yourself and relax!

Cranberries

Cranberries are much more than a traditional food served during the holiday season. Recent studies prove cranberries' efficacy in treating urinary-tract infections. It has been known for a long time that cranberries acidify the urine. Bacteria cannot survive when the pH changes. But there is another way that cranberry fights urinary-tract infections. It contains a polysaccharide called *mannose*, which decreases the ability of the bacteria to adhere to the cells lining the urinary tract. The bacteria will adhere to the mannose from the cranberry rather than to the surface of the cells. These bacteria then get flushed out with the urine. Both cranberries and blueberries, which are in the same genus, prevent bacteria from adhering to the cells on the bladder wall.

Additionally, cranberries are excellent as a general health tonic, balancing the acid-base (pH) levels in the body. Many dogs eat far too much protein and grain, causing an increase in the body's acidity. Cranberry makes the body's environment a healthy alkaline one and the urine a healthier acid. Adding some stewed cranberries to a meal helps promote a healthier, more alkaline state. Fresh and frozen cranberries are four times as potent as cranberry juice cocktail, while cranberry juice concentrate is twenty-seven times as potent.

Dandelion

Rather than being troubled by all those dandelions on your lawn, use them to make a healthy tea infusion and detoxify your dog's liver. Dandelion is a somewhat recent addition to the field of herbal medicine, first appearing in Europe in the mid-fifteenth century. The earliest known mention of dandelion as medicine was in seventh-century China. The Chinese use the entire plant, whereas Western herbal medicine tends to use either the root or the leaf.

Dandelion is a powerful diuretic and is one of the best sources of potassium. Pharmaceutical diuretics drain potassium out of the body and deplete potassium reserves. The dandelion root works as a very effective diuretic, removing excess fluid from the body, and it replaces potassium lost in the process, serving as a wonderful example of how a complete herb works. Dandelion can be used for easing fluid retention, especially with heart problems.

Dandelion reduces congestion in the liver and can even help with jaundice. Both the roots and the leaves can be used for medicinal purposes. The leaves work as a digestive and liver tonic. The root is used as a cleansing tonic for gallstones, jaundice, constipation, and liver detoxification. Dandelion also increases gastric secretions to aid in digestion.

The nice thing about these herbs is that they can be used preventatively. Some chopped dandelion in a meal works to clean a relatively healthy liver and make it even healthier.

A few fresh leaves can be chopped and added to a tasty meal for your dog. They can taste bitter, so add them sparingly at first. Dandelion leaf juice can be made in a juicer, and a quarter of a teaspoon can be given three times a day for a medium-sized dog. The fresh juice is a more powerful diuretic than an infusion, which is prepared from dried leaves. A tincture can be purchased in liquid form in health food stores. A few drops given a few times a day can aid in removing excess fluid in dogs with heart conditions. Dandelion capsules and extracts also can be found in health food stores.

Do not use dandelions from lawns that have been sprayed with herbicides. That would counter our goal of healing the body. Unsprayed leaves can be harvested at any time during the growing season. The fresh leaves are often sold in supermarkets in the produce department. Commercially available dandelion is less bitter than what grows on your lawn.

More Dandelion Ideas

Place 2 to 3 tablespoons of dandelion leaves in 1 cup of water and bring to a boil. Simmer gently for fifteen minutes and let cool. Give a tablespoon of the liquid three times a day to a medium-sized dog. An infusion or tea can also be made by pouring hot water over the leaves and allowing the mixture to steep for five to thirty minutes.

Echinacea (Purple Coneflower)

The Native Americans used this herb to treat fevers, wounds, and even snakebites. It was commonly used by the Native Americans of the Great Plains region of North America for its powers of healing wounds and boosting the immune system.

Of course, the early settlers caught on and used echinacea for colds and infections. Later, a German researcher, Dr. Gerhard Madaus, brought some seeds over to Europe and conducted scientific research on the herb, which proved its immune-stimulating properties. Today, echinacea is the most important over-the-counter remedy in Germany.

Echinacea is the well-known herbal remedy that many start to take the minute they feel a cold coming on because it is effective against both bacterial and viral attacks. Many people grow the purple coneflower, from which echinacea comes, as a decorative plant in their gardens, completely unaware of its healing properties. You may very well have admired this common long-stemmed purple flower in a garden without knowing it was the source of the popular herb.

Echinacea Immune Booster

To boost the immune system, place 1–2 teaspoons of the root and one chopped flower in 2 cups of water and bring it slowly to a boil. Let this simmer for ten to fifteen minutes. A medium-sized dog can have 1 tablespoon per dose, given three times a day. Do not worry about adjusting for size.

The root is the most commonly used part of the plant for infections and inflammation. It can be especially helpful for recurring kidney and bladder infections.

While some people take echinacea all winter with the intent of warding off the flu, its best use is at the very start of a fever or infection. When my twin boys were babies and a fever or cold came on, I would go to my garden and pick one coneflower plant, root and all. After simmering both the root and flower for ten to fifteen minutes, I would cool it a little and add some honey. Each of the boys would drink a cup and go to sleep. When they awoke, their fevers would be gone.

Echinacea can also be used topically, as demonstrated in studies with guinea pigs that showed an increased rate of healing. An infusion made with the root can be applied to minor scrapes and cuts.

Some say the fresh plant is much more effective than the dried herb, and I would fully agree. That is why it is so nice to have it growing in your garden. Of course, echinacea comes in all forms in the health food store: liquid tinctures, tablets, and capsules.

Fennel

Fennel is a wonderful digestive aid and has been used for this purpose in Australia and Spain for hundreds of years. Fennel seeds, when taken after a meal, assist in digestion. The seeds have also been used for years to expel intestinal parasites. Tea made from fennel helps rid the body of toxins and helps cleanse the body's cells and tissues. The plant itself can be chopped finely and added to a home-cooked stew for your dog. The seeds can be made into a tea or added to the meal.

Fennel Tea

To make a tea, pour 2 cups of boiling water over 2 teaspoons of fennel seeds. Let steep for fifteen minutes, then add ¼–½ cup of the cooled mixture to your dog's meal. Refrigerate the leftover tea and use for future meals.

Lavender

The lavender plant is known for its relaxing and soothing effects on the spirit. An important use for lavender with dogs is for reducing the buildup of excess sebum, or skin oil, on the skin. Lavender works like a charm for some of those lovable yet greasy and smelly dogs. You see, bacteria begin to grow in the excess sebum, and the bacterial growth in a greasy coat is responsible for that musty old-shoe odor that some of our dogs seem to have.

A lavender rinse after a bath, or spraying some lavender tea on the coat, reduces the sebum, works to decrease the bacteria, and keeps that odor at bay. As an added benefit, it is an anti-inflammatory and analgesic, so it decreases itchiness as well. It is beneficial for skin irritations or wounds because it promotes tissue regeneration and speeds wound healing. As an added benefit, the delicate purple or white flowers are beautiful to look at and smell great!

Lavender Rinse

Add a ½ cup of chopped lavender to 4 cups of boiling water to make a rinse. Let it steep for thirty minutes and then strain and place in a clean jar or spray bottle. Refrigerate any that you will not use within five days. Rinse your dog with the tea after his bath, and use the spray bottle to keep him fresh in between.

Parsley

Parsley is a herb rich in minerals and is an aid to digestion. Its use in meals helps maintain a good pH level that your dog needs for disease prevention. It also freshens the breath, and we all know one or two dogs who could really use that! Parsley works to detoxify the body and is excellent for the urinary system—the kidneys and bladder. It works as a diuretic to remove water retention in the body and is a good addition to each meal for dogs with heart conditions and fluid retention. Parsley is easy to add routinely to each meal; a teaspoon or more can be finely chopped and added to home-cooked food. Parsley adds chlorophyll, which is essential to good health.

Rosemary

Rosemary originated in France and the United States. A small amount of fresh rosemary can go a long way. This herb has an absolutely beautiful aroma, and it is lovely to sit near a flowering plant in the summer months. It would be great to place a bench or a table and chairs next to your herb garden because the aroma in itself has a healing effect on the body and soul.

Rosemary, used topically, has an antifungal, antibacterial, and antiseptic effect. Inhaling the steam from a tea made of rosemary is good for sinus infections. Adding ¼ teaspoon of rosemary to 2 cups of home-cooked food is adequate for flavoring. This herb also helps digestion.

More Rosemary Ideas

Throw some bits of rosemary and lavender on your floor and vacuum them up as you clean. They will, as they sit in the bag, give off a pleasant scent as you vacuum.

Rosemary is excellent to add to a rinse for your dog's coat because it promotes hair growth and brings out the luster and color tones in the fur. Rosemary rinses are also great for dogs with flaking, dry skin.

To make a tea, pour 2 cups of water over 2 teaspoons of finely chopped rosemary. Let steep for fifteen minutes and use as a rinse for the coat.

Sage

Sage is another herb that has a wonderful healing fragrance. It can be used as an addition to the everyday diet by adding a ½ teaspoon of chopped fresh sage to a stew or casserole. It can also be used as a tea to rinse the mouth because of its healing effect on gingivitis. To make a tea, pour 2 cups of water over 2 teaspoons of chopped sage, let it steep for fifteen minutes, and refrigerate. You can even add some of the tea to your dog's water bowl and simply allow him to drink it. Start out with small amounts in the water and, if he likes it, gradually increase the amount of tea.

Sage works to strengthen the body in general and has the effect of balancing estrogen levels. It would be good to add this herb to the food of a spayed female who is experiencing urinary leakage while sleeping.

Thyme

Myths, legends, and rhymes all seem to have been inspired by the humble thyme plant. The ancient Egyptians used it when embalming their dead. Even today, the oil of thyme, *thymol*, is an ingredient in embalming fluids. Thyme evolved in the Mediterranean, but it has spread all over the world and is used by many diverse cultures in their cuisine. Thyme comes in an amazing diversity of flavors, ranging from oregano to cinnamon, lemon, and caraway. Common thyme or any other cooking thyme is excellent to use to flavor stews and casseroles for your dog.

Thyme has antibacterial effects. Thyme oil and its components have been suggested as food additives to more naturally extend the lives of processed foods. Vapor that contains the essential oil has been shown to inhibit airborne fungus and bacteria. Thyme has proven antispasmodic and respiratory effects and has historically been used for bronchitis, as an expectorant, and for laryngitis.

You can dry thyme by hanging it upside down for a week. The leaves can be saved for seasoning your dog's food, or you can mix them with dried rose petals for a lovely potpourri.

Additions to the Recipes

Garlic, chamomile, fennel, parsley, rosemary, and sage can all be added to the home-cooked recipes that you make for your dog. Add from ¼ to ½ teaspoon to a full recipe because the fresh herbs go a long way. If the herbs are dried, double the amount. Parsley can be added more freely, as it is bland and very good for maintaining the body's proper pH level. Garlic can be either fresh and chopped or cooked with the meal. Fresh chopped garlic would be added in a smaller amount than cooked garlic. One clove of raw garlic per day is plenty for a medium or large dog; give a small dog no more than half a clove per day.

Herbs for Healthy Skin

The herbs from your garden can be used in healing rinses that can be applied after a bath or sprayed on to keep the skin and coat healthy and to reduce irritation or inflammation. Herbs can be used as treats in your own bath, too.

Allergy Rinse or Spray

2 tablespoons chopped lavender leaves
2 tablespoons chopped echinacea root
2 tablespoons chopped chamomile flowers and leaves
2 tablespoons chopped calendula (marigold) florets (flower petals)

Place all of these ingredients in an enamel or glass pot. Pour 8 cups of boiling water over them. Let the pot sit on the stove on very low heat for fifteen minutes. Remove from heat and let the mix sit and cool for another forty-five minutes. Strain and use as rinse, or fill a spray bottle with the mixture and apply as desired.

The type of coat your dog has will decide the best way to use this rinse. Dobermans, Dalmatians, Dachshunds, and other dogs with short coats would benefit from both the after-bath rinse and regular "freshen-ups" with the spray. Collies, Newfoundlands, and other long-coated dogs would benefit from the after-bath rinse and the spraying of any problem areas after the fur has been parted.

Oil-Controlling Rinse and Spray

1 whole sliced lemon, including skin and rind
4 tablespoons coarsely chopped lavender leaves
1 tablespoon chopped calendula

Pour 6 cups of water onto all ingredients in an enamel or glass pot. Bring to a boil and simmer for twenty minutes. Remove from heat and allow the entire mixture to sit overnight. Strain the liquid and store in a clean glass jar in the refrigerator. Use as a rinse after shampooing, and spray on your dog's coat as needed.

Healthy Shiny Fur Rinse and Spray

2 tablespoons chopped rosemary leaves
2 tablespoons chopped lavender leaves
2 tablespoons apple cider vinegar

Place ingredients in glass or enamel pot and add 6 cups of water. Bring to a boil, and, after a brisk boil is achieved, immediately remove from heat. Let the mixture sit for a few hours and then strain and store. Use as a rinse after shampooing.

Herbal Indulgences for You

A Relaxing Bath

Finally, for you—an after-gardening treat. Take ½ cup of chopped lavender leaves and flowers and add to 2 cups of boiling water. Let this boil for a minute or so. Remove from heat and let sit for twenty minutes. When ready, strain the lavender from the water. You will be using the scented water in your bath.

While the lavender is steeping, make yourself a relaxing tea. Pour 1 cup of boiling water onto 1 tablespoon of chamomile flowers. Let this sit for three to five minutes, strain, and add a scented honey to sweeten.

Put on some of your favorite music. Pour the lavender water into the bath you have drawn, place your chamomile tea on the side of the tub, and relax in the scented warmth, sipping your tea and listening to your music. You deserve it!

An Invigorating Bath

For a more invigorating bath, use rosemary in place of lavender. Take 1 cup of chopped rosemary leaves and add 2 cups of boiling water. Let this boil for about a minute and remove from heat. Allow to steep for twenty minutes.

While the rosemary is steeping, make yourself an invigorating tea. Put 1 teaspoon of grated fresh ginger, the juice of a lemon, and 1 teaspoon of honey into a mug or cup. Fill the cup with boiling water.

Put on your favorite music. Strain the rosemary from the water and pour the scented water into the bath you have drawn. Place your tea on the side of the tub and relax in the water. This combination will invigorate you.

7. The Benefits of "Supplemental" Health Insurance

We all want our dogs to live long, healthy, and happy lives. This quest causes responsible dog owners to research nutrition in pet foods and pet supplements. Nowadays, there are so many choices and so many claims, it's tough to know what's the best product to buy for your dog. There's just no reason to purchase a supplement that does not contain everything your dog needs to stay healthy and vibrant. Selecting the right supplement can bring your dog's quality of life from *nutrition holes* to *whole nutrition.*

Vitamins and minerals are the tools that maintain and clean out your dog's cells. Your dog's body has trillions of cells in it that make up tissues, which in turn make organs. A cell can be compared to a microscopic house that's always under construction. Vitamins and minerals are the hammers, nails, mops, and detergent that keep the house clean and in working order. They run all of the metabolic processes and are the tools the cells use to maintain good health every single day. The tools available to your dog need to be complete and balanced, so you need to know how to compare labels and understand ingredients so that you can purchase a quality supplement. Vitamins and minerals work together, and, if they're not balanced, containing all of the ingredients needed to get the job done, the job simply doesn't get done.

It's pretty common for dog owners to purchase individual ingredient supplements, such as glucosamine, trying to prevent a particular problem in the future. They think of it as health insurance for the future. Yet, how would your house stay in good shape if you had only a hammer but no nails, a mop but no cleaning products? I think we can agree it would be an awfully messy house. When caretakers purchase only a few items and not a complete supplement, it's tantamount to short-changing the cells out of their life support.

In a perfect world, dogs and their human friends would get all the nutrients needed for a healthy life from a balanced diet. Although no supplements can take the place of real food (no, you can't just pop a pill every day and be healthy), the truth is that our food supply just ain't what it used

DR. LINUS PAULING, who discovered vitamin C, is one of the few people to have been awarded two Nobel Prizes. He received the second one for his work on ending the testing of nuclear weapons.

to be. Studies done in both the United States and Britain have revealed how commercially grown foods have been stripped of much of their nutrient value, apparently due to commercial farming techniques that rely on agricultural chemicals and nitrogen-based fertilizers. These practices have largely succeeded in wearing out the soil used for crop cultivation. The depleted soil lacks nutrients, both vitamins and minerals, for plants to pull in. The result is produce that might look beautiful and be in bountiful supply but contains fewer vitamins and minerals than the fruits and vegetables grown years ago.

That's why I strongly recommend that your dog be given a complete and balanced supplement. A good supplement gives your dog the help he or she needs to stay healthier. I like to think of them, in fact, as a form of "supplemental" health insurance for pets, providing whatever extra nutrients your dog needs to maintain optimal health. Supplements become especially important at this time of shrinking food value.

The government's recommended daily allowance of vitamins and minerals has established what is needed to stay alive rather than stay healthy and live for a long time. Most of us who take supplements do so in order to stay much healthier and significantly extend our life span. We routinely supplement significantly above the government's recommended daily allowance (RDA). We should do the same for our dogs because they're in the same situation that we're in. We're all exposed to far too many toxins and far too much empty processed food.

Vitamin C, for example, provides us with just one telling example. The more we learn about the benefits of vitamin C, the more we have come to appreciate how important it is in helping keep us alive and well. Besides boosting the immune system, this vital antioxidant plays a powerful role in detoxification, ridding the body of all of sorts of heavy metals, pesticides, and toxins to which we're exposed daily. Vitamin C helps keep our metabolic innards clean and sparkly, prevents disease, dramatically boosts our immune systems, and retards the aging of cells. Those are enormous health benefits from one easy-to-obtain and inexpensive vitamin.

The amount of daily vitamin C that our government recommends is not even near what researchers, such as Nobel Prize winner Dr. Linus Pauling, recommended. Rather, it is based on the amount necessary to prevent scurvy, a condition that long ago afflicted sailors who ate *absolutely no vegetables or fruits for months*, even years, while out at sea. After it was discovered that the tiniest bit of vitamin C would remedy their situation, sailors would pack some limes and lemons for their journeys—which is how British sailors came to be called "limeys."

The government's RDA of vitamin C is not designed to provide you with enough of this essential vitamin to prevent chronic diseases, to keep your body from degenerating, to ensure optimal functioning of your enzyme pathways and biochemical processes, or to enable you to feel healthy and alert. It is also not enough to allow your system and organs to meet the increased demands placed on them by environmental toxins and stress or to promote longevity.

Although vitamin C can benefit your dog in the same ways it benefits you, dogs are typically given none. Because, unlike humans, dogs manufacture their own vitamin C, it is assumed that the amount their bodies make is sufficient to meet their requirements. Yet that assumption, too, is obsolete, since dogs are routinely exposed to a toxic overload that Mother Nature never anticipated from such factors as dog food, lawn treatments, flea and tick prevention, heartworm medication, heavy metals in the diet, and excessive vaccinations.

If you've ever wondered why it is that a "health care crisis" should exist in a nation as supposedly advanced and affluent as the United States, perhaps one answer can be found in the US Food and Nutrition Board's recommended daily allowances for various nutrients. These, as it turns out, have been set at levels only high enough to prevent the clinical manifestations of certain known deficiency diseases, such as the aforementioned scurvy. The same holds true regarding the vitamin and mineral intake of your pets, who have also become the victims of nutritional standards and requirements that are grossly inadequate. This is borne out by the fact that many dogs' coats and energy levels improve whenever even a poor-quality vitamin supplement is administered to them. Even though the owners may think their dogs are receiving good basic nutrition from the food they consume, what they're really getting is a diet so deficient that the addition of anything with some extra nutrient value is enough to make a noticeable difference.

If we hope to keep both ourselves and our pets healthy and free from disease, we simply can't rely on government "subsistence requirements" for vitamins and minerals. Nothing better exemplifies the old adage about an ounce of prevention being worth a pound of cure than the need for such nutrients above and beyond what we derive from dietary sources. But before you buy the first vitamin supplement you see, you should be aware that all vitamin supplements are not created equal.

Most people don't know this, but ingredients can vary in their activity level. As one example, cranberry can have activity levels ranging from 10 to 70 percent, but the milligrams noted on the bottle will be the same. If one bottle states 50 mg of cranberry, and that ingredient is 70 percent active, it's that much better than a bottle with 50 mg of 10-percent-active cranberry. The rub is that you can't discern this from a label. The best way to get around this is to purchase from a reputable company and/or look at the difference the product makes in your pet's health and vitality. Ingredients from poor sources have poor efficacy.

Unfortunately, many vitamins prepared especially for dogs are similar in quality to commercial dog food. Typical of this kind of supplement is the poor-quality vitamin mixture thrown together with ingredients such as powdered bonemeal, oyster shell, and nutritional yeast. Calcium that can be readily utilized comes either in a water-soluble form produced by plant cells or is attached to amino acid chains that can be absorbed by the gut. Organic plant-cell calcium is readily available, yet canine vitamin manufacturers and

Ten Tips on How to Choose a Good Supplement

1. Your dog should like the vitamins, either as a treat or as an addition to his food. If you need to chase your pet around to get him to take his daily supplement, both you and your pet will quickly tire of it.

2. The milligrams (mg) and international units (IU) of each vitamin should be listed on the label. This information tells you exactly what's in the vitamin so that you can compare apples to apples.

3. The vitamins must be complete. If a few inexpensive components are placed in a flavored mix, your pet is getting flavor and not a complete formula.

4. The vitamins must be correctly balanced. Vitamins work together, and if they are not balanced with all the ingredients needed to get the job done, the job simply doesn't get done.

5. The sources should be bioavailable. The source of the ingredient and the quality of the ingredient are also important factors because the vitamins and minerals need to be in a form that your dog can assimilate and absorb. For example, calcium is best absorbed from an acidic formulation or as a water-soluble calcium from leafy greens.

6. The flavorings and formula should be designed with respect to the high incidence of allergies in pets. Brewer's yeast, the inexpensive by-product from brewing beer, is often used as a flavoring. It does have some nutritional value, but it is one of the top foods to which dogs are allergic.

7. The vitamins in the supplement should incorporate the most recent research in their formulation. For example, vitamin D_3 has been found to be deficient in many people and is important for mood and immune function.

8. The vitamin should be designed with the biochemical needs of canines in mind.

9. A vitamin with ingredients that help decrease the toxic load of today's environment would further promote your pet's health.

10. The quality and the sources of the ingredients, human-grade being the best, must be considered.

even many veterinarians have continued to recommend bonemeal as a healthy additive. To be properly utilized, calcium also needs supportive minerals in specific proportions, as well as an acid medium—important details that are neglected by many dog-vitamin manufacturers. Furthermore, bonemeal contains toxic cadmium and lead, which are readily absorbed by your dog, while the calcium is not.

Many vitamin and mineral supplements intended for human consumption are also poorly formulated and derived from inferior sources. Then, too, many vitamin and mineral supplements, both those intended for pets and those intended for humans, contain binders, fillers, sugars, coloring agents, and flavorings that can compromise their ability to be utilized. Even something as simple as an enteric coating can prevent an elderly person or an individual with decreased digestive enzymes from being able to properly assimilate the ingredients. Such ingredients may even cause allergic reactions in sensitive individuals, human and dog alike.

With supplements, you usually get what you pay for. While higher cost doesn't necessarily ensure better-quality vitamins, the very cheap ones are most likely to be of inferior quality. A good rule of thumb is to go with a known, established, reliable vitamin company whose products are found in health food stores. The vitamins that I often find in commercial pharmacies do not impress me.

The best forms of vitamins are those that are closest to what occurs in nature. They may be available from alternative medicine practitioners, as well as in health food stores. And, unlike in the old days when different vitamins and minerals had to be taken at different times of the day to avoid conflicting characteristics, many excellent multivitamin supplements today contain all of the necessary vitamins and minerals in forms that will not interfere with each other. They are also from good sources and are easily absorbed. Now, that's real progress!

There are more inherent problems with the quality of doggy vitamins because most vitamins don't taste very good. Therefore, the average vitamin or mineral supplement for dogs contains large quantities of nutritional yeast and powdered liver to improve its flavor and small, if not negligible, quantities of vitamins and minerals. It is also a fact that pet vitamins usually come from poor-quality sources and preparations.

The best pet vitamins are composed of high-grade human-quality ingredients prepared in ways that are extremely appealing to your pets. I have designed a vitamin and mineral supplement that fills all of the nutritional needs of dogs. This human-grade supplement, which includes superfoods, is then microencapsulated in order to hide all of the unpleasant tastes of certain vitamins and minerals. Importantly, the microencapsulation process protects the ingredients from degrading. This thin coating protects the power of these vitamins and minerals because the air cannot reach them and degrade them. You may have experienced your B vitamins beginning to smell rather sour and rank a short time after opening the bottle. That's because they begin to oxidize and degrade the minute they are exposed to air.

Deserving Pets

For many years, I used human vitamins in my practice because I appreciated the quality of the ingredients and how complete and carefully balanced they were. Sometimes my clients would hide them in cream cheese for their dogs. The problem was always the small dogs for whom the pills were too big and the veteran expert pill-finders and pill-spitters. Finally, in frustration, I decided to create a pet supplement of my own, one that utilized human-quality vitamins and minerals and was palatable for even the fussiest pooch. In Deserving Pets supplements, I used a brand new nanotechnology to create a supplement that contained all human-grade balanced and complete vitamins and minerals and superfoods in a special formulation that tasted like a treat. To my delight, the formulation created even more dramatic changes than the high-quality human vitamins. That proved my hypothesis: our dogs were getting so much disease and cancer because their bodies were not getting all the tools they needed. Every dog deserves a healthy and long life, and this is why supplementation is so very important. You can learn more about Deserving Pets at www.deservingpets.com.

Prebiotics

Lots of folks supplement their pets with extra *probiotics* for digestion. Yet, many pet owners do not know that *prebiotics* are even more effective than probiotics in building up the good gut bacteria. Prebiotics are foods that allow specific healthy changes in both the composition and activity within the community of friendly bacteria. Prebiotics also confer benefits to the host's well-being and health. Prebiotics are nondigestible food ingredients that promote the growth and proliferation of "good" gut bacteria. In other words, prebiotics are the health food for probiotics. Prebiotics have been shown to work faster than probiotics in restoring healthy intestinal balance by giving the friendly bacteria the materials that they need to grow and multiply. Kale, dandelion greens, and chard are good examples of healthy prebiotics that can be added to any dog's diet.

When a first-rate supplement is given, the difference in coat, energy level, and health is readily apparent. Before we move on to some vitamins basics, let's talk a bit about superfoods.

Your mother knew what she was talking about when she told you to eat lots of fruits and veggies. Research on cancer and nutrition in people has shown that eating fruits and vegetables—especially "superfoods" containing phytochemicals—significantly decreases the risk of cancer. Since phytochemicals work at a cellular level, and canine cells function exactly the same way as human cells, these foods can also help prevent cancer, along with many other diseases, in your dog.

What Phytochemicals Do

Phytochemicals are organic compounds found in plants. They both prevent and fight disease and have been used as medicines for millennia. When Hippocrates said "Let food be thy medicine," he probably never imagined his words would be proved in scientific laboratories 2,000 years later!

The potential for cancer begins when carcinogens damage and alter the DNA in cells. This modification remains latent—in other words, it just sits there and does not form cancer—until some very specific conditions promote the creation of a cancer cell. The tumor-suppressor gene p53 then plays a vital role in the body's struggle to stave off cancer by creating proteins that instruct the cell to either halt the growth cycle or self-destruct. If this fails, the immune system still has its opportunity to step in to eliminate cancer growth. Research has proved that proper nutritional support with phytochemicals helps prevent a cell from developing into a malignant cancerous growth.

You see, certain phytochemicals help cells dump carcinogens and toxins much more quickly, thus decreasing the potential for permanent DNA damage. Other phytochemicals support more general cell functions while some give the immune system a super boost.

Kale: The dark vibrant greens in kale leaves are rich in carotenoids, which travel throughout your dog's body (and yours!) to scavenge free radicals and clean up "after the party." Kale is also rich in elements that reduce the risk of cancer. Scientists have found that certain specific compounds found in kale—glucosinolates, cysteine sulfoxides, and sulforaphane—clear carcinogenic substances more quickly. One study found that when dogs with cancerous tumors were fed kale, their tumors were smaller and grew more slowly than those in dogs not fed kale.

Nutrition by Color

To ensure that your pet receives a wide range of phytonutrients, include foods from each color group. For example:

Orange	Pumpkin, carrots
Green	Kale, parsley, broccoli, alfalfa, dandelion
Red	Cranberries, apples
Red-Purple	Beets
Blue	Blueberries

Broccoli: Compounds found in broccoli act as modulators to the immune response system with antiviral, antibacterial, and anticancer activity. Broccoli has a sizable quantity of sulforaphane that boosts your dog's protective cellular enzymes and flushes out the toxins that cause cancer. A study at the University of Michigan found that sulforaphane targets specific cancer cells that aid in tumor growth.

Berries: All berries are packed with phytochemicals that work to prevent cancer. Red raspberries, blueberries, and strawberries contain ellagic acid, found to slow and sometimes stop tumor growth. Black raspberries contain very high concentrations of phytochemicals called *anthocyanins*; these slow malignant cell growth and curtail the blood supply to cancerous tumors.

Increasing phytonutrients in our pet's bodies helps them fight off disease, making them healthier and more resilient to illness. It's become a known scientific fact that eating these superfoods results in better health and disease prevention.

Superfoods have so many health benefits, and more are being discovered every year. I firmly believe in being proactive. In the long run, the end product will be healthier dogs.

The ABCs of Vitamins

What exactly is a vitamin? My dictionary defines a vitamin as "any of a group of organic substances *essential* in small quantities to normal metabolism and health, found in natural foodstuffs and also produced synthetically." Both your body and your dog's body work via "metabolic pathways" consisting of all of the tiny biochemical processes that, when taken together, make the whole body work efficiently and, more importantly, stay healthy and free of disease. Vitamins and minerals keep your dog's many and varied metabolic pathways working well and keep that fuzzy body functioning at optimal health.

You and your dog share the need for a variety of vitamins because different vitamins perform different functions to help promote overall health and keep the body's metabolism running smoothly. The basic vitamins include A, B, C, D, and E.

Vitamin A

Vitamin A is good for your dog's coat and eyes, possibly reducing the risk of cataracts. It has antioxidant properties and helps protect against cancer. It is naturally assimilated from animal fats, egg yolks, and cod-liver oil.

A word of caution: a fat-soluble vitamin A supplement should never be taken at doses exceeding 20,000 IU daily. You need not worry about that, however, with water-soluble vitamin A, as you cannot overdose on a water-soluble supplement. And while it's true that extremely high doses can be damaging to the liver if taken over long periods of time, taking that high a dose on a day-to-day basis is hard to do and needn't be of concern to most of us.

Carotenes are the water-soluble and therefore safer forms of vitamin A. Beta-carotene consists of a double molecule of the vitamin that is converted into vitamin A in your dog's body, which then eliminates whatever part the dog can't use. It is found naturally in orange and yellow fruits and vegetables. Interestingly, while dogs can convert beta-carotene into vitamin A, cats can't.

The B Vitamins

These vitamins, which include B_1, B_2, B_3, B_5, B_6, B_{12}, folic acid, biotin, choline, inositol, and PABA, are often referred to as stress vitamins because they help alleviate the effects of stress on the body. Each has specific functions, such as aiding in red blood cell production and muscle functions and helping support the nervous and cardiovascular systems. B vitamins are found naturally in grains, leafy vegetables, beans, molasses, yeast, eggs, fish, and organ meats.

B_{12}, to cite just one example, is utilized by cells to promote growth and remove waste products and, in your dog, to help build new nerve, muscle, intestinal, and immune-system tissue. But the B_{12} content in even healthy food may no longer be adequate for this purpose, having decreased dramatically in the past forty to fifty years (in some foods, by as much as 80 to 100 percent). This is largely due to the decrease of certain B_{12}-producing bacteria in soil, water, and food and the fact that the soil has also been depleted of the cobalt needed to synthesize this important vitamin.

Because of this decrease in naturally occurring B vitamins, it is especially important to include them in any supplements for dogs. Because they dissolve easily in water, excessive amounts are excreted from the body—something that may be indicated by your dog's urine being more yellow than normal. Some people might call this expensive urine, but I call it good insurance. In any event, your dog will not be harmed by taking too many B vitamins.

Vitamin C

Perhaps the best known of antioxidants, vitamin C can help ward off or shorten the duration of viral infections, reduce the risk of cancer, and protect the cells of your dog's body from toxic overload. It can also help alleviate canine allergies, chronic infections, and periodontal disease. Like the B vitamins, it is water soluble and nontoxic, with any excessive amounts being eliminated from the body (although a higher-than-recommended dose can bring on diarrhea). Dietary sources of vitamin C include many fresh fruits and vegetables, and supplements are often derived from rose hips.

Extra vitamin C is especially important for a dog suffering from an illness because then the body requires more of it than usual to help fight off infection, and it becomes rapidly depleted. Even an allergy can quickly use up your dog's supply of vitamin C. That's why dogs who suffer from allergies should get higher doses of vitamin C every day to help their condition. Repeatedly dosing a dog with this vitamin during a viral infection can do a great deal to bolster the animal's immune system, increasing both interferon and white blood cell function. Giving your dog extra vitamin C before and after a vaccination can help prevent vaccine-related reactions and health problems.

Some canine health foods use vitamin C as a preservative, but not in any amount remotely sufficient for supplementation. I recommend a buffered vitamin C ascorbate that uses calcium, potassium, sodium, magnesium, or zinc as a buffering agent. (The Ester-C form of the vitamin is generally less palatable and more expensive.) The dose you should administer depends on the dog's size and general state of health. Small dogs can receive up to 250 mg once or twice a day, while larger dogs can be given up to 1,000 mg a day. To keep the dog from developing diarrhea, doses should be increased gradually.

Vitamin D

Found in fish, egg yolks, and butter, as well as in cod-liver oil, vitamin D is commonly referred to as "the sunshine vitamin" because exposure to sunlight's ultraviolet-B radiation tends to produce it in a human's body. Considered a hormone—a unique distinction in the vitamin world—it helps your dog's body absorb and use calcium, supports the immune system, and is necessary for good bone development. There is also evidence that vitamin D might help reduce the risk of colon, breast, ovarian, and prostate cancers, research having shown that statistics for such cancers are lower among people who live in sunnier climes. It is also a fat-soluble vitamin that is stored. You want to find the D_3 form of this vitamin for your dog because the other forms are not as effective. Milk is fortified with the D_2 form, and this is not the form of vitamin D you want to get in the liver.

Vitamin D

Optimal vitamin D serum blood levels dramatically reduce the risk of most serious diseases in people by an astonishing 50 to 80 percent. These diseases include osteoporosis, osteomalacia, hypertension, and a range of cancers from breast and colon to deadly melanoma skin cancers. Vitamin D boosts the immune system dramatically in humans and dogs.

Vitamin E

This vitamin, which occurs naturally in grains, nut oils, and leafy dark green vegetables, is an important antioxidant that protects your dog's cells and tissues. From 100 to 200 mg of vitamin E can be given daily, depending on the size of your dog, and it can be combined with vitamin C for extra effect. Vitamin E gets an important boost from vitamin C, creating a powerful one-two preemptive punch against cancer and other chronic diseases. The natural form of vitamin E works far better than the less expensive synthetic versions.

Mineral Wealth for Your Dog's Health

In addition to serving as a buffer for acids in the body, minerals carry the electrical charges that implement nerve impulses. Since there are almost twenty minerals that aid and promote your dog's metabolic processes, we cover here only the most important ones, the *macrominerals*.

Calcium

Although you may be aware of calcium's importance in strengthening bones and teeth, you may not know of its crucial role in nerve conduction and the muscles' ability to contract. It can be derived from foods such as dairy products, salmon, sardines, and tofu.

Calcium, however, requires an acidic environment to be properly assimilated and is not absorbed well from bonemeal or powdered oyster-shell supplements. Far more useful is calcium that is derived from plant cells or that has been attached to an amino acid chain. Your dog's body will absorb the organic forms of calcium (calcium citrate, calcium lactate, and calcium orotate) far better than it will the calcium carbonate found in oyster shells.

To work effectively, calcium supplements should also contain the mineral magnesium and vitamin D, both important in promoting calcium utilization. Calcium and magnesium should be served up in a 2:1 ratio.

Magnesium

A calming antistress mineral, magnesium, along with calcium, has a sedative effect that is helpful in promoting restful sleep. It is also needed by the nervous system to regulate nerve impulses and conduction. Food sources include nuts, legumes, whole grains, dark green vegetables, meats, seafood, and dairy products.

Taste Test

Supplements that are concentrated for maximum effect and added to food in a way that does not sufficiently disguise their taste tend to defeat their own purpose. It really doesn't matter how beneficial a vitamin and mineral supplement is if you can't get your dog to eat it.

Potassium

Potassium, which is found in a variety of foods, including turkey, chicken, salmon, cod, sardines, many fruits and vegetables, and dairy products, helps regulate the acid-alkaline balance in your dog's body. It is contained within cells and can be depleted in cases of severe vomiting and diarrhea, causing your dog to become weak and lethargic.

Selenium

Selenium, a trace mineral, is essential to good health but is required in only small amounts. Selenium is incorporated into proteins to make selenoproteins, important antioxidant enzymes. The antioxidant properties of selenoproteins help prevent cellular damage from free radicals, which in turn helps prevent the development of chronic diseases such as cancer and heart disease. Other selenoproteins help regulate thyroid function and play a role in the immune system.

This mineral is very important for your dog's thyroid and heart health and for cancer prevention. The selenite form, called sodium selenite, is the only form that has been shown to directly stop tumor growth. The more common form, selenomethionine, is stored in the liver, whereas sodium selenite goes directly to the tumor.

Plant foods are the major dietary sources of selenium in most countries. Selenium also can be found in eggs, some meats, seafood, and grains or in plants grown in selenium-rich soil.

Antioxidants: Preventing Internal Wear and Tear

That our pets' bodies (as well as our own) are exposed to so many more environmental toxins and pollutants these days—just think of all those pesticides and herbicides on grass that dogs are likely to come in contact with—greatly increases their need for regular antioxidants as part of a supplement program.

Antioxidants can deter aging by helping your dog's cells and organs resist damage. It's a form of preventing internal wear and tear. Antioxidants are substances that inhibit the destructive effects of oxidation. Oxidation is a process that begins when toxic substances in our environment cause damage to cells, producing unstable molecules with loose electrons known as "free radicals." These seek to bind themselves to other molecules. A buildup of free radicals helps speed the effects of aging by altering cellular DNA codes and damaging internal organs and skin. Antioxidants work by neutralizing the free radicals before they can cause any damage. You can think of them as a "first line of defense" against an increasingly toxic world and a tool to help your dog stay younger longer.

Some of our familiar vitamins and minerals are powerful antioxidants, including vitamins A, C, and E and the mineral selenium. Vitamin C is an antioxidant with additional benefits because it helps to prevent disease, dramatically boost the immune system, and retard the aging of cells.

Antioxidants

Vitamins	Minerals	Herbs	Nutrients
Vitamin C	Zinc	Ginkgo	SOD
Vitamin E	Selenium	Hawthorn	Bromelain
Vitamin A		Rosemary	Pycnogenol
Beta carotene			Quercetin

While vitamin C can benefit your dog in the same manner it benefits you, dogs are typically given none. Buffered vitamin C powder for human use is fine for dogs, and you can give from 100 to 1000 mg a day depending on the size of your dog. It's a vitamin, so the dose is not absolute, but start low and work your way up to allow your dog to acclimate and avoid loose stool.

Another antioxidant you may be familiar with is coenzyme Q_{10}. It plays a key role in the production of ATP (adenosine-5'-triphospate), the energy molecule of the body. There are two commercially available forms of what is commonly known as CoQ_{10}. The most commonly available one uses ubiquinone. However, research in both animals and humans has shown that the ubiquinol form is much better absorbed and thus better utilized. CoQ_{10} is a very important antioxidant for dogs with liver or heart problems because these two organs need high levels of ATP to function. CoQ_{10} in ubiquinol form is available online and at health food stores. A dog should get from 10 to 50 mg a day.

The antioxidant glutathione is produced naturally in the liver via the synthesis of certain amino acids. Diminished glutathione levels have always been associated with aging; however, in today's toxic world, low levels of glutathione are no longer reserved for the aged. Glutathione is a master antioxidant that enhances healthy growth and promotes immune activity. It protects against cancer and aids in the synthesis and repair of DNA. In addition, it is a powerful liver detoxifier and enables the elimination of unwanted toxins and heavy metals. It also supports kidney function. The rub is that glutathione cannot be given as an oral supplement because it is simply digested before it can do any good. The good news is that certain foods, such as eggs, trigger the production of glutathione. Asparagus has high glutathione levels whereas broccoli, brussel sprouts, cauliflower, apples, and watermelon also help raise glutathione levels. Just like kids, dogs don't always eat their vegetables, so here are some tips to encourage your fussy four-legged kids. Most dogs like broccoli stems, apple slices, and watermelon. Also, a medley of the veggies mentioned can be chopped and mixed into a healthy antioxidant omelet. Another option is a preventive supplement that can be powdered on your dog's food every day, making it easy to give your dog everything he needs.

Feeding your dog healthy organic vegetables, fruits, and free-range eggs and creating variety in his diet will ensure that he gets health-supporting, antiaging antioxidants every day. No matter how you choose to provide your dog with what he needs for a healthier life, both you and your dog will reap the benefit of more quality time together.

One can think of the dog's body as a sort of biological or inner terrain, akin to soil. Good soil will grow strong, healthy plants; poor, depleted, or undernourished soil will not. That's the way it is with your dog's biological terrain, and that's why I have placed such emphasis on good diet and good supplements in this book. The terrain of every body needs healthy supplies to fuel the healing machine. When properly applied, holistic medicine can be a powerful healer, providing gentle but effective guidance that can remedy many diseases and health problems without the side effects so often associated with more conventional forms of medicine.

Your dog's body has a system of multifaceted built-in protective mechanisms designed to ward off pathogens and other internal threats and to repair any damage. Unfortunately, although the immune system works in powerful, even miraculous, ways to promote healing, it is often unwittingly sabotaged by a lack of support. Not only does poor-quality nutrition frequently deprive the immune system of the vitamins, minerals, and enzymes it needs to perform at peak capacity, but the reliance on drugs, often reflecting our lack of trust in the body's remarkable capabilities, also tends to weaken it.

When your dog's body is given the software needed to run its systems and the guidance needed to correct the "programming errors" that cause disease, it moves rapidly to heal itself. There are many holistic modalities and techniques available, but they all have the same common denominator in that they greatly increase the body's ability to heal and cure *itself*. It's that simple. Holistic health works with the nature of healing.

Part II

The Nature of Health

8. Rediscovering the Natural Path

Brilliant discoveries over the span of many millennia afforded humankind numerous workable approaches to healing. For instance, as far back as 6,000 years ago, the Egyptians were using herbs to heal infections and treat disease. Acupuncture has been practiced in the Far East for 5,000 years. But depending on the place and period in which they were practiced, the various styles of healing might have been considered either fashionable or treacherous.

Nostradamus, the famous French physician and astrologer, practiced medicine in the sixteenth century. He began treating plague victims with a new and unusual medicine—ground rose hips. Rose hips happen to have a high vitamin C content, but vitamin C was yet undiscovered in the Middle Ages. Nostradamus read books banned by the Church, and, from them and his own experience, he learned how to use natural products to successfully cure diseases. This very success put his life in danger, however, for curing a disease known to be fatal put one in league with the devil. Only his close relationship with Catherine de Medici, the Queen of France, kept him safe. Catherine's son, King Charles IX of France, appointed Nostradamus as his court physician in 1560.

Healing in America has traveled a varied path. The ways and methods for healing have changed greatly over the centuries as herbs and homeopathic remedies gave way to pharmaceutical drugs and aggressive treatment of disease symptoms rather than a more naturalistic approach. Then, toward the end of the twentieth century, people began to realize that so-called conventional medicine was creating as many problems as it claimed to fix. People once again sought medicines grown by nature rather than manufactured by man and looked to other cultures and times for treatment options.

Holistic Therapies and the Body's Wisdom

Today, terms such as *conventional, holistic, alternative, homeopathic, allopathic,* and *complementary* abound when reading about, writing about, or discussing medicine. *Conventional* clearly refers to the use of surgery and pharmaceutical drugs. By contrast, *holistic* is used almost too broadly, for it portrays a range of approaches from sophisticated and learned modes of healing such as acupuncture and homeopathy to simpler methods such as eating organic foods, exercising, and getting massages. In its most basic sense, *holistic* means choosing to work with the body's innate intelligence to promote balance, strength, and restoration. Sometimes that simply means choosing a healthier diet and taking daily vitamins. Sometimes it means the approach that an owner takes in

Treating the Whole

Holistic medicine describes a system of diagnostics and treatments for the whole patient, not just a patient's particular disease.

an effort to save his beloved dog from a deadly disease such as cancer or kidney failure.

Alternative means not using the conventional approach of surgery and drugs. Ironically, although pharmacological drugs are dubbed *conventional medicine*, medical practices such as homeopathy, acupuncture, and herbs were around long before these drugs were and are employed widely in many parts of the world.

Homeopathy refers to a method of healing in which very small amounts of substances that have no side effects are given to create a cure. At the very popular advent of homeopathy, most of the medical schools were homeopathic, thus the term *allopathic* was coined to refer to treatment that differed from the popular and common homeopathic protocols.

My favorite word, by far, is *complementary*. I hope we have approached a time in history when this term can fully describe the nature of medicine. *Complementary* means that the wonderful medley of styles of healing, both new and ancient, can be used together to treat people. There is a time and place for each and every one of them.

The ability to combine the best options from different healing disciplines is known as *integrative health care* and *complementary medicine*. Although the holistic aspect of this is commonly referred to as *alternative medicine*, I believe that both treatment and prevention of disease should begin with holistic care and that the so-called conventional techniques should be used as alternative methods. This approach is often difficult to implement, however, because many of my clients come to me in desperation, after all else has failed. That's when things get tricky. It becomes my job to balance the holistic with the conventional in an already compromised and drug-dependent dog. If the owner had opted for holistic treatment when the dog's problem first developed, it might never have turned into a monster illness.

All holistic therapies work synergistically. Of course, pharmaceutical drugs may be needed on occasion. A critically ill patient may need them to stabilize him, after which holistic products are quickly brought into play. I still find it amazing how much holistic therapies can do to alleviate illness. There is just so much available in the holistic realm, with more surfacing all the time. I see holistic medicine as a vast rain forest teeming with green healing plant life. By contrast, conventional medicine is a tiny weed-filled lot in a crowded city. That tiny lot offers you steroids, antibiotics, and a few more things. The rain forest offers a vast array of holistic options, with more and more incredible holistic products becoming available all the time.

In deciding what approach to use on my canine patients, I have never excluded any option that I thought would help them obtain better health. I like to think of all of these techniques as composing a literal body of knowledge about how to heal disease. While some are time honored and others relatively recent discoveries, all utilize the inborn knowledge within the body and work with that innate intelligence to create good health.

I use pharmacological drugs when I deem it necessary, and I have saved lives with them. If symptoms such as an erratic heartbeat or high blood sugar call for it, the correct drug should be used to help the sick individual compensate. Conventional medicine has come up with some impressive techniques and technologies for detecting and diagnosing disease.

Pharmaceutical drugs work differently than holistic products, however. Pharmaceutical drugs typically alleviate symptoms; they rarely cure. At best, they buy time while the body heals. Taking an analgesic for a headache kills the pain while the body works to heal itself. Someone suffering from migraine headaches truly appreciates the relief, but the drug does not correct the actual problem. In all too many cases, the illness becomes chronic because the real source of the problem has not been found and corrected.

In fact, treating only the symptoms can curtail the body's ability to completely heal. When a dog injures a knee, the pain forces him to rest it. When we give our dog a pain-killing anti-inflammatory drug, his knee will feel better, and he will run on that knee and injure it further when instead he should be resting it. The dog's owner thinks that things are just fine because the dog is running around and is not in pain. The consequence, however, may be expensive knee surgery. In addition, both steroids and nonsteroidal anti-inflammatory drugs (NSAIDs) have been irrefutably proved to retard healing.

Natural medications promote healing, so the pain is relieved as the joint heals. Allowing the body to heal at its own pace is the best insurance against chronic disease. The holistic approach assumes that the body is intelligent and that symptoms occur for a reason. This is not to say that an illness or disease should be left untreated or that you can assume your dog will just heal on his own. Rather, holistic treatments can be powerful tools that complement and enforce the body's innate ability to rebalance and restore itself, thus allowing the body to overcome the disease or injury. Too many of us have forgotten that the body's inherent wisdom, along with a little help from some holistic friends, can recreate true health.

Typically, many patients with chronic problems refill their pharmaceutical prescriptions over and over again, month after month. Patients depend on their medications, and this is very good for the pharmaceutical companies' bottom line. Dispensing a pill that would actually cure your high blood pressure or arthritis would be very bad for business.

As already mentioned, holistic medical treatments can be used together and can be used along with conventional medical treatments and drugs. Often, I see animals with such severe diseases that they may need some of both. Sometimes, they are already on conventional drugs and cannot be taken off them until we can get the holistic modalities working.

If you are fixing a house that has structural damage, you'll need to put new beams in place to hold up the roof before you remove the old, faulty beams. In the same manner, it's necessary to get a dog's body back working on its own steam before removing the crutches provided by pharmaceuticals. This requires a good working knowledge of the healing capabilities of various holistic options and their synergistic effects—how they interact with each other and with whatever conventional medication the animal is receiving. Just as important is the knowledge of how our dogs' bodies change in response to different therapies.

There is an innate wisdom always at work within our bodies and those of our dogs. Without any conscious thought, the cells work at a furious pace toward order and health. They are well acquainted with the actions necessary to continue in their pursuit of life. For thousands of years, humankind has worked to support the inherent objectives of these cells, augmenting and supporting their ability to heal.

Pharmaceutical drugs, while they have their most definite place, cannot compete with thousands of years of documented natural supportive methods of healing. These age-old discoveries are even more important now because they are needed desperately to help our dogs and us deal with all of the toxins in our environment. In many situations, pharmaceutical drugs should be sought if natural therapies, taken in a timely fashion, fail, and when truly necessary. In this scenario, conventional drugs become the "alternative medicine."

In this chapter, you'll get a primer in each of the techniques that holistic medicine uses to root out the underlying causes of many chronic health problems rather than simply addressing the symptoms. As I've said, I like to think of these techniques as a literal "body of knowledge"—that is to say, the body's innate knowledge about self-healing, with the role of holistic medicine being to reawaken the body from a drug-induced slumber. Holistic methods give that "spark of life" more fuel to generate energy and heal while they also balance.

Acupuncture: The Needlework That Restores

The Chinese have practiced the holistic technique of acupuncture for more than 5,000 years. The procedure, which involves inserting very fine needles into specific points on the body to relieve pain and treat disease, was part of a remarkably sophisticated and accurate science of healing developed in ancient China. The principles of Chinese medicine, for instance, which were published in the period from 400 to 200 BC, included a discussion of how the heart controlled blood flow through the body, something accepted by Western medicine when William Harvey made the same "discovery" 2,000 years later.

The practice of acupuncture, in fact, predates the production of metals, the original needles having been made of stone and fish bones. But it wasn't until 1972, when President Richard M. Nixon paid his historic visit to China, that interest in this ancient art of using needles to treat pain and disease arose in the United States. It came about serendipitously, in fact, when *New York Times* reporter James Reston required an emergency appendectomy while covering the American table tennis team's trip to China that preceded the Nixon visit and subsequently wrote about how acupuncture had been used to relieve his pain.

A particular acupuncture method is employed in China that enables the patient to have surgery without medical anesthesia. The patient may be awake for the surgery because the acupuncture procedure handles any physical pain. As a result, the president's personal physician became interested in observing the procedure. By the following year, acupuncture had been declared an experimental medical procedure by the American Medical Association's Council on Scientific Affairs.

Acupuncture's popularity extended to animals as well, having been used on animals in China for nearly as long as it has been in existence. Today, veterinary acupuncture is recognized as a legitimate medical treatment by the American Veterinary Medical Association. Extensive certification courses are available for veterinarians. And while the idea of inserting needles into certain points on an animal's body to induce healing may still sound far-fetched to some skeptics, its results have often proved to be remarkable, even in treating conditions that appeared hopeless.

Acupuncture has shown to be effective in alleviating a whole range of metabolic, traumatic, arthritic, and neurological problems, including infections, immune disorders, heart problems, arthritis, liver disorders, kidney failure, hip dysplasia, anemia, paralysis, back problems, gastrointestinal problems, and asthma. It also has no side effects because it does not involve introducing anything toxic into the body. Veterinary acupuncture is a healing science that deals with the individual animal as a living, energetic being, rather than simply as a catalog of signs and symptoms.

Why Being Punctured Spells Relief

Acupuncture points lie along *meridians*—series of interconnecting channels through which the body's energy flow is conducted. The flow and balance of the energy that runs the body is referred to as *Qi* (pronounced "chi") in Chinese medicine and is directly influenced by the positioning of the needles so as to promote deep healing.

Modern medicine has come up with a couple of explanations for this phenomenon. The neurophysiological theory holds that the stimulation produced by the needles results in the release of hormones and neurotransmitters, such as serotonin. These chemicals, along with the body's natural opiates, endorphins, and enkephalins, are always found in larger amounts directly after an acupuncture treatment. Their release probably accounts for the euphoric feeling that subjects appear to experience. This includes my canine patients, who usually

The Story of Max the Dachshund

Before introducing you to some new ways of helping and healing your dog, allow me to tell you a real-life story to help put this all together. This short story is about a short dog named Max, a Dachshund.

As is true for many Dachshunds, Max had back trouble. He had a very long back and very short legs. And he liked to jump. While playing with his brother, Max got bumped, and he yelped. One of his discs bulged out, putting pressure on the large nerve that forms the spinal cord.

After Max hurt his back, his owner took him to her local veterinarian, who gave Max steroids (prednisolone) to relieve the pain and swelling. Strict crate rest for a month was also recommended. Max would seem to feel better for a while, but the problem would return. Then his back legs became paralyzed, and he could not urinate on his own. His veterinarian discussed expensive back surgery but said that it was probably too late for that to help. Fortunately for Max, he still had some feeling in the tips of his back toes, but just a little.

Max had a bulging disc in his back. The pressure from the swollen disc had destroyed some of the nerve tissue in his spine, which is why he couldn't walk. He had been taking steroids because they suppress the inflammation in the spine, helping keep the nerve tissue from becoming even more damaged. Although this is the usual conventional treatment for this kind of problem, the symptoms are suppressed and the real cause of the problem is not addressed. For Max, steroids were necessary, and they helped keep the swelling down until Max could be treated holistically.

A dog's back is like a suspension bridge between his hips and his head. While our spine is a vertical pole, a dog's spine runs parallel to the ground. Imagine placing a dozen dominoes side by side so they make a long column. Now push on each end and watch where it gives. The dominoes toward the middle begin to bulge out. When the pressure between the top and bottom of a dog's spinal column is uneven, the vertebrae (segments of the backbone) can become misaligned. This puts pressure on the discs, which form cushions between the vertebrae. Max's back is extra long and prone to problems. It's just the way Dachshunds are put together. Other breeds with long backs, such as the Basset Hound, Petit Basset Griffon Vendéen, and Welsh Corgi, can also be prone to back problems.

pull their owners into my clinic after a few such treatments and who seem to find the therapy genuinely relaxing and enjoyable.

Another hypothesis is the bioelectric theory, which suggests that electrical currents run along the body's nerve pathways and that stimulating these currents has an impact on the system as a whole. To better understand such an effect, imagine that your dog's body contains an electrical current that runs into each organ and system. Visualize each of these as a separate room of a house that is lit by electricity. Now imagine that some of these rooms are only dimly lit due to a poor electrical connection. As a result, the immune system can't do as good a job of cleaning these particular rooms as it does in the rest of

Max's owner brought him to see me, and I began treating him. First, I used a special laser on the affected area to relieve pain and inflammation. Next, I carefully injected some homeopathic remedies into acupuncture points near the injury. As a result, Max's muscle spasms decreased. The muscles on either side of his back had gone into spasms in an attempt to protect his spine, and this had only made his pain worse. Now these muscles were more relaxed, and I was able to adjust his back with a spinal adjustment. I gently moved his vertebrae back into the correct position. Max already looked brighter and more relieved. I carefully placed acupuncture needles along the sides of his spine; I also placed four more tiny needles in some special points on his legs. This relieves blockages and reinstates the harmonious flow of energy along the spine.

Max went home with Chinese herbs and homeopathic remedies, which work to keep any swelling to a minimum, alleviate pain, and promote rapid healing. He returned for his follow-up spinal adjustments and acupuncture treatments. With each treatment, the mobility and strength in his hind legs improved. Control of his bladder returned, and Max can now urinate on his own. As Max improved, the remedies were changed to those that help rebuild the nerves that lead to his bladder and hind legs. Finally, Max received nutritional supplements to strengthen his spine.

If Max had contracted a bladder infection during his course of treatment, I would have put him on antibiotics or a Chinese herbal preparation because, considering his condition, they would have been necessary. His systems had been weakened by the painful illness and the use of steroids, and I would not want the infection to spread. I would also have dispensed cranberry. The antibiotics would have been dispensed with probiotics (friendly bacteria) and followed with holistic preparations to prevent any further bladder infections.

Max is running and playing again. His brother is still bumping him, and Max still likes to jump. But now his owner practices preventive holistic health care. Every few months, she brings Max into my clinic for a checkup. We give him acupuncture and a spinal adjustment. Max loves this treatment. As far as he is concerned, it's his day at the spa!

the house. However, once the electrical system is repaired, rewired, and balanced, and the dirt is more easily visible, the system can come in and make a clean sweep of the areas in question. Acupuncture harmonizes the electrical circuits running through your dog's body so its healing mechanisms can function the way they are supposed to.

Certain misconceptions can make dog owners apprehensive about having their pets undergo acupuncture. They worry about the pain that the needles may cause, but they are surprised to see how fine the needles are (a reporter who once visited my clinic had expected them to be the size of knitting needles!) and to learn that inserting them involves very little, if any, discomfort. The

The practice of acupuncture is based on both the natural and scientific aspects of healing. In China, acupuncture is sometimes referred to as the "poor man's medicine" because it is so inexpensive to administer.

actual treatments last from ten to twenty minutes after the needles are in place and can be performed in a variety of ways. The most commonly used method of stimulating acupuncture points involves simply leaving the needles in place and allowing them to do their work.

Variations on the Therapy

There are variations on acupuncture therapy and how it is administered. These variations include electroacupuncture, aquapuncture, moxibustion, laser acupuncture, acupressure, and gold bead implants.

Electroacupuncture: Needles are attached to an electrical acupuncture device that stimulates the points more aggressively with a small amount of current. This method is most often employed on dogs suffering from paralysis or back problems.

Aquapuncture: This involves injecting an aqueous solution, which may contain B vitamins or a special injectable homeopathic preparation, into the acupuncture points. This method demonstrates how holistic therapies can be combined for maximum effect.

Moxibustion: Specific herbs are burned on the acupuncture points. These herbs, through the smoke, penetrate the skin and serve to relax the area being treated. Moxibustion is an especially good technique to use on a dog whose muscles are stiff and rigid, as occurs with arthritis.

Laser acupuncture: When performed with many of the newer lasers, this treatment can prove to be very deep-acting and beneficial.

Acupressure: This involves the manual massaging and stimulating of acupressure points. No needles are inserted; rather, a gentle pressure is applied to the acupuncture points.

Gold bead implants: This method effects a more prolonged stimulation of the acupuncture points by implanting them with various metals. In my practice, I commonly use solid gold beads, inserting them into the acupuncture points while the dog is under sedation or anesthesia. This is a procedure that's easy to perform, effective, and very safe. I commonly use this technique to treat young dogs suffering from hip dysplasia. Many young dogs have come to me with such severe hip problems that their veterinarians had recommended either hip-replacement surgery or euthanasia. These same dogs are now running and playing.

Acupuncture's Fountain of Youth

In whatever form it takes, acupuncture can be especially helpful in reinvigorating older dogs, which is why I often refer to it as the "fountain of youth." I first became aware of its remarkable rejuvenating powers when I became a certified veterinary acupuncturist and began using the technique on many of my regular canine patients. In many cases, it was almost as if they'd started aging in reverse. Ten-year-old dogs began to look and act as if they were six. Their eyes became brighter and their whole demeanor became more youthful. Many times, a dog's owner and I have watched this phenomenon with no small amount of astonishment.

Acupuncture treatments are normally administered once a week for the first few treatments, although dogs suffering from paralysis or back problems need to be treated more often. With each session, the body readjusts itself and heals a little bit more. Cumulatively, this therapy works to restore your best friend to health and harmony, eliminate any pain and discomfort that he might be having, tone up his internal organs, and help him live a longer and happier life.

Homeopathy: Helping Your Dog Heal on His Own

Homeopathy is a very individualized therapeutic approach. The same illness causes a different reaction in each different dog. Here's a situation for you to think about: Four different dogs have itchy skin problems. Two go to a conventional veterinarian and receive drugs, such as steroids and antibiotics. These drugs work to suppress the symptoms, and both dogs are prescribed the same medications. The other two canines go to a veterinarian who practices homeopathy. The veterinarian asks the owners all sorts of questions about their respective dogs. One dog likes the heat, and his itching gets really bad after midnight. The other dog avoids heat, actively seeks the cold, and gets much itchier after his baths. The dogs each get a different remedy, each remedy chosen for the dog's individual case.

Homeopathic preparations are easy to obtain for home use because they are sold in some pharmacies, in most health food stores, and by mail order from homeopathic pharmacies. They are referred to as "remedies" and can be used to address all kinds of conditions, from sprains and injuries to a variety of chronic health problems. Homeopathic remedies have a long track record of proven effectiveness.

Homeopathic remedies have no toxic side effects. They are inexpensive and, most importantly, they are very safe. According to the World Health Organization, homeopathy is the second most commonly used method of health care in the world. The Homeopathic Pharmacopoeia of the United States is fully recognized by an Act of Congress. The Homeopathic Pharmacopoeia has uniform, specific methods of preparation for remedies, and it works in conjunction with the US Food and Drug Administration (FDA) to assure quality and consistency. This means that no matter where or from what manufacturer you buy a homeopathic remedy, it will have been made in the same way, with consistent manufacturing procedures.

Let's Start at the Very Beginning

The innovative German physician Samuel Hahnemann founded this powerful and safe system of medicine known as homeopathy over two centuries ago. It all started in 1790, when he was translating a medical text into German. He disagreed on the reasoning put forth to explain the action of an extract of the bark of a Venezuelan tree, the cinchona, which was successfully used to treat malaria. Upon experimentation, Hahnemann discovered that drinking a tea made from the bark would produce, for a short time, the very same symptoms that one would get from malaria. Once again, as so often happens among the twists and turns on the historical road of healing, he "rediscovered" an old medical principle espoused by Hippocrates: "Like cures like."

Early Veterinary Homeopaths

In 1813, a veterinarian named Wilhelm Lux of Leipzig, Germany, was recognized for his use of homeopathic remedies in treating colic in horses. In 1886, Frederick Humphreys published his veterinary manual on homeopathy for animals in the United States.

The Law of Similars

Called the Law of Similars, "like cures like" is one of the basic principles of homeopathy. It maintains that a substance administered in large doses, provoking specific disease symptoms in a healthy person, will treat those specific symptoms when administered, in minute doses, as a homeopathically prepared remedy. For example, what happens when you slice an onion? Your eyes and nose will run as if you had an allergy or cold. In homeopathy, one of the remedies used for a cold or allergy will be made from—that's right—onions! However, the method of preparation is not as simple as presenting an allergy sufferer with a glass of onion juice. A homeopathic remedy is prepared in a very special and precise way by a method of repeated dilution and shaking (succession). A homeopathic remedy stimulates the vital force, the life force, to react vigorously and cure the disease. The remedy has no actual toxicity or effect on the physiology of the organism because just about all of its physical substance has been eliminated through a process of dilution. The remedy produces a stronger disease picture, although wholly energetic, for the vital force to react to. The remedy has taught the body to handle the disease, and the result is, again, a stronger and wiser body.

In a similar fashion, the syrup ipecac, which will induce vomiting, is made into a remedy to treat someone who is nauseous and vomiting. Homeopathic formulas, unlike conventional drugs, do not directly attack the disease or condition. Instead, these highly diluted substances trigger the body's own self-regulating and self-healing mechanisms, enabling the body to handle the illness on its own.

Dr. Hahnemann encompassed the whole philosophy of homeopathy in this simple statement: "The highest ideal of therapy is to restore health rapidly, gently, permanently; to remove and destroy all whole diseases in the shortest, surest, least harmful way, according to clearly comprehensible principles."

In keeping with that description, you can expect homeopathic remedies to be just as safe for your pet. Remember, homeopathic remedies have no toxic side effects. Rather than suppressing symptoms, they are designed to encourage your dog's own defense mechanisms to effect a cure. This will also help your dog's further ability to fight off disease and pathogens.

A homeopathic remedy, then, can be described as one that stimulates the body's natural defense mechanisms by specifically stimulating the body's vital force to heal. This type of healing also serves to ensure improved immunity and health.

An Enduring Alternative

During the first half of the nineteenth century, homeopathy thrived in both Europe and the United States, earning itself a solid reputation during Europe's cholera epidemic of 1832, when homeopathy's recovery rates proved to be higher than those of the conventional physicians of the day. Homeopathy was endorsed by several renowned nineteenth-century Americans, including poet

Henry Wadsworth Longfellow, novelist Nathaniel Hawthorne, and industrialist John D. Rockefeller.

In fact, many notable and famous people have supported homeopathy, including Mahatma Gandhi, who said, "Homeopathy cures a larger percentage of cases than any other method of treatment and is beyond doubt safer and more economical, and is the most complete medical science."

While homeopathy gained converts throughout the world and has remained popular in Europe and India, its following in the United States was eclipsed for a time with the advent of medical politics that promoted newer, more profit-driven types of treatment at the expense of natural ones. In recent years, however, the benefits of homeopathy have come to be rediscovered by millions of Americans who have been alarmed by the high risks and side effects of conventional medicine.

But what's in it for your dog? The answer is that homeopathy offers as much to your pet as it does to you. That's because in homeopathy, everything that applies to people applies equally to animals. The 2,000+ remedies it offers are considered just as effective for humans and animals alike, and the selection criteria are also the same. Here's another point to consider: while homeopathic remedies were developed out of experimentation and research studies, none has ever involved animal testing. Such research was done instead on healthy individuals who volunteered their services.

How Homeopathic Remedies Work

Homeopathic remedies are prepared from a wide range of animal, vegetable, and mineral substances, including insects, poisons, and modern medicines, such as antibiotics. Quite frankly, homeopathic remedies can be made from just about anything, although about 80 percent come from plants, some as familiar as lily of the valley and poison ivy, and some as rare as the St. Ignatius bean from the Philippines. No matter what substance may be involved, however, because of the method of preparation, a homeopathic remedy will never have a toxic side effect. For example, some remedies are made from things as toxic as cobra or rattlesnake venom, but because of the method of preparation, they are rendered harmless. As a result, homeopathic preparations are some of the safest and least toxic medications available today.

The Dilution Solution

When Dr. Hahnemann initially set out to determine the minimum doses required to bring about improvement, he found, much to his surprise, that the more he *potentized* a remedy, the more powerful it became. He thereafter began systematically diluting, then *succusing*, or vigorously shaking, each of the substances he wanted to test. After this process was complete, the remedy was considered *potentized*, meaning that the liquid involved had retained the memory, but none of the toxic effects, of the

Homeopathic Remedy Preparation

A preparation to be used as a homeopathic remedy may be diluted using ratios of either 1:10, known as an X potency, or 1:100, referred to as a C potency. This distinction is important for you to know when you purchase such remedies. A remedy is listed by its name, followed by the number of times it is diluted and potentized and its dilution ratio. To illustrate, the remedy Arnica 6c is composed of the herb arnica, which has been diluted and potentized six times using a factor of 1:100, whereas the remedy Bryonia 30x is made from the herb white bryony, which has been diluted thirty times at a ratio of 1:10.

Potentization

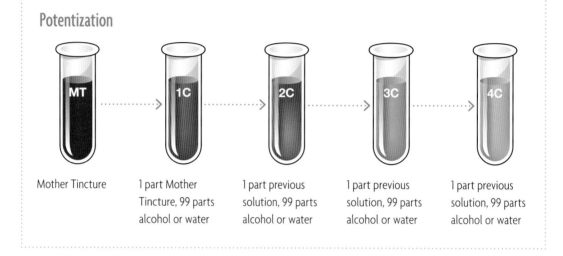

| Mother Tincture | 1 part Mother Tincture, 99 parts alcohol or water | 1 part previous solution, 99 parts alcohol or water | 1 part previous solution, 99 parts alcohol or water | 1 part previous solution, 99 parts alcohol or water |

substance from which it was made. By stimulating a body's natural defenses without adversely affecting them, the energetic capacity imbued in this memory creates a powerful tool to promote natural healing.

Prescriptions for the Individual

There are so many homeopathic remedies currently available that just the commonly used ones fill entire books—and there is quite a collection of books out there that discuss them in detail, should you be up for some reading. Later in this book, I'll acquaint you with some of the remedies commonly used for treating certain ailments, but for now, I'd like to touch on what these remedies can accomplish and the factors that go into selecting them.

Homeopathic remedies can be used for a variety of veterinary purposes. Within homeopathy itself, there are many avenues available in addition to the rigid classical approach, in which only one remedy at a time is used. Homeopathic remedies can also be used for treating acute emergencies or first aid situations such as shock, trauma, and bee stings. Interestingly, the homeopathic remedy Apis mellifica, made from the common honeybee, is the remedy of choice for bee stings. Another homeopathic approach is organ drainage, with the aim of eliminating the toxins from organs such as the liver, kidneys, and spleen. Specific remedies work with each organ. There exists yet another, more modern, avenue of homeopathy referred to as homotoxicology. Without denying the basic principles of homeopathy, it uses a more scientific explanation and clinical language that is easily understood by today's doctors. Homotoxicology introduces new classes of homeopathic remedies produced on the basis of the most recent scientific discoveries.

An interesting true story illustrates how homeopaths learned from every avenue and developed many remedies to deal with a plethora of problems. In colonial times, the child of a settler had a disease then known as dropsy. His belly was filled with fluid, and he was dying. Some Native Americans, learning of the child's illness, killed a few honeybees, toasted them on a fire, and had the young boy take them. The fluid passed, and he lived. Today, the remedy Apis, prepared in a standard homeopathic fashion, is commonly used for edema and swelling and to promote urination.

Homeopathic remedies are also used to cure deep-seated chronic diseases, which usually require extensive study to determine the precise remedy that is indicated. In this situation, the healer takes the patient's full history, including all mental, emotional, and physical symptoms. Each individual responds differently to an illness, and this is very important in choosing the correct homeopathic remedy. How an individual responds to an illness is just as important as the illness itself in deciding which remedy to take.

Every homeopathic remedy has its own picture of disease, which was carefully recorded during its proving. Each remedy in the *Materia Medica* contains a description of the symptoms and modalities associated with it, set out under the systems of the body. One of the characteristic features of a homeopathic *Materia Medica* is the inclusion of modalities, meaning which things make the patient feel better or worse. These can include cold, heat, movement, rest, and even the amount of attention that the patient seeks when ill or the mood that the patient is in. We also find mental symptoms in the *Materia Medica* relating to the temperament, emotions, and feelings of the patient.

Consider, for example, how two people might respond to being afflicted by the same cold virus. One seems to require constant attention and a lot of fussing and have no thirst, even though suffering from a fever. The other wants to be left alone to lie in a quiet room and, despite being very thirsty, snaps at the person who brings him a drink. The first individual might need the remedy Pulsatilla, which suits individuals who want to be loved and pampered when sick, while the second might be best off with Bryonia, which suits the patient who feels better when lying quietly. (Of course, many more of the symptoms and modalities are often taken into account when choosing the appropriate remedy.)

Administering Remedies

Remedies come in the form of tiny white pellets that can be tucked into your dog's lower lip fold to melt. They also come in liquid form, and you can place a few drops on your dog's gums. Additionally, a few pellets can be placed in a small amount of spring water and stirred, and this water can be given as a remedy.

Homeopathy Simplified

Homeopathy has particular rules associated with using it, which can be confusing and put off prospective students. But for many simple and common accidents and illnesses, it's really pretty simple to use. The following are some important facts about working with homeopathic remedies:

- Homeopathic remedies need to melt on the gums, so they should not be hidden in treats or food. A dog has a built-in pouch on the side of his mouth, and the remedies can go right in there.

- Your hands should be clean, and you can touch the pills and put a pinch of tiny white pellets in your dog's mouth.

- Remedies come in tiny white pellet or liquid form. Either form can be placed directly into your dog's cheek pouch area. If the pellets are large, you can crush them in a small folded piece of paper and then slide the powder into your dog's mouth.

- It's not important if you give one drop of the remedy or five, or one homeopathic pellet or three, because homeopathy is an energy medicine, and there is typically none of the physical substance left in the remedy. One tiny white pellet could treat an elephant, and ten pellets could treat a mouse. That's a hard one to digest, if you'll excuse my pun, but people are always worried about how much and how often to give the remedy. The amount is no big deal, and you give it until your dog gets better. If the remedy is not working at all, stop giving it. We're all just too used to antibiotics, which have to be calculated to the weight of the dog and must be given at the same times each day. This is simply not the case with homeopathy.

- Because homeopathy is an energy medicine, the remedies should not be stored next to heavy electromagnetic appliances, such as televisions and computers, or left in the hot sun for a long time.

In another example, a dog with arthritis who is very stiff after lying around and who is especially bothered by damp, cold weather might need the remedy Rhus toxicodendron (commonly known as Rhus tox). Conversely, an arthritic dog whose condition is made worse by exercise and warmth and who prefers to lie on a cool floor might benefit from Bryonia.

As you can see, the remedy Bryonia was prescribed for both a cold and arthritis. What is the common denominator? Both patients who were prescribed Bryonia feel better when they are resting and would rather not move about.

Each remedy has its own personality—a whole "picture" associated with it, including many detailed symptoms for which it can be used. This is why two dogs with the same illness can be given different remedies, and why a particular remedy can be used for different illnesses. Remember the scenario presented at the beginning of this section? The two itchy dogs who visited the homeopathic veterinarian were given different remedies, as one loved the cold and the other craved heat.

The fact that mental and emotional factors need to be assessed in addition to the physical presentation of the disease changed the way I practiced veterinary medicine. I had to notice the dogs more than their owners and open up a true line of communication with my patients.

My patients responded in kind. The dogs I treat make it evident that they consider me their friend, and I can tell how much they appreciate the fact that they matter to me and are being recognized as individuals.

Combination Remedies

Not all homeopathic remedies are derived from a single substance. Products containing combination remedies are formulated to treat different problems when the best option isn't always evident. These remedies are often sold in health food stores, and, while they are geared mainly toward human health, veterinary versions are also available. However, the human products are just fine to use on animals. Dogs and people have a lot of the same problems.

Combination remedies have been designed to treat such ailments as asthma, diarrhea, arthritis, and the like; to improve the health of particular organs such as the liver or kidneys; to detoxify the body of such substances as heavy metals or pesticides; or to alleviate nervousness and other emotional problems. Many of the remedies they contain complement each other and work synergistically for maximum effect.

How to Use Homeopathic Preparations

Doses of homeopathic remedies are not adjusted for size or weight as, let us say, an antibiotic or herb would be. In homeopathy, the potency, or number of times the remedy was diluted, and the frequency of the dose are what matter. In most cases, as soon as the symptoms improve, the remedy has done its job and thus is discontinued.

Everything that touches the remedy should be clean and odor free. Remedies may be obtained either in a water-based liquid, which is often preserved with a little alcohol or vinegar, or as small medicated white pellets that are coated with the remedy. Dogs usually do not mind the taste of these preparations, which need to be dissolved directly on the blood vessels—on the gums, in the mouth, or inside the lips. Remedies need to melt on the mucous membranes of

More about Bryonia

The homeopathic remedy Bryonia is made from a flowering plant called white bryony, which grows in England. Bryonia is indicated for conditions, including cold and flu, in which the patient is tired and irritable and does not want to move. It is also good for arthritis that worsens after exercise and in which the patient feels better after and when resting.

What Dose Should I Give?

Unlike drugs, homeopathy does not work by body weight (e.g., give 500 mg per 25 pounds of body weight). With homeopathy, the original physical substance is sequentially diluted, and this is why there is a number after the name of the remedy. *Arnica* 6x does not mean that you have to give it six times. It means that the remedy has been diluted six times. To confound you even more, the more dilute the remedy, the more powerful it is, so very highly diluted remedies are usually available only to doctors. The potencies most commonly available to consumers are 6x and 30x (diluted 1:10 either six or thirty times) and 6c and 30c (diluted 1:100 either six or thirty times).

the mouth and therefore should not be hidden in food. If using a liquid preparation, the liquid is dropped under the lip, onto the gums. If using the pellets, they are easily inserted into the lip fold and allowed to absorb—which is much easier than having to pry your dog's mouth open to push a pill down his throat.

It requires an open mind to follow a path that is not in complete accordance with the conventional wisdom taught in medical and veterinary schools. I have never excluded anything that I thought might help my canine patients achieve optimal health. Homeopathy, I have found, works beautifully alongside sister therapies such as acupuncture and various other treatment options described in this book. In fact, whether used alone or with other therapies, homeopathy usually works well even when combined with conventional drugs. Many of my new patients, for instance, come to me in very bad condition and would not survive if abruptly taken off the pharmaceuticals that have been prescribed for them. I give them the benefit of appropriate holistic treatments while slowly weaning them off the medications on which they have become dependent. It all works together for the benefit of your pet.

Flower Power: It Really Works

Ask who Bach was, and the answer you're most likely to get is that he was a famous prolific Baroque composer. But there was another Bach, a homeopathic physician known for his ability to soothe the emotions of both man and beast—not through beautiful music but through evocative floral essences. I'm referring to Dr. Edward Bach, the British physician, bacteriologist, and immunologist who in the 1930s discovered what have become known as the Bach flower remedies. These are a series of thirty-eight special preparations, all but one derived from the essence of a wildflower or tree blossom, designed to treat different emotional states from depression to nervousness to aggression to hyperactivity to apathy.

Having administered these remedies to dogs suffering from emotions such as jealousy and fear, I can vouch for their effectiveness in many cases. The owners of a puppy who whines may find that the Bach flower remedy chicory makes the house a lot more tranquil. A tendency to bite might be nipped in the bud with a little Bach flower remedy snapdragon. Bach flower remedies are usually available through health food stores, and books explaining what each remedy treats are interesting to read and easy to find.

The production of flower remedies has grown exponentially. You can find numerous companies around

Bach Flower Remedies

Here are some popular Bach flower remedies and what they're used for:

Agrimony	is used to restore inner peace.
Cherry plum	helps remedy uncontrollable behavior or compulsiveness and helps restore control.
Honeysuckle	helps remedy homesickness and an inability to cope with present conditions, and it helps dogs adjust to present circumstances.
Impatiens	remedies irritability and restores patience.
Mustard	remedies depression and gloominess and restores courage.
Star of Bethlehem	helps to soothe grief.
Sweet chestnut	remedies extreme mental and physical distress and restores endurance.
White chestnut	remedies restlessness and preoccupation and restores the ability to rest.
Bach's Rescue Remedy Pet	which combines Star of Bethlehem, clematis, rock rose, impatiens, and cherry plum, is recommended in any situation in which a pet feels grief (the loss of a canine sibling or owner), anxiety, stress, or fear over situations such as going to a new home, going to the veterinarian or groomer, or during thunderstorms or fireworks.

the world making flower remedies from their indigenous plant life. The real beauty of Bach flower remedies or any other flower remedies is that they're easy to figure out, and you can administer them at home. And they have no side effects or undesirable repercussions should the wrong one be used for a particular condition.

The Backbone of Health: Chiropractic

Your dog's brain takes in millions of bits of information about what is going on in his body. All of this information is carried on a cable made up of billions of nerve wires that run down a dog's back. This cable—the spinal cord—sends messages to all of the organs and muscles of your dog's body and acts as a relay center, both sending and receiving data.

Ancient Greeks looked at people's backs and noticed the regular bumps formed by the spinal column. They thought these bumps looked like thorns, so they called them *spina*, which is the Greek word for "thorn."

The delicate spinal nerves are protected by special bones called *vertebrae*. The vertebrae of the spine are stacked up like a pile of bagels whose holes are all lined up. People have a vertical spinal column because they stand upright on their legs, and dogs have a horizontal bridge of vertebrae.

The neck vertebrae hold up the head. The vertebrae that sit just under your dog's head are called the *atlas* because the Greek god Atlas held up the globe of the earth the way the atlas of the spine holds up the globe of the head. Vertebrae are present all the way down your dog's spine; they end at the sacrum, which connects to the hips on either side.

Between each vertebra are pads called discs, which act as little cushions, or shock absorbers, so your dog's vertebrae won't bump into each other when he walks, jumps, and plays. They are, in fact, jellylike fluid-filled sacs. Displacements of the vertebrae that cause discs to bulge into the center of the spine's canal can pinch the spinal cord and the nerves that branch out to the body from the spinal cord.

A sequence of events comes into play when a dog begins to feel discomfort in his back. First of all, his vertebrae are no longer aligned, presenting a mechanical problem. In an attempt to stabilize and protect the area, his muscles might tighten or go into a painful spasm. Last of all, the nerves exiting his vertebral column might be compressed and inflamed. Minor back problems, if left untreated, can escalate into debilitating and dangerous disc problems.

Disc displacement will alter the flow of the vital communication between your dog's brain and body. If severe, the displacement can also be a very painful experience for a dog and may even cause paralysis. A backache acts as a danger signal for people, alerting them to a possible pinched nerve. A dog's back may hurt him, but he has no way to tell his owner. I have seen many agility dogs and working dogs who stop performing as they used to because of a pinched nerve and spinal pain. After an adjustment or two, they returned to their normal selves.

A paralyzed dog has experienced a severe injury to his spinal cord. Correcting the positioning

of the vertebrae deals with the root of the problem, while drugs or holistic preparations act to minimize swelling and pain. I have seen hundreds of dogs with severe disc problems who have recovered through the use of adjustment, acupuncture, homeopathy, and Chinese herbs.

The science of spinal manipulation is based on the fact that the spinal cord and massive nerve network that emanates out from it carry communications essential to health and life from the brain to the organs of the body. It is the unimpeded function of the nerves and nervous system that helps maintain health and alleviate pain and discomfort. The nervous system has dynamic, intelligent impulses that work to impart natural health.

Veterinarians who practice spinal manipulation care are becoming more common and are much needed. Life seems to provide many opportunities for injuries. Dogs at play leap and bump each other; agility dogs jump, crawl, and twist; and Dachshunds, well, are just Dachshunds. One very careful Dachshund was tentatively walking on a pile of frozen snow to go potty. The top frozen crust broke, and he fell down into 4-foot deep snow. His owners rescued him and, being "in the know," rushed him in for an adjustment. And did he need it!

Prolotherapy

You may never have heard of this particular therapy, but it is my treatment of choice for dogs with knee injuries. Prolotherapy stimulates the repair process after an injury. It is an effective treatment for chronic back, joint, and musculoskeletal injuries.

Ligaments and tendons are the fibrous tissue that connects bone to bone and bone to muscle in a joint. If you look at a fresh ligament, it appears as a white sheet or band. There is virtually no blood supply to ligaments, so they heal very slowly. When they finally do heal, they are never as strong as they used to be and are more prone to reinjury.

Prolotherapy has been around for a long time. Once again, Hippocrates, the father of medicine, took the first step. He stabilized the shoulders of javelin throwers by inserting hot needles into the joint capsules to provoke scar tissue. In 1835, several medical doctors researched the use of irritating substances to provoke healing. The term *prolotherapy* was coined in 1950. Since then, much research has been done, and decades of clinical experience have also been reviewed. It was found that prolotherapy had a profound regenerative effect and that the ligaments of rabbits were stronger and larger than they had been before they were injured.

By 1970, the use of prolotherapy had been nearly perfected, and by 1980 a great deal of research demonstrating both microscopic and clinical regeneration and improvement had been done. Additionally, many medical doctors have documented years of clinical success with prolotherapy. One important research discovery was that nonsteroidal anti-inflammatory drugs (NSAIDS) cannot be used in conjunction with prolotherapy because their use seriously slows healing.

With prolotherapy, injections are made into the ligaments around the joint and, if needed, into the joint itself. This stimulates the ligaments to regenerate and encourages new cartilage growth in the joints. In the hands of a holistic-minded veterinarian, this therapy is key to stimulating the growth and repair of collagen, ligaments, and connective tissue. This treatment causes marked relief of pain from hip dysplasia, back problems, and knee problems. Prolotherapy causes the ligaments and surfaces in these areas to be rebuilt and strengthened.

Once again, as with so many holistic-minded modalities, prolotherapy stimulates the body's own natural healing and repair mechanisms. After the tissues are rebuilt, there is a stronger, more supported area as well as less pain. The bottom line is that it works—and works very well. Prolotherapy speeds healing exponentially, and the result is an even stronger ligament!

For many years, I would treat dogs with anterior cruciate ligament injuries (knee injuries) with numerous acupuncture treatments. The rate of improvement would depend on the severity of the injury. Often, the patient would reinjure the knee by overusing it as soon as his discomfort went away, and then he'd be back to holding his leg up in pain. Owners who were not in the habit of taking their large-breed dogs out on a leash would be pulled around by their dogs for weeks and have to go to all extremes to keep their dogs from jumping and playing, as letting a dog with a knee injury out in the yard to romp or relieve himself off lead was a big no-no. But what could we do? Ligament injuries just took a long time to heal.

Now, I just do a quick prolotherapy treatment and tell the owner to keep the dog quiet for a few days. If the dog is of a sensitive disposition, I will give a little sedative. It is a fast procedure, so the more stoic dogs are done with the treatment in no time. The injections contain a local anesthetic, dextrose, and a few other healthy ingredients. As far as ligament injuries go, prolotherapy is "the bee's knees." Veterinarians who practice prolotherapy are rare, but a course to learn it has been made available in recent years. The American Holistic Veterinary Medical Association (AHVMA) or holistic veterinarian Dr. Roger DeHaan, DVM, MTS, CVC, CNHP (www.aholisticvet.com) in North Carolina may serve as a referral source. The website www.getprolo.com also has valuable information on this form of therapy.

A Holistic Return

You wouldn't be the first person to wonder how such long-recognized therapies as homeopathy, which has remained popular in Europe and India over the centuries, and acupuncture, the value of which has been known for many centuries in the Far East, could disappear from the face of healing in the United States. The answer is that when antibiotics took center stage, all other treatment options were dismissed as obsolete or unnecessary—even though many of these new "wonder drugs" would themselves end up fitting that description.

Initially, the effect that antibiotics had in halting the progress of certain all-too-common diseases was so profound that it seemed as though the panacea for all ills of man and beast had been found. During World War I, soldiers suffering from wounds and a variety of infections were effectively treated with these new drugs, as were civilians afflicted with once life-threatening ailments. Before long, the fields of human and veterinary medicine began putting all their eggs into one basket, with antibiotics becoming a newfound source of wealth for both doctors and drug companies.

As a result, antibiotics became overused, prescribed for ailments they could not relieve (such as viruses), which eventually led to the creation of more and more strains of antibiotic-resistant bacteria. Infections from resistant bacteria that do not respond to familiar antibiotics are becoming more and more common. In addition, these drugs, while valuable in certain applications, tended to weaken or destroy, by their mode of action, the immune system, the body's first line of defense.

Many of our most feared, crippling, and lethal diseases are those that don't respond to antibiotics—not only viral infections but also cancer, heart disease, and autoimmune diseases. Such chronic and debilitating ailments have become rampant in both the human and pet populations.

That's why our rediscovery of holistic products and procedures is such an important development. While conventional therapies tend to take over the healing function and decrease the body's ability to heal itself, holistic treatments work with the body to fortify and encourage its own healing powers. The holistic experience creates a wiser and stronger body, more able to maintain and retain health. The end result is a healthier patient with a stronger immune system. The most important thing we can do for our dog is keep his body strong with inherent health.

Working Wonders

As millions of Americans discover the benefits offered by the various types of holistic medicine, it is becoming more apparent to them that these same techniques can work wonders for the health and well-being of their companion animals. Unlike conventional medicine, which often uses dogs and other animals for research and testing, holistic therapies are completely "animal friendly." My patients have always seemed to love their treatments. It's a nice change to see dogs rushing their way into a veterinary clinic rather than dragging their owners back to the car.

9. Eliminating Allergies

ow we're going to look at allergies in detail. The easiest way to understand allergies is to understand the immune system. If we look at our immune system and compare it to a computer, we can see how it remembers and reruns a program, recognizing an invading "bug" many years after the original infection and gearing up against it, knowing just what to do. Your immune-system computer registers various enemies, never to forget their identities. You probably feel secure that you'll never get measles or mumps as an adult if you had them as a child. You know that your immune system has compiled its own file on these attackers and will never again let them make inroads into your body.

In the case of allergies, however, the immune system also begins to register certain good guys as enemies. Common and innocuous substances such, as a simple food or a tree pollen, become identified by the immune system as threats to the body. Where did the body learn to react so ferociously when an allergen is introduced? If the entirety of a body's construction is geared toward survival, then where is the sense in a child dying from a bee sting or a peanut? One small bit of peanut in a candy bar or even just breathing in peanut dust is all that it takes to initiate severe allergic reactions in some children—reactions so exaggerated that they actually become life-threatening. Why do peanuts cause this particular child to suffer when all of his friends are eating peanut butter and jelly sandwiches for lunch? Because his internal computer has been corrupted to behave in a self-destructive manner. Allergies in their mildest forms are merely nuisances. But, for some, contact with an allergen could result in death.

A similar, if not quite as severe, situation exists with other typical allergies. The immune systems of some dogs, not unlike virus-corrupted computers, have registered simple foods, vitamins, pollens, molds, and many other substances as threats that call for some type of response. Simply being fed a food allergen may not be enough in itself to get a dog's immune system hopped up to the point at which itching or diarrhea occurs. However, when seasonal pollens and molds are added to the mix, the total number of allergens present will reach concentrations high enough to exceed the dog's threshold and will cause allergic symptoms such as chronic itching. Foods play a big part in the overall allergic reaction when it does occur, with the pollens acting as the straw that breaks the camel's back.

Why would a dog's internal computer program go haywire? One likely explanation is that vaccinations have worked to confuse his immune system and cause this exaggerated response. The immune system, you see, was never designed to ward off simultaneous incursions by several different agents. I know of no recorded cases in which a person was exposed to polio, smallpox, measles, mumps, and whooping cough all at one time. The immune system's design is compatible with the laws of statistics, meaning that the immune system isn't set up to handle such a multipronged attack because the chance of any one virus occurring is so low. But such an attack on the immune system is exactly what multivalent combination vaccinations simulate. The immune system is being asked to register and fight off, all at once, all of the vaccine components. For a dog, this means distemper, parvovirus, leptospirosis, adenovirus, hepatitis, bordetella, and perhaps also coronavirus, rabies, and Lyme disease. In addition to antigens and viruses, vaccinations contain formaldehyde and mercury. Neither the human nor the canine immune system was designed to have multiple disease organisms, antigens, and toxic substances injected into the body at one time, as is the case with vaccines.

Even more significant in these vaccines are the tiny bits of chicken and cow material left over from the chicken embryo and bovine serum in which the viruses are incubated. Unfortunately, when these food products are introduced to the body with the invaders, that's how the body's internal computer is likely to subsequently identify them. Just imagine yourself living in a house on the prairie and being attacked by a gang of a dozen outlaws. As you prepare to defend yourself from the invaders, would you try to differentiate between them to decide if perhaps some were benign? Or would you register them all as enemies? For your survival, you'd likely do the latter, and that's exactly what the immune system is prone to do.

It's not a coincidence that the first foods usually removed from the animal's diet are chicken and beef, kissing cousins to the egg and bovine serum used to incubate vaccine viruses. A "hypoallergenic diet," typically consisting of lamb and rice, is likely to be substituted. But the proteins in lamb are not so far removed from those in beef, and because the dog is usually fed the same thing every day, he'll soon develop an allergy to lamb, too. The concerned owner may switch the dog to wild game, such as venison or rabbit, but these foods, too, soon begin to trigger the immune system to put up a fight. After going through a veritable dietary petting zoo, the hypoallergenic food of last resort is a special predigested protein. At best, all of these changes in diet tend to be only short-term fixes for the true underlying problem.

The dog's immune system—just like a misfiring computer program—will find more and more substances to become allergic to. As the years pass, the two-week summer allergy becomes a three-month allergy and finally results in year-round itching as your dog's allergies increase.

Itching to Get to the Root of It

The increased frequency of vaccinations is only part of the explanation for allergies. What else caused

The Allergen Equation

The intensity of an allergy might be the result of a synergistic effect of two or more allergens combining. Your dog might have a severe allergic reaction to yeast, for instance, and mild reactions to corn, wheat, and soy. And while you might make a point of not feeding him anything that contains yeast, a food with a combination of the latter items might produce a reaction just as severe, if not more so. The fact that these three ingredients are present together will increase the allergic response, even though the allergy to each of them individually is not nearly as severe as the one triggered by yeast. The number of allergens in your dog's environment plus the intensity of the allergy to each substance equals the total allergic reaction.

Another factor that influences the occurrence of allergic reactions is seasonal change. During the winter in some northern climes—when grass, weeds, trees, and pollen become dormant and covered over—many allergy-prone animals may experience some relief, while others may actually suffer an increase in allergic reactions to dust, molds, and debris from heating systems. In autumn, romping in fallen leaves increases a dog's exposure to such potential allergens as fungus, mold, and mildew.

Every season has its own allergy triggers, which affect different dogs in different ways. Whereas an allergy trigger might cause our eyes to itch and water, the same trigger is more likely to affect a dog by irritating the area above the tail, along with other areas of his body. If we experienced allergies as dogs do, we'd probably be going around scratching our butts while complaining about how bad the ragweed is this year!

the immune system, so brilliantly designed to ward off pernicious invaders, to come to mistake innocuous substances for sources of imminent peril and, in so doing, wreak such havoc inside the body it is supposed to protect?

One thing is apparent: the incidence of allergies and asthma has been on the rise in recent years. Veterinarians of a half-century ago, for instance, encountered far fewer animals suffering from allergic reactions. But, in those days, feeding table scraps to dogs was much more common, and vaccinations were far more limited in scope.

Along with the increase in vaccinations, there has been the increased exposure to environmental toxins, potent pharmaceuticals, and chemical additives in the food supply. Pesticide use, for example, has proliferated in recent years, and both dogs and children are particularly likely to be exposed to toxic residues on lawns, which may also cause far more serious health consequences.

Unfortunately, nature did not design the immune systems of mammals to cope with the array of synthetic poisons to which we and our pets are constantly exposed. Such factors could well account for many of the allergies we see in dogs (and people) today, as well as the fact that an allergic dog is more likely to breed progeny with the same problems. Root causes aside, the fact to remember is that allergies tend to intensify and widen with time unless aggressive measures are taken to nip them in the bud.

One point being overlooked is that the best way for an allergy to develop and grow in intensity is through repeated and frequent exposure to something. Doctors, for instance, commonly become allergic to the powder or the latex in latex surgical gloves. This would not happen if they didn't routinely use them. Or a woman who works in a hair salon may develop allergic lesions on her hands when exposed to hair dye, while someone who works at a newsstand may become similarly sensitive to newsprint and ink. As the immune system increasingly responds to such routine exposures, it also develops allergic responses to other items in the environment, such as dust, molds, fabrics, pollens, weeds, grasses, and trees. So you can see why feeding your beef-allergic dog the same lamb kibble day after day after day can result in the dog's developing a new allergy to lamb. It should be apparent by now that there's something wrong with the basic approach to treating allergies.

It All Adds Up

Conventional kibble, in particular, can perpetuate the allergy cycle because, in addition to being consumed on a daily basis, it contains various dyes, preservatives, and poor-quality proteins that can serve as red flags to a malfunctioning immune system. By varying your dog's diet and not feeding him the same food day in and day out, you'll not only provide him with more balanced nutrition and make him a happier camper, but you'll also reduce the opportunity for food allergies to develop. Variety in your dog's diet—for example, fish one day, lamb the next, and dairy the third—will also allow you to isolate, and then remove, those food items to which your dog might be allergic.

Skin Allergies

A dog afflicted with skin allergies may develop itching anywhere from his head to his tail. That's because he has more mast cells than you do. These mast cells release compounds that cause itching and are distributed over a dog's entire body. Mast cells release histamines in response to certain triggers, and this starts the actual irritation and itching. Just as your mother told you in the case of mosquito bites, "The more you scratch, the more you itch." I've tried telling this to my allergic canine patients, but they just don't seem to get the message, opting instead to literally chew holes in themselves!

When the immune system begins acting like a fire department responding to a bunch of false alarms, it is diverted from its intended task, which is to fight bacterial infections, viruses, cancers, and other alien invaders. What allergies do is exhaust the body's inherent defenses, cause imbalance and disharmony, and lead to the production and retention of toxins.

What Doesn't Work

To make matters worse, the drugs routinely used to treat allergic reactions act to suppress the overburdened immune system. The use of corticosteroids, for instance, can send that devoted but confused immune system sprawling. In addition to being toxic to your dog's liver, these drugs throw the body's pH balance out of kilter, with all of the resulting problems. Steroids, while relieving the symptoms, only entrench the problem more deeply in your dog's body, making it more toxic. Typically, if the allergens are still present after a few days to weeks off the steroids, your dog will need to go on them again. Steroids do not cure the problem; rather, they simply suppress the immune system's ability to function.

Antihistamines are the least toxic of the pharmaceutical options, but they are also the least effective when it comes to reducing itching and may not help severely allergic dogs at all.

The worst offender is a very powerful immune system inhibitor. Atopica is a product that touts its efficacy with dogs who have allergies and other dermatological conditions. You now know that allergies result from an incorrect response of the immune system to foods and environmental substances. For many years, steroids such as prednisolone were used to decrease the ability of the immune system to function and thus relieve allergies. It's when steroids can't and don't work that Atopica is prescribed. Why does it often work so well? What does it do? How does it work?

Atopica is cyclosporine. Cyclosporine is a mycotoxin. Mycotoxins are harmful products produced by fungi. They are chemical in nature and are immune suppressing. Fungi rely on the mycotoxins that they produce to kill any bacteria, other fungi, viruses, and anything else that might compete with them. They suppress the immune system of dogs, cats, and humans. Some examples of mycotoxins found in nature are aflatoxins, the most potent carcinogen on earth, and ocharatoxins—both produced by an *Aspergillus* fungus. Other medical mycotoxins include Adriamycin, a chemotherapy drug, and Lovastatin, a cholesterol-lowering drug.

The immunosuppressive effects of cyclosporine were discovered in Switzerland in 1972, and it was used successfully in preventing organ rejection in kidney transplants and later in liver transplants. Apart from transplant medicine, cyclosporine is used for a variety of skin conditions in both humans and pets. Of course, in transplant patients it suppresses the immune system so they do not reject their transplants.

The side effects of this drug include headaches, nausea, vomiting, diarrhea, shaking hands, swollen and bleeding gums, cancer, kidney failure, hypertension, easy bruising, hearing problems, yellowing of skin and eyes, loss of consciousness, vision changes, swollen glands, immune suppression, and dizziness. Interestingly, these aren't side effects at all, but rather symptoms of poisoning caused by mycotoxin. Farmers are familiar with the deleterious effects that mycotoxins can have on animals that eat moldy grain containing mycotoxins, and the symptoms coincide. In fact, *death* is one side effect listed on the feline prescription.

The literature for humans states that their risk of infection will be higher when they are on this drug and to avoid people with contagious diseases or infections. Of course, your pet will have the same increased risk for infection and cancer. This is why it's just so important for you to understand and learn natural methods for treating allergies.

To complicate the situation further, conventional allergy-testing methods, which consist of either injecting allergens into the skin or a blood analysis, too often prove inadequate. One reason is that the actual number of allergens for which testing is done tends to be rather paltry, especially when compared with the thousands of potential allergy triggers in food and the environment. While efforts are being made to improve the reliability of these tests, they now stand at less than 50 percent accurate. This means that, basically, it's a toss-up as to whether the results are correct. Combine that with the small number of antigens tested, and it's no wonder that allergy vaccines do not work in many cases. It's simply a matter of statistics, and, when the dice are thrown right, the hyposensitization therapy (in which vaccinations of antigens that are serially increased in concentration are given to decrease sensitivity to an allergen) does afford improvement. In instances in which allergens are identified and removed from the dog's environment, diet, or both, relief is likely to be only temporary. The underlying problem won't be solved because the dog's immune system is on a sort of witch hunt, seeking out and finding new things to respond to with allergic reactions. The dog's internal computer system is often busy finding more and more items to which it will become allergic.

Holistic Treatments

Rather than simply attempting to identify and remove the growing list of substances that trigger your dog's allergies, a much more efficient remedy would be to fix the faulty immune system, the computer that has gone awry in your dog's body. And that's where holistic solutions, especially homeopathy, Nanbudripad's Allergy Elimination Technique (NAET), and other allergy-elimination techniques, can be especially effective. An easy way to understand these methods is to make the parallel of installing a virus-search program on your computer to clean up any glitches.

Nellie's Story

Nellie, a wonderful Golden Retriever who is a patient of mine, is a true testament to the curative powers of holistic healing methods. Here is Nellie's story—one dog's odyssey through the medical system in search of allergy relief.

When Nellie was a little more than a year old, she began doing things to relieve her itchiness like licking her paws and running her face along the carpets. The dog's owners, who are very attentive, took her right to a veterinarian, who diagnosed an allergy and started her on a daily regimen of the steroid prednisone. But even on a very high dose, Nellie didn't improve. The owners then tried antihistamines, but they didn't help either. Nellie was then tested for a thyroid condition and put on another drug, called Soloxine, along with more steroids and antibiotics, and she seemed to improve for a while. The steroids caused her to drink water constantly, so her owners tried to cut back on them, which only led to Nellie's becoming very itchy again.

A year later, her owners decided to try another veterinarian, who prescribed a new steroid and more antibiotics. Soon, Nellie's chest hair was gone, and her skin had become thick and greasy. Her paws didn't look so good, either. They then went to a third doctor, who took a blood sample and sent it away to determine what exactly Nellie was allergic to. This doctor also gave the owners a serum that they injected under the dog's skin every week. The vet did not anticipate improvement for at least nine months, but after a year, Nellie still was no better.

Sparing no expense, Nellie's owners' next stop was a veterinary school, where this time Nellie was given a skin test for allergies. From this test, another serum was developed and she was put on the new serum as well as antibiotics and antihistamines. Nellie's condition worsened. The fur was gone from her paws, which had developed black skin with red irritated areas. It was the same under her neck, which also had begun to ooze. She still itched all the time, her skin burned, she had no energy, and her owners were getting desperate and disillusioned.

Then, just as it seemed as though Nellie would be doomed to a life of irritation and misery, her owners heard about my practice. Not particularly hopeful, Nellie and her owners visited my office, and I immediately started her on homeopathic remedies, a rotating diet, and an allergy-elimination technique. The improvement was noticeable after the very first visit! As the treatments progressed, the itching diminished, the fur grew back under her neck and paws, and her skin returned to normal. After a few months, the scratching ended altogether, and Nellie's coat returned to its lustrous, good-as-new condition.

Methods for treating allergies include allergy-elimination techniques, adjusting the diet, limiting vaccinations, checking thyroid function, providing vitamins and supplements, using topical preparations, and administering homeopathic remedies.

Allergy-Elimination Techniques

The typical scenario the owner of an allergic dog follows is *the path of avoidance*—avoiding foods to which the dog is believed or suspected to be allergic. It's a lifelong job. The problem is compounded by the fact that, typically, the allergic dog will subsequently become allergic to ingredients in the *special* food because of the repeated exposure. Then it's on to a new food with another novel protein.

It simply doesn't have to be that way. If you've been running this gamut for years, it may be hard to conceive that allergy-elimination techniques exist that do away with your "food-eluding expeditions" by transforming an allergic dog into a nonallergic dog. It may seem too good to be true that you can turn these chronic problems around, but, in the hands of a competent veterinary practitioner, it's quite probable. So let's find out how that is.

Whatever the reason—karma, kismet, or serendipity—the manner in which this very workable technique was discovered was indeed fortuitous. Dr. Devi Nambudripad, a chiropractor and an acupuncturist, was very ill with allergies all her life. She was allergic to almost everything under the sun, and she lived exclusively on polished white rice and broccoli. One day she decided to "take a walk on the wild side" and eat a carrot. She started to pass out so she quickly placed needles into some of her own acupuncture points to keep herself from going into shock, and she simply fell asleep holding the offending carrot in her hand. She felt a supreme feeling of well-being when she awoke forty-five minutes later. She researched her experience and found that when you hold an allergenic substance within your body's electromagnetic field while receiving a treatment for

the adverse allergic reaction, the system somehow self-corrects. Dr. Nambudripad found that the body corrects itself simply by recognizing the electromagnetic signature of an item while being encouraged, by stimulation of acupuncture points, to start the process of healing, repairing, correcting, and harmonizing. She subsequently developed and refined this therapy that she dubbed the Nambudripad Allergy Elimination Technique (NAET). This noninvasive method uses a special combination of chiropractic treatment, muscle response testing, and acupuncture to reprogram the brain and nervous system.

After first identifying an allergy trigger through muscle response testing, the practitioner goes about correcting the source of a blockage or imbalance in the body that is causing the allergy. This is done by a technique that corrects the immune system's misperception of the allergen. This, in effect, enables the body to heal itself by restoring the unrestricted flow of such energy—a sort of corrective reprogramming that harmonizes and therefore normalizes the body's reaction to the allergen. Each treatment teaches your dog's body that an allergen, whether it be pollen or a food, such as beef, is a friend rather than an enemy.

Because I felt NAET was needed in the field of holistic veterinary medicine, I introduced the topic at the 1998 American Holistic Veterinary Medical Annual Conference when it was virtually unknown. When we enter the realm of energetic holistic medicine, we leave the field of biology and enter the field of physics. Every day, new research in physics challenges old beliefs about how the body works and heals. Even though the Chinese recognized energy pathways, called acupuncture meridians, more than 6,000 years ago, it's taken the advent of new scientific methodology to recognize how changes in the energy fields affect and determine health. The autonomic nervous system has an integral role in recognizing what the body's computer has deemed an enemy. It then calls into action the various components of the immune system to defend the body against the perceived enemy.

Allergies in pets occur because what should be considered "friends of the body" (beef, chicken, fish, etc.) get logged in as enemies, just like the peanuts that cause a deathly allergic reaction in certain children. Allergies in our pets are more commonly seen nowadays because there are simply more ways to confuse the body's systems and increase the items that are logged in as enemies. Nature never designed these systems to be exposed to so many vaccinations, chemicals, and pesticides on a routine basis.

Allergy-elimination techniques correct the autonomic nervous system's perception of the allergic substance so that it is no longer perceived as a threat. It all happens within the realm of physics on an energetic level and translates into physical healing. The NAET practitioner has the energetic resonance of each allergen in a vial. *Applied kinesiology* is utilized to determine your pet's reaction to the resonance of that allergen. Once an allergen, such as pollen, beef, or eggs, is recognized, the vial is placed directly on your dog while specific acupuncture points on the body are lightly stimulated. This readjusts the autonomic nervous system's perception of the substance, and the allergic reaction to it is eliminated. It may be amazing to learn that something so simple can work so well, but the proof is in the rewarding results.

The inventor of applied kinesiology is Dr. George Goodhart, a Detroit chiropractor. After he held his first seminar in 1974, many other practitioners began using the technique with great success to determine the causes of problems that had previously seemed to defy diagnosis. Over the ensuing years, this method of testing for triggers of various conditions blossomed into a major diagnostic art, with many more medical professionals, including veterinarians, adopting it in their practices. (*Your Body Doesn't Lie* by Dr. John Diamond is an excellent source on the subject.)

A few visits are usually sufficient to eliminate food allergies, while follow-ups are generally needed to successfully rid patients of allergies to grass, pollen, weeds, trees, flowers, dust, fabrics, mold, vaccines, and anything else that triggers a response. Other forms of treatment that are based on this technique have since been developed.

In my practice, the first step is identifying what substances the patient is allergic to. In the first comprehensive assessment, approximately 500 vials specifically designed for this purpose are checked using applied kinesiology. I decide the order of treatment of the allergens and create a program for the patient. The vials are mailed to the pet owner's home with clear instructions on how to gently massage easy-to-find acupuncture points and complete the treatment in the comfort of home.

Allergies can surface as skin problems, ear infections, chronic diarrhea, vomiting, picky appetite, and asthma. These problems often become chronic lifetime problems and need continual veterinary oversight and medication. Whether these allergies are the mildest or the most extreme, they have a drastic impact on a pet's comfort and happiness. Allergy-elimination treatments that have since stemmed from NAET don't just relieve the symptoms but remove the source of the torment. These treatments have helped many pet owners and their best friends live happier and fuller lives.

Adjusting and Rotating the Diet

Dogs are often allergic to items present in food. There are certain food items that the majority of allergic dogs react to: nutritional yeast, wheat, beef, chicken, eggs, and corn and fish oils. The by-products in many commercial foods may also promote allergies. Changing the food can help, but if the same diet is given every day, the dog's immune system will eventually perceive the products that the dog eats daily as allergens to which it needs to react.

To avoid this problem, feed your dog a rotating diet of three different hypoallergenic home-cooked meals. Jars of baby-food meat or healthy deli cuts without preservatives can be handy to use in a pinch. Typical proteins include lamb, venison, salmon, and duck. On the first day, you might feed lamb, white rice, and chopped parsley and carrots. A sample diet for the second day might include venison, cooked white potatoes, and chopped kale or greens. The menu for the third day could be cooked oatmeal and salmon. Rotate these three diets on a regular basis.

Malassezia

Malassezia occurs when the organism *Malassezia pachydermatis*, which is a normal yeast found on the skin and in the ear canals, overgrows and causes itching and inflammation of the skin. It can also cause a brown, sweet-smelling substance in the ears. Malassezia is commonly found on the thickened, denuded areas of the skin of dogs with chronic allergies. Often it is found in areas that sunlight cannot reach, such as the belly, lower neck, and underarms. The allergy and the yeast infection play off each other, each one contributing to the other's ability to cause a problem. Typically, the yeast would not be there if it weren't for the allergy, and its presence makes the itching worse and causes the skin to become thickened and dark. Learn how to treat it in Part III, Fungal Infections.

Limiting Vaccinations

Routinely giving cocktails of vaccinations containing six or more diseases encourages your dog's immune system to react incorrectly. Read the Chapter 10 to learn all about the dos and don't of vaccinations.

Checking Thyroid Function

Thyroid problems may contribute to the allergic symptoms your dog exhibits. Checking the thyroid requires a simple blood test that tests the thyroid hormones T4 and free T4. Free T4 is the active tiny fraction of unbound total T4. These two readings will help determine whether your dog's thyroid is underactive. If you have a diagnosis of hypothyroidism, your veterinarian will want to prescribe supplemental thyroid medication. Often, after a dog's thyroid problem is corrected, allergies and secondary infections subside. When a thyroid problem is found and corrected, holistic therapies also seem to work more quickly. While this may differ for every dog, every bit helps. The thyroid is a master gland, and it regulates the performance of many important organs as well as the immune system.

Providing Vitamins and Supplements

Vitamin C is an important vitamin for dogs with allergies. Dogs with allergies rapidly use up their stores of self-made vitamin C. Allergic dogs definitely need extra vitamin C to help decrease their allergic responses and to help remove toxins from the body. Vitamin C is even more important for dogs who are on steroids or who have been on antibiotics. The dose of vitamin C ranges from 250 mg to 2,000 mg once or twice a day, depending on the size of your dog.

Too much vitamin C all at once will cause loose stools. Always increase the dose of vitamin C gradually to avoid diarrhea. While some dogs may do well on 2,000 mg of vitamin C twice a day, some may be able to tolerate only 500 mg once a day. After the lower dose is well tolerated, the dose can be slowly increased.

Vitamin E works in conjunction with vitamin C. Both vitamins act as antioxidants. A recommended dose of vitamin E is from 200 to 400 IU once a day for any size dog.

Omega-3 fatty acids have been found useful in relieving allergic skin conditions. Other sources of omega-3 fatty acids are evening primrose oil, borage seed oil, and black currant seed oil. Hemp oil and olive oil, along with coconut oil, are also good sources of healthy fats.

Other helpful supplements include an antioxidant combination containing CoQ_{10}; a dose of 30 mg can be given once a day. Zinc can also be helpful with certain skin conditions. Zinc picolinate is the best form, and 10 mg can be given once a day. Quercitin, a nutraceutical found in health food stores, assists in the temporary relief of allergies by reducing the release of histamine from the mast cells, thus minimizing the allergic response.

Using Topical Preparations

Dogs with allergies often chew at themselves incessantly. The more they chew, the more they itch—just like that mosquito bite. It is very important to put an end to the scratch-itch-scratch-itch cycle that is created. There are many topical preparations that can help soothe the irritated area and decrease the inflammation:

- Black tea or Japanese green tea prepared as a very strong brew is applied to the inflamed area for three to ten minutes to soothe it. The rest of the brew can be stored in refrigerator and used later.
- Calendula tincture can be applied to the irritated areas either full-strength or diluted 1:1.
- A cotton ball soaked in witch hazel can be placed on itchy areas a few times a day.
- Aloe vera can be applied to the area one to three times a day. The gel from the fresh plant works the best.
- Baking soda can work wonders! Mix 1 teaspoon of baking soda with a little water to make a paste. Place the paste on the areas that are itchy or reddened. Leave the paste on for a few hours and then wash off.
- Prepare a baking-soda spray by mixing 1 tablespoon of baking soda with 8 ounces of water. Put the mixture in a spray bottle and use as necessary. Shake before using.
- Oatmeal poultices are easy to make. The powder, mixed well

with water, is placed on the area for a short time. Colloidal oatmeal, found in pharmacies, can be used as a tub bath or poultice.

- Preparation H cream contains no harmful ingredients and works to stop itching and burning. It can often prove helpful with itchy skin.
- Cabbage leaf is an old-time remedy used to remove heat and inflammation from an area. Pound one cabbage leaf until the surface is broken and the juice oozes out. Hold this leaf on the inflamed area. The leaf will begin to get warm as it soaks the inflammation out. Remove the leaf after several minutes.

Administering Homeopathic Remedies

Homeopathic remedies need to be chosen in relation to the symptoms they produce. The type of reaction that occurs in relation to the problem is important when deciding on a remedy. Some dogs itch less and feel better when they are warm. They may sit out on an asphalt driveway and bake in the sun. Some dogs desperately need a cool environment and will lie on the tiled bathroom floor or sit by the air-conditioner vent.

You should begin to see results with the following remedies in two to ten days. If no relief is gained or if the dog gets worse, discontinue the remedy.

- Sulphur 6c. This remedy is indicated in dogs who prefer a cool environment. The skin can be red and the itching intense. The skin can also have an unhealthy, leathery look to it. This remedy is given twice a day for one week.
- Arsenicum album 30c. This remedy is used with dogs who prefer the heat. The skin can be dry and flaky, and the coat can appear lusterless and dry. The dog who needs this remedy may also be thirsty and restless. Dose at twice a day for two weeks.
- Graphites 30c. This remedy is good for dogs who get hot spots with their allergies. These areas can ooze a sticky yellow or honey-colored substance that causes the fur to stick to the area. Give this remedy four times a day for one week and use calendula tincture topically as well. You may need to shave the fur in this area so that the hot spots can get some air and dry up.

Apply the calendula several times a day, reducing the frequency as the area improves.

- Rhus toxicodendron 30c. This remedy is made from poison ivy, and we all know how itchy a poison ivy reaction can be! The dog who needs this remedy will often have a pimply vesicular rash with much itching and redness. Warmth lessens the severity of the symptoms. Dose at three times a day for two to four weeks.

Administering Remedies

Homeopathic remedies are easy to administer. As previously mentioned, the tiny white pellets are meant to be tucked into your dog's lower lip fold to melt. If you are using a remedy in liquid form, simply place a few drops on your dog's gums. An alternative is to dissolve a few pellets in a small amount of spring water, stir, and then give the water to your dog as a remedy.

Discontinue the remedy after the problem resolves. Homeopathic remedies work to assist the body to heal. When this is accomplished, the remedy is stopped.

- Grindelia 30c. This homeopathic remedy can be given up to three times a day, as needed, to help decrease the intensity of the itching.
- Psorinum 200c. This remedy is excellent for conditions in which the skin appears unhealthy. The coat may have a noticeable musty odor, the skin is commonly dry, and the itching is intense. This remedy should be given once a day for one week. If symptoms reappear later, give the remedy again for one week.

10. Injecting Doubt into Annual Inoculations

*Y*ou've received your postcard from the vet's office reminding you that it's vaccination time again. But didn't you just go through this same routine last year? If your dog needs to be vaccinated so often, why, you might wonder, don't you need to have that polio vaccination you received as a tiny baby repeated annually?

Should you dare to query, you will probably be lectured about the validity and importance of vaccines. Who are you to question professionals who do this every day? Folks have been made to feel confused under these circumstances and have ended up being embarrassed into having combination vaccines injected into their pets in spite of their doubts about the vaccines' safety or necessity.

Vaccines are widely accepted and highly regarded in our society. Having an unvaccinated dog is often seen as a sign of neglect and abuse. And while vaccinating your new puppy may protect him from dangerous infectious diseases, improperly vaccinating or overvaccinating will have ramifications for his health in adulthood. Vaccines can initiate serious and chronic health problems such as autoimmune disease, allergies, and irritable bowel problems. That's why it's wise to understand vaccines and make the correct choices for your new family member. Historically, vaccines were started far too early and were given too frequently. The recommended vaccination schedule for puppies was to start at six weeks and vaccinate every two weeks until they were fourteen weeks old. Some folks even started at four weeks. This antiquated schedule now has been found to contribute to health problems. Vaccinating too early and too often actually prevents the vaccines from having their desired effect. First of all, the maternal antibodies in the mother's milk identify the vaccines as infectious agents and destroy them before a four- to nine-week-old nursing puppy can benefit. Additionally, vaccinations too closely spaced interfere with a puppy's immune system response because immune components from the earlier vaccine nullify the following one. To prevent nullification, the ideal interval between the first vaccine and the next booster shot is three to four weeks.

Nowadays, all veterinary schools are proponents of more careful vaccination protocols. If expert advice is what you need, be aware that many experts working at prestigious veterinary schools are speaking out against the regimen of yearly vaccines as well as questioning the validity of giving certain vaccines at all. Before I share my own opinions, let's consider some of the official positions taken by various veterinary institutions. *Kirk's Current Veterinary Therapy (now in its twenty-fifth edition)*, a major reference book for veterinarians, states that the practice of giving annual vaccinations "lacks scientific validity of verification" and goes on to note that "immunity to viruses persists for years or for the life of the animal."

In 2006, the American Animal Hospital Association's Canine Vaccine Task Force recognized that vaccination decisions must always be made on an individual basis, based on risk and lifestyle factors. Updated and new information, including serologic testing, vaccine adverse event reporting, and medical and legal perspectives, was taken into consideration. It was the opinion of the task force that vaccines against canine distemper, canine adenovirus-2, and canine parvovirus produce excellent immune response and can be used in extended-interval vaccination programs and at the discretion of the veterinarian.

In 2007, the American Veterinary Medical Association Committee report stated that the annual revaccination recommendation frequently found on many vaccination labels is based on historical precedent, not scientific data. The American Animal Hospital Association's Canine Vaccine Task Force stated in 2003 that "Misunderstanding, misinformation, and the conservative nature of our profession have largely slowed adoption of protocols advocating decreased frequency of vaccination."

Furthermore, serology testing and challenge studies indicate that the duration of immunity for the canine distemper and canine parvovirus vaccines has been demonstrated to be a minimum of seven years. As a result of all of this scientific research, most of the veterinary schools in North America have changed their protocols for vaccinating dogs. These veterinary schools, along with the American Veterinary Medical Association, have looked at studies that show how long vaccines

last and have concluded that annual revaccination is unnecessary. Quite simply, there is no scientific documentation to support the supposed need for yearly vaccinations. At the same time, research shows that these same vaccinations subject a dog to the potential risks of allergic reactions and immune-mediated disease.

In 1995, C. A. Smith, in the *Journal of the American Veterinary Medical Association*, explained that vaccination is a potent medical procedure with both benefits and risks for the patient and that revaccination of patients with sufficient immunity does not add measurably to their disease resistance and may increase their risk of adverse post-vaccination events. She also stated that adverse events may be associated with any of the ingredients in the vaccine mix. Possible adverse events include anaphylaxis, immunosuppression, autoimmune disorders, and transient infections.

When your dog receives his DHLPP vaccination, it includes distemper, hepatitis, leptospirosis, parainfluenza, and parvovirus. In many cases, dogs also receive vaccinations for coronavirus, bordetella, Lyme disease, and rabies at the same time, which means that he's getting from *five to nine* inoculations all at once. This is the equivalent of a person's getting immunized for encephalitis, measles, mumps, hepatitis, polio, whooping cough, tetanus, Lyme disease, and flu all at the same time.

The devastating effects of such cocktail vaccinations on humans—in this case, Gulf War troops— were described in H. McManners's article "Scientists Link Gulf War Illness to Vaccines and Drugs," which appeared in the June 22, 1997, edition of the *London Sunday Times*:

> The drug cocktail suppressed one part of the body's immune system, known as Th1, which combats viruses and cancers. At the same time, Th2, a part of the immune system, which normally reacts mildly against pollen or house dust mites, was made hypersensitive to outside irritants. The double effect meant that the soldiers were more likely to succumb to common diseases, while also suffering extreme allergic reactions to harmless elements in the atmosphere.

A further report documenting the relationship between vaccinations and Gulf War syndrome, published in the British medical journal *Lancet*, opened the door to massive legal claims filed on behalf of the ailing veterans.

There's just not much motivation for profit-driven veterinary drug companies to research vaccine-related problems in pets or the true duration of immunity to vaccinations. But such research has been done with children in numerous countries. Although manufacturers of drugs for humans attempt to isolate cases of vaccine injury as unusual and a tragic consequence of progress, they don't seem to have any interest in attempting to discover whether kids who have received no vaccines at all are healthier than those who do.

A Japanese study done in 2000 ("The Effect of DPT and BCG Vaccinations on Atopic Disorders," published by H. Yoneyama, M. Suzuki, K. Fujii, and Y. Odajima in the Japanese allergology journal *Arerugi*) looked into that question and found asthma cases in vaccinated

Guidelines for Vaccinations

Whenever you choose to vaccinate your dog, follow these guidelines:

1. Make sure your dog is in optimal health at the time of each vaccination.

2. Never administer vaccines to a dog who is on a corticosteroid (e.g., prednisone, prednisolone, dexamethasone, and especially Atopica) or any other immunosuppressive drug.

3. Do not allow vaccinations to be given to a dog suffering from cancer or any severe illness, such as liver problems or kidney failure.

4. Do not allow your dog to have unnecessary vaccinations.

5. Do not allow ineffective vaccines such as bordetella (kennel cough) to be administered annually on the assumption that it will provide your dog with twelve months of immunity. The effectiveness of this vaccine is very short lived, so it would need to be given within three months of boarding if it is required by the kennel.

6. Do not allow your dog to have vaccines that have not been proved to be either safe or effective.

7. The dose of vaccine given should correspond with the approximate size of the dog.

8. Do not have your dog inoculated with his first puppy booster until he is at least nine to twelve weeks of age. Just keep him away from public places and unknown dogs for a bit longer.

9. The interval between the first vaccine and the booster shot should be three to four weeks; otherwise, the shots can interfere with each other. Upon being infected with the vaccine virus, cells increase their production of interferon; therefore, if the second vaccination is administered too soon (within a week to ten days), it will be less effective. Delays of longer than eight weeks should likewise be avoided. The exception to this rule is the rabies vaccination, which is given once at three to six months (later being better) and then a year later, with subsequent shots administered on whatever schedule your municipality requires.

10. Give your dog the homeopathic remedy Thuja 6x (available at most health food stores) at a dose of twice a day for two weeks following any and all vaccinations. This should help reduce any chronic damage from the vaccine.

11. If your pet experiences discomfort (swelling, redness, or pain) at the site of the inoculation, give him the homeopathic remedies Ledum 30x and Hypericum 30x (commonly available at health food stores) four times a day for three days.

12. If your dog experiences a mild fever after a vaccination, administer the homeopathic remedy Belladonna 6c four times a day until his temperature returns to normal for an entire day. Also contact your veterinarian.

13. If your dog begins to develop any swelling around the face or muzzle following a vaccination, give him the homeopathic remedy Apis 200c every fifteen minutes. You can also give the over-the-counter drug Benadryl; check with your vet for the dosage. If the swelling persists, get him to your veterinarian ASAP, as he may be suffering from anaphylactic shock, which can cause the throat to swell until it constricts the airways, causing asphyxiation. Your veterinarian can give him an injection of steroids, which usually handles the problem uneventfully.

14. The best vaccination protocol is one combination puppy booster after ten weeks of age and then a booster three to four weeks later. The next booster would be a year later, and this booster, being administered after the age of six months, will most likely provide lifetime immunity to parvovirus and distemper.

15. Instead of having your dog revaccinated for distemper and parvovirus the year after his "one year" vaccine, use blood titer tests to determine whether or not immunity persists. The owners of show dogs or therapy dogs may want yearly titers to satisfy themselves and others that their pet is immune. Titers are reliable and dependable.

Exception to the Rule

Guidelines from the AMVA state that a veterinarian can, in the case of any dog with an illness, opt to write a note to the township stating that the dog cannot be vaccinated at that time due to illness.

children to be ten times higher than in those who had not received any shots. In addition, more than 50 percent of the vaccinated kids had either asthma, rashes, or chronic runny noses, compared with less than 10 percent of the unvaccinated children. Fifty years ago, before vaccines became an annual ritual, the incidence of allergies, autoimmune disease, and cancer in the canine population was a mere fraction of what it is today. Since then, vaccine manufacturers have encouraged the veterinary establishment to use their products whenever and wherever possible, and as a result have evolved into multibillion-dollar enterprises. But they've also been successful at something else— evading responsibility for the damage their products cause. In recent years, vaccine companies have become indemnified. This means that you can't sue the manufacturer if your pet becomes severely ill or dies due to a vaccination, although occasionally the medical expenses might be reimbursed to demonstrate the "goodwill" of the company.

By and large, the public has learned to blindly accept the notion that it is essential for dogs to be inoculated every year with a combined vaccine. Owners who want their dogs to stay healthy are told that is what it takes and are sent regular reminders that these "important" shots are due. Yet veterinary journals, medical textbooks, and veterinary schools have all spoken out against this practice, emphasizing that there is no justification for many of these vaccines to be injected annually.

If you, like me, have cried during the movie *Old Yeller*, you may be wondering about the rabies vaccine. Rabies is contagious to all mammals, including humans, and is an awfully frightening, fatal disease. Research is currently being done to assess the exact duration of immunity following the vaccination. Qualified laboratories also perform vaccine titer tests for rabies that will inform you if your dog has retained immunity from his last vaccine. However, for the time being, owners are obligated to have their pets vaccinated for rabies on a schedule as determined by state and local laws.

While attitudes are gradually changing toward canine vaccinations, especially the necessity of administering so many so often, you have to realize that many people are still trapped in a conventional rut. You must therefore expect to encounter opposition if you express a desire to cut back on your dog's immunization program and be ready to stand your ground, politely but firmly.

Veterinary schools are now at the forefront of change. For daring to go against the conventional wisdom when the health of patients is at stake, they deserve to be commended. If they can do it, you can, too. Holistic veterinarians take a stricter stance, with many recommending that it's best to wait as long as you can before beginning to vaccinate your dog. Some veterinarians recommend starting at nine weeks; others advocate as late as twenty-two weeks. I personally recommend waiting until at least ten weeks of age, ideally twelve or fourteen weeks if you possibly can. The second vaccine should be given twenty-one to twenty-eight days after the initial vaccination. I like the second vaccine to occur at sixteen weeks of age or older.

First Vaccination	Second Vaccination
12 weeks	16 weeks
14 weeks	17 weeks
13 weeks	16 or 17 weeks

Immune-Mediated Disease

Studies show that some breeds, such as the Akita, Cocker Spaniel, German Shepherd Dog, Golden Retriever, Irish Setter, Great Dane, Kerry Blue Terrier, Dachshund (especially the longhaired variety), Poodle, Old English Sheepdog, Scottish Terrier, Shetland Sheepdog, Shih Tzu, Vizsla, and Weimaraner, as well as breeds with white or predominantly white coat color, have an increased frequency of immune-mediated disease. A significant number of these animals had been vaccinated within thirty to forty-five days of the onset of their autoimmune disease.

This information comes from an article by W. Jean Dodds, DVM, "Vaccination Protocols for Dogs Predisposed to Vaccine Reactions," which appeared in the *Journal of the American Animal Hospital Association*. Dr. Dodds is known for her research on animal vaccinations and her Canine Minimal Vaccine Use Protocol.

The next question to address is what vaccines are important to give. Combination vaccines are commonly available, each with different mixes. Distemper and parvovirus are the important viruses with which to vaccinate your puppy. Dr. W. Jean Dodds of Hemopet is a forerunner in research on the duration of protection of the various vaccine viruses and on the medical problems created by vaccines. Dr. Dodds does not recommend vaccinating against coronavirus because it is a very rare, mild, self-limiting disease that infects only puppies younger than six weeks of age. The kennel cough vaccine protects against only two of the possible six causes of kennel cough and should only be given prior to boarding. Additionally, its duration of immunity is only three months, if it even works at all.

Many veterinarians believe that the Lyme vaccine for dogs is controversial and unnecessary when tick prevention is practiced. It is listed as a noncore vaccine on the American Animal Hospital Association's canine vaccine guidelines. Dr. Meryl Littman, Associate Professor of Medicine at the Ryan Veterinary Hospital at the University of Pennsylvania, does not recommend the Lyme vaccine. Doctors and researchers have been concerned that this vaccine has the potential to create immune-mediated problems, the very same reason that the Lyme vaccine for people was considered too risky.

If this is uncharted territory for you and you're going to worry that a minimal vaccination schedule might not protect your new puppy, ask your veterinarian to run a vaccine titer test (a simple blood test that proves immune memory) that can measure your dog's antibodies to distemper and parvovirus. A positive titer proves that your dog's immune response will be adequate.

The new adage to follow when planning your dog's vaccination schedule is "less is best." Puppies can be socialized and play with other healthy dogs. No one wants his or her pup to develop allergies, autoimmune disease, or chronic gastrointestinal problems. With vaccination schedules, an ounce of prevention is truly worth that pound of cure. We want our dogs to live healthy and long lives, and *carefully* vaccinating them will give them that extra edge.

Let your veterinarian know how you feel about vaccines and make sure that your preferences are documented in your dog's records. Get your veterinarian to agree that he or she will not give your companion any inoculations without your prior consent. Make it clear, also, that you'd like a vaccine titer test done once a year (if that is indeed your preference); use copies of the titer tests to prove standing immunity for your pet if he is to be boarded or admitted for surgery.

Boarding kennels are slowly beginning to accept titers as alternatives to vaccinations. If the people who operate your kennel don't accept titers, educate them. (Don't be afraid to quote Dr. Khalsa!) If they still insist on requiring shots, maybe you should find another kennel or hire a dog sitter. There are folks out there who do dog sitting and house sitting for a living, including many who are bonded. My dogs prefer to stay at home when the family is away, anyway. If you have multiple animals, as I do, this can be a solution that will both reduce the risk of your pets contracting diseases and save you money.

Doggy daycare facilities should be handled the same way. Try to acquaint them with the latest thinking of the veterinary schools, or ask them to do some research on their own. Dog training schools may likewise need to be enlightened. Therapy-dog facilities do generally accept titers, although they usually require an entire set of tests.

The point is, don't be reluctant to let the people most involved with your dog know what you want and how you arrived at that determination. In addition to making things a lot easier for you, it just may help increase the speed at which "the times…are a-changin'."

Duration of Immunity

The AAHA and AVMA reevaluated their vaccination schedules, thanks in part to the work of Dr. Ronald D. Schultz. The AAHA's Canine Vaccine Task Force warned vets in the March/April 2003 issue of the *Journal of the American Animal Hospital Association* that "immunological memory provides durations of immunity for core infectious diseases that far exceed the traditional recommendations for annual vaccination."

Dr. Schultz concurred, stating, "This is supported by a growing body of veterinary information as well-developed epidemiological vigilance in human medicine that indicates immunity induced by vaccination is extremely long lasting and, in most cases, lifelong."

According to Dr. Schultz, "The recommendation for annual revaccination is a practice that was officially started in 1978. This recommendation was made without any scientific validation of the need to booster immunity so frequently. In fact, the presence of good humoral antibody levels blocks the anamnestic response to vaccine boosters just as maternal antibody blocks the response in some young animals. The patient receives no benefit and may be placed at serious risk when an unnecessary vaccine is given. Few or no scientific studies have demonstrated a need for cats or dogs to be revaccinated. Annual vaccination for diseases caused by CDV, CPV-2, FPLP, and FeLV has not been shown to provide a level of immunity any different from the immunity in an animal vaccinated and immunized at an early age and challenged years later. We have found that annual revaccination with the vaccines that provide long-term immunity provides no demonstrable benefit."

Dr. Schultz published the following chart, which displays the minimum duration of immunity for canine core vaccines based on more than 1,000 dogs, in a March 1998 *Veterinary Medicine* article titled "Current and Future Canine and Feline Vaccination Programs." Both challenge (exposure to the real virus) and serology (antibody titer results) are included in the chart.

It is important to note that this is the minimum duration of immunity (DOI) based on the duration of the studies; at the time of the article's publication, longer studies had not yet been done on some of these vaccines. Dr. Schultz says, "It is possible that some or all of these products will provide lifelong immunity."

Dr. Schultz has done further studies with similar results, finding that the vaccines tested consistently not only provided protection for a minimum of four to five years, but it did so in 100 percent of the dogs tested.

Vaccine	Minimum Duration of Immunity	Methods Used to Determine Immunity
Canine Distemper Virus (CDV)	5–15 years	challenge/serology
Canine Adenovirus-2 (CAV-2)	7–9 years	challenge-CAV-1/serology
Canine Parvovirus-2 (CPV-2)	7 years	challenge/serology

11. Cancer Prevention and Treatment

For loving dog owners, cancer is the most feared disease. It's a sad fact that cancer is the primary cause of death in dogs older than two years in the United States; one in three (some statistics say one in two) dogs will get cancer. That's truly significant. Whether it's called cancer, the Big C, a malignancy, the silent killer, a tumor, or a growth, it's just plain frightening.

Unless the mass is bulging out noticeably from the skin, most cancer grows invisibly, inside the body. Many of the symptoms and signs that tell the owner and the veterinarian that something is very wrong are discovered only after the cancer is well established. The later the cancer is found, the more time the cancer cells have had to spread. Unfortunately, there is no "tumor marker testing" for dogs (as there is for humans) for early detection of certain types of cancer. Additionally, it's common for routine blood tests to show normal results even when cancer is present.

Malignant tumors are made up of cancerous cells. As they break away from a malignant tumor, these cancer cells can invade nearby tissues and organs. Cancer destroys life by invading an essential organ, where the disease grows out of control. Different types of cancer have different behaviors. Some cancers grow only locally, while others, such as lymphatic cancers, in which cancerous cells enter the bloodstream, spread rapidly to multiple areas in the body.

The spread of a malignant cancer is called *metastasis*. In contrast to a cancerous tumor, a benign mass does not spread and does not cause degenerative changes.

Most cancers are named for the type of cell or the organ in which they begin. There are numerous types of cancers, and there are many ways to treat each type. While cancer treatments are based on detailed research into the causes of cancer, it can often be a trial-and-error process to find which treatment works best for an individual patient. Often, several mechanisms used in combination prove more effective than just one. The best choice to make about conventional or holistic treatment (or both) depends on the kind of cancer and how far the disease has progressed as well as what medical treatment the patient has already received.

Cancer takes a terrifying toll on both young and old dogs. Most types of cancer, once found, are difficult to stop. Cancer is an illness for which the proverbial ounce of prevention is definitely worth that pound of cure.

The Start of Cancer

The potential for cancer begins when carcinogens damage and alter the DNA in a cell. This damaged DNA sits and waits, like a seed on the ground waiting for water, until the conditions that promote the creation of a cancerous cell are just right. When a cancerous cell then starts to divide, your dog has a built-in mechanism to stop it. The tumor-suppressor gene p53 monitors the biochemical signals in cells that indicate that DNA mutation and division is in progress. The p53 gene instructs the cell to either halt the growth cycle or self-destruct. Your dog's body is set up to nip cancer in the bud; if the p53 gene fails (there can be genetic reasons for this), the immune system will kick in and attempt to eliminate the new cancer growth.

Once cancer gets a toehold, each type has its own special behavior. Some excrete substances that help them hide from the immune system, while others encapsulate themselves and become what could be considered something akin to an individual life-form. Some forms are very aggressive, while others grow slowly.

With every passing decade, the number and concentrations of carcinogens to which our dogs are exposed increase. Nowadays, exposure to toxins and carcinogens is unavoidable, but we can certainly work to decrease our pets' exposure to these toxins. It's important to learn about what's out there in the environment and how we can avoid carcinogens.

Flea- and Tick-Prevention Products

One way to reduce our dogs' exposure to carcinogens is simply not to buy and use carcinogenic products on our dogs. Dr. Dobozy of the Environmental Protection Agency's (EPA's) pesticide division states that one of the laboratory effects of fipronil in Frontline includes thyroid cancer and altered thyroid hormones. While the company creates the impression that its product does

not migrate into the body, radiolabeled fipronil was found in several organs and in the fat of dogs and was also excreted in their urine and feces. Bio Spot flea and tick control, Defend EXspot treatment, and Zodiac Spot On all contain either or both of the active ingredients permethrin and/or pyriproxyfen. Permethrin has been implicated as a carcinogenic insecticide, causing lung cancer and liver tumors in laboratory animals. Pyriproxyfen is a newer chemical, but testing has shown adverse effects on laboratory animals and their offspring.

Natural Lawn Care

Lawns should be treated as naturally as possible. While we all imagine that a good rain will wash toxic ingredients down into the earth, it actually forms a thick mist of the herbicides, fertilizers, and other lawn-care chemicals that rises a few feet off the ground. It's exactly the right height for dogs to easily inhale those toxins.

Exposure to a carcinogen typically occurs many years before the cancer appears. Often, exposure never escalates into a cancerous growth. Imagine how potent the carcinogens are that create cancer within several months in a laboratory setting!

I'm simply mentioning the foregoing commonly used products in relation to cancer. Unfortunately, this does not mean that the rest of the products—those I did not mention—are safe. According to the Center for Public Integrity, which collected data through the Freedom of Information Act, the pyrethrins (naturally occurring compounds from the chrysanthemum plant) and pyrethroids (the synthetic counterparts) caused double the fatalities (1,600) from 2002 to 2007 than the nonpyrethroid compounds.

The first thing we can do to protect our pets is find a good natural product (such as Ticked Off by Deserving Pets) that will keep those pesky fleas and ticks away and try to minimize the overall use of toxic insecticides. We can then expand our horizons to lawn chemicals, weed killers, herbicides, and cleaning agents. Take it upon yourself to research items such as dryer sheets and room deodorizers in terms of their cancer-causing ingredients. I think you'll be very surprised. If I went into all of the carcinogens that we expose ourselves and our dogs to on a daily basis, this would be a truly depressing chapter. The information I have already divulged is shocking enough.

Early Spaying and Neutering

Research now shows that early spaying or neutering actually increases a dog's cancer risk. A 2002 study established that there is an increased risk for osteosarcoma in both male and female Rottweilers sterilized before the age of one year. Another study showed that the risk of bone cancer in sterilized large purebred dogs was twice that of large purebred dogs who were not neutered. Additionally, a study at Cornell showed that both male and female dogs neutered at an early age were more prone to hip dysplasia. As an aside, research also indicates that the removal of the sex organs in both male and female dogs at an early age can cause growth plates to remain open.

Owners of female dogs are often advised to spay their pups before the first heat cycle in order to avoid mammary cancer. I have never offered that advice to my clients. In my thirty years of practice, I have never seen one of my patients who follows holistic care get mammary cancer,

Reducing the Risk

To recap, some of the steps you can take to help reduce your dog's risk of cancer are:

- Reduce the use of flea and tick products and find natural substitutes, such as Ticked Off.

- Maintain your lawn and yard with minimal or nontoxic herbicides, insecticides, and chemicals.

- Learn more about the detergents, fabric softeners, soaps, and cleansers that you use and begin to use products that do not contain carcinogens.

- Don't spay or neuter your dog too young. I recommend waiting until your dog is a year or eighteen months old.

- Minimize vaccinations.

although I have treated many patients who came to me with mammary cancer. Additionally, I have never clinically found neutering to lower the risk of prostate cancer in male dogs. The College of Veterinary Medicine at Michigan State University did a small study in which they stated the same. Urinary incontinence, hypothyroidism, and a host of behavior problems have also been associated with early neutering.

Overvaccination

At the end of the last chapter, we discussed how overvaccination and vaccinations with cocktails of multiple viruses compromise and confuse your dog's immune system. The shame of it is that the vaccines are often unnecessary to start with.

Research has shown that up to 15 percent of different types of cancer are caused by viruses, and vaccines are easily contaminated with viruses and submicroscopic particles that can promote cancer. For example, a virus believed to contribute to a type of cancer called fibrosarcoma can contaminate some rabies vaccines. Other cancer-associated viruses can potentially contaminate tissue-culture media used to grow vaccines.

In another example, it has long been known that feline vaccine-associated sarcoma is a malignant tumor associated with the FeLV (feline leukemia virus) vaccine and rabies vaccine, with the tumor occurring at the site of the injection. Veterinary students are now being taught to inject these vaccines into a cat's or kitten's hind leg so the leg can be amputated if a tumor appears.

So what does this have to do with dogs? Allow me to explain. As I've mentioned, when your dog gets vaccinated, you are getting much more than you pay for. Both killed and live viruses that cause diseases in other species often contaminate the vaccine broth, which leads me to share the following true story: Parvovirus was an unknown disease until about 1980, when it broke out at the same time in Japan, England, and the United States. The feline panleukopenia virus had been a contaminant within the canine combo vaccine for some time. In 1980, it jumped species, changing so that it could infect dogs and resulting in the new disease called parvovirus. In fact, during the initial outbreak, veterinarians were using the feline panleukopenia vaccine to protect dogs from the new disease. It would be just as easy for viruses that cause cancer in cats to jump species and create cancer in dogs.

If you must vaccinate your dog, make sure that his immune system is performing optimally at the time of vaccination.

The Invisible Carcinogens

It simply makes sense that microwave towers, cell phones, and other wireless technology, such as smart meters, can impact your dog's body once you understand that all bodies are bioelectric. A body contains electrons that keep an electrical current flowing, and inside every cell are mitochondria, the "power plants" of the cell that respond to the body's natural electromagnetic fields. The International Agency for Research on Cancer recently stated that nonionizing radiation could cause cancer in humans.

The good news here is that our dogs don't talk on cell phones. You see, studies show that cell phones are a definite cause of brain cancer. In fact, in certain countries, young children's use of cell phones is restricted or prohibited. Our dogs', as well as our, DNA gets damaged by the invisible but toxic radiation emitted from cell towers, cell phones, and other electromagnetic devices. DNA is a biological Internet, and it serves as an interface—a crossing point—between cells and the frequencies in the environment. I like to think of it as a responsive and sensitive instrument.

According to Russian scientists, DNA not only is responsible for the construction of our bodies and our dog's bodies but also serves as data storage and communication. The alleles in DNA follow the rules of regular grammar and syntax, meaning that they are put together in a logical way, similar to the way that words are put together to form sentences.

What did it mean when the World Health Organization, on May 31, 2011, placed the nonionizing radiation coming from wireless smart meters on the Class 2-B carcinogen list?

Cell Phones and Tumors

Joel Moskowitz, PhD, is the director of the Center for Family and Community Health in the School of Public Health at the University of California, Berkeley. The Center for Family and Community Health is one of thirty-seven Prevention Research Centers supported by the Centers for Disease Control and Prevention. Dr. Moskowitz was involved in a review of twenty-three case control studies on mobile phone use and tumor risk, involving 37,916 participants. The meta-analysis, published in the *Journal of Clinical Oncology* in October 2009, revealed that the more robust studies showed that using a mobile phone for a decade or longer was associated with increased risk for developing a brain tumor.

Furthermore, scientists have observed DNA chain breaks from levels of nonionizing radiation lower than those emitted by wireless smart meters. In fact, many insurance companies will not cover cell phone manufacturers and wireless carriers—60 percent refuse to insure purveyors against future health damage suits.

The Role of Diet in Preventing Cancer

There is solid evidence that improved nutrition strengthens the immune system and helps prevent cancer. Believe it or not, we'll all get cancer multiple times in our lives. But before those tiny cancer cells get a firm hold, our immune system takes charge of the situation and cleans it all up, unbeknownst to us.

While you're reading this, the antioxidants in your dog's body are countering the destructive forces of free radicals, discussed in Chapter 7. His immune system is locating and destroying abnormal cells. His genes (DNA and RNA) are making proteins to repair damage done by carcinogens. These natural processes are helping your dog fight cancer, but they need a helping hand themselves. You can help by feeding your dog a healthy, cancer-fighting diet.

Vast numbers of studies show that excessive fat intake and a deficiency of important vitamins and minerals are related to higher rates of certain cancers. Figures from the National Cancer Institute show that 35 percent of all cancers can be attributed to dietary imbalances. The consumption of meat, poultry, fish, dairy, fats, and processed foods has steadily risen over the past decades, in step with the rising cancer rates. Thus, diet plays an important role in both cancer prevention and cancer formation.

Carcinogens in the environment and in dog food work to alter genetic information and turn normal cells into potential cancer cells. Just as planted seeds must be watered for them to grow, cells with damaged DNA need a certain diet to make them turn into true cancer cells. Although the genetic makeup of a dog factors into his susceptibility to cancer, I believe that not only poor diet but also overvaccination combined with environmental toxins play a definite role in causing cancer.

The National Cancer Institute states emphatically that many cancers can be prevented by making appropriate lifestyle changes. The following sections discuss the kinds of changes that I believe need to be made.

Benefits of Fruits and Vegetables

Blueberries: Source of a range of nutrients, including anticancer compounds

Broccoli: Rich in antibacterial, anticancer, and antiviral compounds

Carrots: Source of anticancer compounds; rich source of beta-carotene

Cranberries: Protects urinary tract, normalizes pH

Dandelion greens: Supports liver and kidney function, rich in potassium

Kale: Source of antioxidants and anti-inflammatory and anticancer compounds

It's important to know the nutritional "tricks of the trade" of preventing cancer. What ingredients in dog foods should you avoid? What foods effectively help prevent cancer? How do cancer-fighting foods accomplish their jobs?

According to a national report, there are more than 175 known carcinogens in the foods that humans eat. Food for animals is regulated much less strictly, and many carcinogens that are banned for humans are used in animal food. Additionally, when the fats in dog food are heated, very powerful carcinogens—nitrosamines—are produced. The coloring agents, nitrites, and nitrates in dog food also contribute to cancer formation. Further, if you cook for your dog, you should wash all fruits and vegetables with a soap designed to remove pesticides from food surfaces.

Aflatoxins

Avoid commercial dog foods that have peanut by-products or peanut husks or hulls in them. Peanuts are often contaminated with a fungus that produces carcinogenic toxins called aflatoxins. Dr. Colin Campbell, author of *The China Study*, received grants from the National Institutes of Health to research the presence of these aflatoxins, considered to be among the most potent carcinogens on the planet, in food. He tested twenty-nine jars of peanut butter purchased at grocery stores and found all twenty-nine to be contaminated with aflatoxins—as much as 300 times the amount judged to be acceptable in food in the United States. Corn is also high in aflatoxins.

Say No to Bonemeal

Don't use bonemeal as a calcium source. First of all, the calcium in bonemeal cannot be absorbed. Second, some bonemeal contains toxic heavy metals, such as lead and cadmium, which are absorbed. Cadmium appears to be the single largest contributor to autoimmune thyroid disease.

This powerful toxic metal depletes the body's selenium because the selenium is used to remove the cadmium. The selenium combines with the cadmium, and both are excreted through the liver. The enzyme that creates active thyroid hormone needs selenium. Selenium is also very important in protecting the cells from cancer. When the heavy metals in bonemeal deplete a mineral that helps protect against and treat cancer and lowers thyroid function, the effect is that of a double-edged sword. Vitamin E in the diet protects against cadmium toxicity.

Avoid Plastic

Store food in glass containers. If you must cook in a microwave, use only glass containers. When you heat food in the microwave in plastic containers or cover food with plastic wrap, the heat in the microwave causes the poisonous substance dioxin, a carcinogen, to leach out of the plastic and into the food. Restaurants are moving away from plastic and foam containers to paper ones.

Dioxins can leach into water that is stored in a plastic bottle or container and left in the sun or in a hot car. Use a canteen or glass bottle for your dog's (and your own) water if you can. Do not freeze water in plastic, either.

Vegetables

Adding vegetables to your dog's diet affords him the benefit of the phytonutrients present in these foods. Studies with humans have demonstrated a reduction in cancer risk in those who ate the most fruits and vegetables. Plants contain generous amounts of cancer-fighting antioxidants and

phytonutrients. Cruciferous vegetables, such as cabbage, kale, bok choy, turnips, rutabagas, mustard greens, and brussels sprouts, contain substances that demonstrate a genuine ability to protect your dog from cancer.

Carotenoids are what make plants colorful. Leafy greens and orange and yellow vegetables, such as squash and sweet potatoes, contain beta-carotene and other phytonutrients that help protect cells from cancer. Broccoli contains compounds that inhibit the effects of carcinogens and boost the production of cancer-blocking enzymes. Research has shown that eating kale helps the cells rid themselves of carcinogens eight times faster. Additionally, dogs with tumors who were fed kale had tumors that grew more slowly (or not at all) than dogs with tumors who were not fed kale.

Some studies talk about as much as a 30 percent lower risk of cancer in people who eat a lot of vegetables and fruit. It is no different for our dogs. The thing is—our dogs are exposed to many more environmental toxins than we humans are, so they need their phytonutrients even more.

Vegetables can be fed raw or lightly steamed, grated and mixed into your dog's food. Organically grown vegetables are the most beneficial because they are far richer in minerals and enzymes.

The Power of Chlorophyll

Chlorophyll is a green pigment found in just about all plants and algae. It's an extremely important compound in photosynthesis because it actually allows plants to absorb energy from light.

A marvelous and amazing fact is that the molecular structure of chlorophyll is almost identical to that of hemoglobin, which is found in red blood cells. Chlorophyll and hemoglobin are identical except for one atom. The hemoglobin in your dog's blood has iron as the central molecule, whereas the chlorophyll in plants has magnesium as the central molecule.

Hemoglobin is responsible for carrying oxygen to all of your dog's organs and cells. When our dogs eat chlorophyll, they're actually helping build the health of their blood because the chlorophyll will help replenish their red blood cells.

Chlorophyll helps to cleanse all of the cells of the body, fight infections, heal wounds, build the immune system, and detoxify all systems, particularly the liver and the digestive system. It also promotes digestive health, which is why many dogs with acute digestive problems tend to go for the grass.

Many of our canine friends can also benefit from chlorophyll's double action in both treating and preventing bad breath. Chlorophyll can eliminate odors in the mouth. It also improves digestion, the most common cause of bad breath in dogs with healthy teeth and gums.

Chlorophyll can increase oxygen utilization within your pet's body. It also breaks down calcium oxalate stones in the bladder. Importantly, chlorophyll reduces the ability of carcinogens to bind with DNA in the liver and other organs.

A study published in *Carcinogenesis* clearly shows that chlorophyll blocks procarcinogens, such as aflatoxins, that damage DNA. The Linus Pauling Institute's Cancer Chemoprotection Program has indicated that natural chlorophylls in the diet offer cancer protection. Chlorophyll also binds to toxic heavy metals, eliminating them from the body before they cause organ damage, such as kidney failure.

Dogs have the right idea when they eat grass, but the sad truth is that they do this because they have no other source of fresh green plants. Wild dogs and cats get their chlorophyll from the intestines of their prey. They also have a plethora of healthy wild plants to nibble on.

Most domestic dogs can't open the fridge and take out the spinach, broccoli, asparagus, and kale that give such a boost to their health. That's why we have to provide healthy additions for them.

Good and Bad Fats

Saturated animal fats have been shown to increase risk factors for cancer. When these animal fats are heated and cooked, the risk factor becomes even higher. Cancer-preventing diets for humans are low in animal fats. Remember, most people buy meat that is much leaner than the meat by-products that are found in dog food.

Keep the level of animal protein, including dairy, to below 20 percent of your dog's diet. If you feed a commercial dog food, don't add animal proteins or dairy to a food that already has more than 20 percent protein. If you cook for your dog, follow the recipes in the Canine Café section and keep the percentage of animal protein low. If you want to feed a raw diet, feed lots of vegetables and add well-cooked grains to provide a healthier, cancer-fighting balance.

Although cooked animal fat is undesirable, not all fats are bad. I recommend olive oil as the only oil to use for cooking because it does not decompose into toxic compounds as other cooking oils do.

The Protein Problem

An estimated 80–90 percent of all cancers in people are preventable by lifestyle choices. This can, of course, also be true for dogs. Dr. Colin Campbell's *The China Study*, published in 2006, proved that a diet with more than 20 percent animal protein posed a higher risk of turning cells with altered DNA into cancer cells. Cancer cells will not grow and multiply unless the right conditions are met. While our dogs cannot live in bubbles to prevent them from being exposed to the carcinogens in the environment, they can eat a diet that will help prevent cells from becoming cancer cells.

Cancer-Fighting Supplements

You know now that a healthy diet is the first step toward cancer prevention, but it's impossible to get enough nutrients through diet alone. I purposely created and developed the Deserving Pets vitamin/mineral/superfood/phytonutrient mix with kale and broccoli along with many other balanced foods, vitamins, and minerals as a product that could help protect our cherished pets from cancer.

Vitamins and Minerals

A good-quality multivitamin/mineral pill is a necessity. Begin with a multivitamin/mineral supplement with high doses of the antioxidant vitamins A, C, and E as well as beta-carotene and the mineral selenium. These nutrients have been shown to protect the cells' DNA from free-radical damage. Such damage is a major step toward the initiation of cancer. Studies have shown that supplemental selenium reduces cancer death rates by as much as 50 percent. Taking 200 micrograms of selenium a day repairs the damage in the DNA molecule to ensure normal cellular function and puts out the "spark" that ignites tumor growth.

Cancer begins when the DNA of a single cell is damaged or mutated, often by a free radical. The cell's normal repair mechanisms must break down for these abnormal cells to replicate into full-blown cancer. Vitamin C works on two fronts to fight cancer. First, it protects cellular DNA from free-radical damage. Second, it enhances the immune response. Although, unlike primates, dogs produce their own vitamin C, supplementation is needed in today's toxic environment. Your dog's diet may contain from 500 to 3,000 extra milligrams of vitamin C daily.

Vitamin E is an important antioxidant in your dog's fatty tissues. We've mentioned that vitamin E and vitamin C complement each other when given together. Vitamin A is also highly recommended as part of a daily supplement; vitamin A is actually used as a cancer treatment in conventional oncology.

Garlic

One of the oldest and most popular botanical medicines is garlic. It is mentioned in ancient Egyptian medical texts. Several compounds in garlic have inhibitory effects on the growth of certain cancer cells. Garlic is one of the most versatile and widely used herbs in the world. It is best given chopped and in the raw form, because the compounds in garlic are easily destroyed by cooking and processing. Chop the garlic fine and let it sit in the open air for ten minutes. This allows a special chemical reaction to occur. Allicin and other sulfur compounds in the garlic clove enhance the immune system, block carcinogens, and inhibit the formation of tumors.

Turmeric

Turmeric is an ingredient that is effective against the progression of cancer. It also has the added benefit of helping your dog's joints and both alleviating and preventing arthritis. This is a very powerful anticancer herb, and it can be used to flavor food. Add ¼–½ teaspoon to your dog's meal.

Thyroid Function

The thyroid gland is located on either side of your dog's trachea. It's the taskmaster of the body. It regulates metabolism and how efficiently all of the organs work, and it also communicates with the other glands in the body, such as the adrenal and the pituitary, to regulate hormones.

When the thyroid gland is functioning as it should, your dog's body is working as a well-oiled machine. An underactive thyroid (hypothyroid) results in a sluggish immune system and suboptimal performance within the body's organs. Humans who have a hypothyroid condition are

Exercise

For so many of us with busy lives, the thought of taking time out to give our dog some extra exercise to help prevent cancer may seem a bit much. I'm going to ask you to look at it this way—when you walk your dog for thirty minutes to stir up his metabolism to help prevent cancer, you're doing the same thing for yourself.

often overweight, but this is not always the case in dogs. Broda Barnes, MD, coauthor of *Hypothyroidism: The Unsuspected Illness*, observed in his clinical practice myriad patients with typical hypothyroid symptoms whose blood values for thyroid tested normal. So when getting your dog's thyroid function tested, it's important to have a good laboratory do the test and to have someone well versed in thyroid medicine interpret the results. I make it a point to send my thyroid tests to the Hemopet/Hemolife laboratory of Dr. W. Jean Dodds in California.

Dr. Barnes presented evidence that suggests a relationship between low thyroid and cancer in humans. In my clinical experience, I have found the same to be true for dogs. As part of a study I conducted for a pharmaceutical company on a natural treatment for cancer, I tested the thyroid function of all dogs accepted into the study. All of the dogs had some type of cancer, and the majority of the dogs tested positive for hypothyroid condition. While the stress of cancer treatment could have contributed to a low thyroid condition, many of the dogs were of breeds that were prone to hypothyroidism. So the question remains: what came first, the chicken or the egg?

Undetected hypothyroidism opens up the door for diseases, infections, and cancer. It's easy to administer supplemental thyroid medicine if necessary, and maintaining good thyroid function is an important step in maintaining your dog's overall health.

Detecting Cancer: Testing Methods

Visible lumps and bumps are the easiest symptoms to recognize; however, often the very visible lumps are benign fatty tumors and sebaceous cysts. Dangerous mast cell tumors within the skin are typically smaller and harder to find under the fur.

Many cancers begin deep inside your dog's body. These growths can go undetected until their sheer bulk causes discomfort and weight loss. Typical signs of cancer may include significant weight loss, increased water intake, and fatigue, but, in many cases, the patient may appear to be in good health until the cancer gets large enough to interfere with organ function.

Blood tests will not necessary tell you that something is wrong. You'd be amazed at how many dogs with cancer have perfectly normal blood tests. Ultrasounds are better tools for diagnosis; they are often able to reveal masses in dogs that cannot be detected by other tests, such as X-rays, which do not reveal nearly as much as ultrasounds do. Tumors can be hidden beside or behind organs and not reveal themselves in X-rays. It is important that any ultrasounds be done by an experienced and competent practitioner if you are concerned about cancer.

The Veterinary Diagnostics Institute (VDI) has developed a three-pronged approach to evaluating the possibility of cancer in your dog. One of the tests monitors vitamin D in your dog. Unlike humans, dogs and cats do not produce vitamin D from sunlight; their sole source of vitamin

D comes from their diets. Recent studies have shown that the vitamin D content in commercial pet food varies significantly by manufacturer. Furthermore, intestinal absorption of vitamin D varies significantly from dog to dog, and by intact status.

Expanding models of vitamin D have generated new terminology of "deficiency," "insufficiency," and "sufficiency" to define the protective effect that increasing stores of vitamin D have against disease. When found inadequate, dietary supplementation is warranted.

VDI laboratories is testing vitamin D in order to bring your pet's levels up to 100 mg/mL. This is exactly why Deserving Pets preventive supplements contain lots of active vitamin D_3 in them. I've researched cancer prevention in depth and know what's needed to prevent cancer in your pets.

Another of VDI's tests is for TK (thymidine kinase) levels; if they are highly elevated, there is a high likelihood that your pet has cancer somewhere in the body or will develop cancer soon. It's important to know that TK levels may also be elevated if your pet has an undiagnosed infection.

VDI's test for CRP (C-reactive protein) in dogs and haptoglobin in cats checks for harmful levels of inflammation. Early treatment and reduction of inflammation in the body is important in preventing cancer.

This is exactly why supplementation with a quality preventive supplement that contains ingredients such as vitamins C, A, active D_3, natural vitamin E, zinc, selenium and biologically active superfoods is so very important to give to your pets every single day. And that's just why I developed Deserving Pets. Statistics say that one in two dogs will get cancer. I was seeing much too much cancer in my practice, and the incidence of this disease was increasing every year.

During a physical exam, your veterinarian should palpate your dog's lymph nodes and abdomen. Once a month, lightly run your fingers over his body in search of any unusual masses on, in, or below the skin. Many older dogs develop benign lipomas, which pose no threat. For concerned owners, I simply aspirate these lipomas with a small needle and syringe and stain them. It's relatively pain free, and when the owners and I view the streak of liquid fat that I place on the slide—and see for sure that it is a lipoma—we're all happy! Suspicious lumps can be aspirated and examined right in the veterinarian's office. Mast cell tumors typically give good samples to be read by a pathologist. It's good to know what kind of tumor is present before it is excised surgically.

Treating Cancer

A point that I cannot stress too strongly is that holistic supplements that work to prevent cancer do not necessarily work to cure cancer. Loving dog owners often come to my clinic after surfing the Internet and visiting the health food store, emptying shopping bags full of cancer-preventing products onto the exam table.

Although all of these products are inherently valuable, many of them are not powerful enough to do the job that needs to be done, and all of them together may give a dog one bad case of diarrhea. It's important to choose the right products—the ones that hit the nail on the head, so to speak.

Once cancer has taken hold, it has a life force of its own to be reckoned with. Holistic guerrilla warfare that is dead-on accurate is necessary to terminate cancer.

The malignancy has to be hit from different angles. Each type of cancer responds differently to the options available. Alternative therapies offer the advantage of bolstering self-healing capacities while avoiding the toxic side effects that accompany conventional medical treatment for cancer. And holistic therapies really can work, depending on the expertise with which they are used. Many of the cancer cases I have successfully treated with holistic medicine were those that were not amenable to chemotherapy, radiation, or surgery. Conventional options were not going to work, and the owners usually had nowhere else to turn.

Cancer in dogs is often recognized later than in humans; therefore, it has progressed further and become more entrenched before treatment of any kind begins. We humans can talk to our doctors about discomfort, so, for example, you can visit your doctor for an uncomfortable feeling in the bladder, and the doctor will explore the problem early on with various diagnostic tests. These tests will detect bladder cancer, if present, and you can begin treatment. Bladder cancer in a dog, on the other hand, is often found after repeated "urinary tract infections" warrant an ultrasound. Prostate cancer follows a similar path. Unfortunately, our wonderful friends cannot tell us that they are uncomfortable, so we find out that there's a real problem only when the symptoms are visible to us. This is why I value diagnostic tests and recommend a yearly blood and urine analysis on older dogs.

Conventional Approach: Chemotherapy

The goal of chemotherapy is to purge the body of cancer. Because cancer cells divide more rapidly than normal cells do, chemotherapeutic agents target these rapidly dividing cells. Of course, there are many other cells in the body that also divide rapidly. Intestinal cells, bone marrow cells, and immune system cells, for example, are also adversely affected by chemotherapy. The bone marrow incubates the immune system, so chemotherapy devastates the immune system at the very time when the body is most in need of its protection.

Chemotherapy has a fairly dismal record of success. Very few dogs are actually cured by chemotherapy. In most cases, a few months' remission is the best outcome. Often, the treatment offers only a month or two more than the amount of time the dog would have lived without chemotherapy. That's depressing.

The dog's quality of life during chemotherapy is another issue. Although some dogs go through it with flying colors, others simply cannot tolerate the treatments. The problem with dogs is that because their cancer is often found at a later stage than it is in humans, dogs' tumors are bigger, more established in the body, and less responsive to chemotherapy. Many types of cancer do not respond at all to chemotherapy.

Chemotherapy can also be very expensive. If your dog is diagnosed with cancer, find out the facts before you decide on a course of treatment. If your veterinarian recommends chemotherapy, ask for the exact statistics, expected survival time, and projected costs.

Natural Relief

For dogs undergoing chemotherapy, there are some natural methods of reducing the unpleasant side effects. As one example, the homeopathic remedy Nux vomica 30c, administered twice a day, helps drain toxins from the body and repair the digestive system.

Holistic Approaches

Veterinarians who use holistic cancer therapies are often dealing with patients who have already been treated with chemotherapy, radiation, or both. By this time, the cancer has spread, and the patient's internal systems have been compromised. Yet, even with all of these barriers, holistic treatment can sometimes succeed. It depends on finding just the right ammunition.

Cancer Salves: In the 1950s, the use of herbal cancer salves for tumor destruction had a 75–80-percent success rate. With the advent of radiation and chemotherapy, this method went underground, yet salves containing herbal preparations have been used to treat cancer for the past 2,500 years.

In my opinion, cancer salves do not cure deep cancer but are reasonable alternatives in many cases of skin cancer. These salves contain ingredients that penetrate and kill the cancer. They are ideal when the cancer is not immediately dangerous and the dog owner is willing to participate in the treatment. I have used salves on mast cell tumors and squamous cell carcinomas on the skin with a good rate of success. In fact, they work brilliantly on small mast cell tumors that are caught early; usually one or two simple applications is enough to destroy the tumor. For mast cell tumors, cancer salves are a very good alternative to surgery.

To use a salve, first shave the affected area so that it is free of fur and then place a small amount of cancer salve on the affected area. Depending on the salve, you will wait anywhere from ten minutes to a few hours before wiping the salve off.

Within a few days, some swelling and redness develops in the area, which can be alarming to squeamish owners. After this, the tumor, or the part of the tumor that the salve has reached, dries up and falls off. Your holistic veterinarian then needs to evaluate the site to see whether the tumor requires another application. Many holistic veterinarians use cancer salves, and I recommend that you work with your veterinarian if you wish to try this technique. Two commonly used cancer salves are Cansema by Alpha Omega Labs and Neoplasene by Buck Mountain Botanicals.

Neoplasene is a holistic treatment that may be used as a salve or dosed internally to treat cancer. When used in salve form, it works differently than other cancer salves. Neoplasene compounds attack the tumor mass by triggering apoptosis in cancer cells while sparing healthy cells.

Ellagic Acid

Found in red raspberries, blueberries, and strawberries, ellagic acid has been found to slow or stop tumor growth. Studies have shown that a cup of fresh raspberries per week can slow certain cancers. Adding some fresh berries to the cottage-cheese diet or to some oatmeal or yogurt is not difficult, and most dogs will enjoy their berries "berry" much!

The cancer cell membrane has a different biochemical makeup than that of a normal cell, and it transfers ions and metabolic products in a very different way. Because of this, the cancer cell is vulnerable. The mix of polysaccharides that form the communication channel on the cancer cell's surface is believed to expose the cell to preferential apoptotic attack by the compounds in Neoplasene. Squamous cell cancer, mast cell cancer, transitional cell cancer, melanoma, osteosarcoma, nerve sheath cancer, hemangiosarcoma, and lymphoma are among the cancer types that have been resolved with Neoplasene treatment. Neoplasene is only available through your veterinarian. (See www.buckmountainbotanicals.net for more information.)

Anticancer Diets: It is accepted as a general fact that a high-fat, high-protein diet works against cancer that has already established itself in the body. It is true that cancer needs sugars and carbohydrates desperately for its metabolism, but it is not true that a high-fat, high-protein, low-carbohydrate diet is the best approach to every dog's fight against existing cancer. To design a cancer-fighting diet, we must look at all of the metabolic facts about cancer.

First of all, cancer cachexia (a wasting of the body that occurs in the course of a chronic disease) results from the high tumor burden that uses up carbohydrates to survive. The body is starved while the cancer uses the body's carbohydrates greedily. In this case, a diet low in carbohydrates will put the cancer at a disadvantage, especially if the cancer patient is thin and does not have fat stores available for the cancer to turn into carbohydrates.

However, this is simply not the case with most dogs who have cancer because many are normal in weight or even plump. Giving such a dog a low-carb, high-protein diet will cause the cancer cells to turn the dog's body fat right into carbohydrates and will keep doing this until the dog is rail-thin. Additionally, the high protein content encourages the cancer cells in a healthy-looking dog to multiply.

Additionally, dogs who have had their tumors removed will have little or no tumor burden to steal their bodies' carbohydrates. So, when placed on a high-fat, high-protein food, they are eating exactly what they shouldn't be eating: a diet high in heated, processed animal fat, saturated fat, and animal protein, which causes an acidic pH and impairs any potential success from holistic cancer treatments.

An ideal diet for a dog with cancer is a low-protein, high-fiber, balanced diet containing 50 percent whole grains, 10 percent beans or apples (for fiber), 30 percent vegetables, and 10 percent fruit, such as berries. The grains are best cooked with kombu or a similar seaweed, available in health food stores. If you can, get organic, nonirradiated foods. The following foods are beneficial ingredients in a cancer-fighting diet:

- almonds, ground (best nuts to fight cancer)
- sprouts of wheatgrass and alfalfa
- egg whites, cooked

- white fish, chicken, and turkey
- whole grains, such as barley, buckwheat, oats, flax, and wheat berries
- brown rice
- molasses
- olive and walnut oils
- apples
- sweet potatoes
- broccoli
- cauliflower
- garlic
- herbs

Tocotrienols: Research has shown tocotrienols, found in vitamin E, to have some very incredible properties. What's important to understand here is their potent anticancer properties. There are eight molecules in vitamin E; one of these, called delta tocotrienol (DT3), has the lowest molecular weight and the smallest head and shortest tail, allowing for greater access to and through the cells and their limiting membranes. Palm oil contains 45 percent gamma tocotrienols; even the larger tocotrienols trigger cancer cell death, block the spread of cancer cells, and decrease the spread of cancer cells.

It's important to note that we are not talking about vitamin E. In fact, it's very important to give your dog tocotrienols apart from other vitamins, particularly vitamin E. Of the eight vitamin E molecules, only two (delta tocotrienols and gamma tocotrienols) act as potent anticancer agents. One product, which contains delta tocotrienols from the annatto plant, has a patent pending from the US Food and Drug Administration (FDA) for use in treating cancer in people.

Carnivora: President Ronald Reagan used carnivora successfully for his colon cancer in 1985. Carnivora, a patented phytonutrient and extract of the Venus flytrap plant, *Dionaea muscipula*, has been used clinically for more than twenty-five years. Biologically active compounds in the extract are essential to a healthy immune system and support healthy cardiovascular functions in the body. At higher doses, the extract has been shown to have immunomodulatory, tumoricidal, antimicrobial, antiviral, antiparasitic, and antibiotic properties. The pharmacology of Venus flytrap extract has been extensively studied and evaluated in both animal and human studies.

Double Helix Water: Specialized waters are a big topic today. You may have heard of Kangen water, structured water, alkaline water, and ionized water, just to name a few. Double Helix Water is none of these.

Garlic and the Magical Reaction

Hippocrates was the first to comment on garlic's antitumor properties. Cooking kills this antitumor activity; the antitumor properties can be destroyed by just one minute of microwaving. The best way to get the most out of garlic is to chop it up and let it sit for ten minutes, during which time the naturally present enzymes in the garlic will start a chemical reaction that produces its cancer-fighting compounds.

Double Helix Water has a story of its own. Double Helix Water is a different phase of water never before discovered. We think of water in its various forms as the vapor in the clouds, rain, a glass of water, snow, or an ice cube. Yet Double Helix Water behaves entirely differently from ice, liquid water, or water vapor.

We know that water can exist as a gas, liquid, or solid. In each of these phases, it's made up of the same molecules, but the space between the hydrogen and oxygen changes. This is the part that gets interesting. In Double Helix Water, the fourth phase of water, the space doesn't change as the temperature changes, thus defying the historical classification of water. Double Helix Water is composed of dry tiny stable water clusters that, when present in water, combine into double helix structures similar in shape to DNA. That's why it's called Double Helix Water. It's actually powdered water. You can send the dry form of Double Helix Water to any lab and the analysis will come up as—water!

You might wonder why this phase of water has never been discovered until recently. The fact is, it couldn't have been found without the advent of the atomic force microscope, which can view the world of atoms. To further complicate the matter, finding this tiny particle in a drop of water is like finding one blade of grass that's being swirled around in a tornado. As researchers began photographing this stable water cluster, they saw it attach to a bacterium and cause it to die. Because of this phenomenon, Dr. Benjamin Bonavida did a series of studies at UCLA, where he found that stable water clusters could combine to form a new structure: the double helix.

What does all of this have to do with healing and health? One in three dogs will get cancer. Autoimmune disease has increased in our dogs exponentially. One hundred thousand new manmade chemicals that Mother Nature never intended have been introduced into the environment. Chronic illness is an epidemic.

Buddy, a thirteen-year-old Yorkie, came to me with five nickel-sized metastases in his lungs. I prescribed Double Helix Water. His mom took Buddy home with his water and began telling all of her coworkers that she was giving him this special water a few times every day to cure his cancer. Her coworkers decided that she was in denial. Together, they waited for Buddy's recheck; a month after starting to drink Double Helix Water, his regular veterinarian declared that Buddy's chest films were clear. The cancer seemed to be gone. Buddy continued to thrive five years after this treatment, despite the fact that he was no spring chicken when he was diagnosed. And many of his mom's coworkers brought their pets to me after they saw Buddy's success.

A short time later, I saw a thirteen-year-old yellow Labrador with a malignant melanoma the size of a golf ball on his gum. After two weeks of Double Helix Water, he was cancer-free.

So, how does this work? Remember when we talked earlier about the fact that DNA changes in the cell, creating a cancerous cell? First, let's reexamine the function of DNA.

DNA provides survival instructions to the body. It keeps us alive and well by taking good notes and storing that information for future generations. One single strand of DNA can store an astounding amount of data—a good estimate being about six gigabits. DNA has a binary code—the same type of code in your computer—and the combinations are seemingly endless. This information is passed from one generation of dogs (and people) to the next.

Linus Pauling once said that we are completely natural organisms, made by Mother Nature. Man-made chemicals that have shown up in the last hundred years simply don't fit into the master plan. Dogs were not created with these chemicals, so there's no information contained in their DNA regarding how to deal with them. Yet these toxins and carcinogens continuously find their way into the food chain. Current research indicates that the stable water cluster in Double Helix Water somehow enables the expression of certain genes. It helps the DNA perform the job it's intended to do.

It's very easy to give to dogs and cats because it tastes just like water. Just use fifteen drops in eight ounces of either distilled or reverse osmosis water. In addition to fighting cancer, I've found Double Helix Water to help with osteoarthritis, autoimmune diseases, diabetes, and any kind of inflammation.

Glutathione: As we have discussed, good or bad health is determined at the cellular level. Glutathione exists in every cell in your dog's body. It protects each cell's tiny but important energy machines, called the mitochondria. Glutathione is a tiny protein compound made up of three amino acids. It may be small, but it is the uncontested king of all antioxidants.

Without glutathione, all of your dog's cells would disintegrate and die from unrestrained oxidation. To understand what oxidation is, think about when a freshly cut apple turns brown, a bicycle fender becomes rusty, or a copper penny turns green. A living cell is different because when oxidation is not kept in check, the cell disintegrates and dies.

Our more well-known antioxidants, such as vitamins C and E, have short life spans. Glutathione has the ability to bring spent antioxidants, such as vitamins C and E, back from the dead, and it

Acetaminophen and Glutathione

You may know that over-the-counter pain relievers containing acetaminophen are toxic to cats, but I bet you never knew why. Acetaminophen rapidly depletes a cat's stores of glutathione, leaving a high burden of toxic metabolites in the liver, resulting in destruction of the liver tissue. The artificial sweetener xylitol can do the same thing in dogs.

When humans overdose on acetaminophen, they're treated with something called N-acetylcysteine (NAC). NAC is a precursor to the formation of glutathione in the body, and it helps replenish intracellular levels of glutathione, thus preventing or minimizing liver damage.

even can recharge itself. Because all other antioxidants depend on glutathione to function, properly doctors respectfully call it the "master antioxidant." Glutathione is the most important, abundant, active, and powerful antioxidant in your dog's body.

Next to water, there is nothing more important than glutathione in your dog's body. Your dog's level of glutathione will affect his health and longevity. Without it, cells would die from oxidation, the immune system wouldn't work, and the liver would fail from toxic overload. The liver is able to detoxify and eliminate herbicides, pesticides, and other toxins from the body only because of the vast amount of glutathione present in the liver. Studies show that half of the dogs with chronic liver disease have reduced glutathione levels in their blood and livers.

Cancer begins with an abnormal reprogramming of the DNA, or genetic material, of the cell, which can result in uncontrolled growth. One theory is that when free radicals form or oxidative stress occurs in the cell nucleus, the DNA may be damaged. Glutathione is an intracellular antioxidant. Antioxidants remove oxidative stress and eliminate free radicals, helping to prevent cancer. Studies show that patients receiving glutathione at the same time as their chemotherapy live longer. Additionally, and no one knows exactly why, people with cancer have low glutathione levels in their bodies.

The tissues within the body make glutathione. That's important to know, because glutathione taken orally is ineffective. While supplement companies may advertise glutathione supplements, the fact is that glutathione is made up of three amino acids and, when taken orally, it's simply digested with the rest of a person's food. What's usually being sold as glutathione is glutathione precursors.

Again, because glutathione is made up of three amino acids, the oral route of administration simply does not work because glutathione is digested. Asparagus contains more available glutathione than any other food. But, once again, the GI tract digests most of it. The best way to administer glutathione is intravenously or intramuscularly. Because that's not practical for dog owners, I typically use a topical gel preparation, which absorbs through the skin when placed on a hairless area. For glutathione that is administered by injection or transdermally, you must get a prescription from your veterinarian.

The Three Most Important Things Glutathione Does in Your Dog's Body

1. Enables other antioxidant supplements to do their job. None of the over-the-counter antioxidants that you administer orally would work without the glutathione that's already present in your dog's body.

2. Fuels your dog's immune system.

3. Aids the liver in detoxifying the body. Your dog has the highest level of glutathione in his liver, and that's no accident. The liver is the major organ in detoxification of heavy metals, herbicides, and toxins. Glutathione is absolutely necessary because of all of the toxins to which our pets are exposed.

The good news is that there are also several glutathione precursors and certain foods that will work to boost glutathione production within your dog's body. A little extra vitamin C on a daily basis will recharge the glutathione already present in your dog's body. The powdered, buffered form of this vitamin is relatively tasteless and easy to sprinkle on a bit of wet food. The suggested dose is 50–100 mg per day. Garlic is a sulfur-rich food, and a little fresh garlic each day supports glutathione production. Kale and broccoli contain compounds that support the production of glutathione naturally in the body. Selenium is an important mineral that helps your dog's body recycle and produce more glutathione. There is also evidence that D_3 increases intracellular glutathione.

The supplement S-adenosylmethionine (SAMe) is converted into glutathione and is easily available at health food stores, on the Internet, and through veterinarians. The recommended dose is 20 mg/kg/day. Another readily available supplement, called N-acetylcysteine (NAC), helps boost glutathione levels in your dog's blood and liver. As mentioned in the sidebar, NAC is also used to treat humans with liver failure from acetaminophen overdose. Finally, exercise boosts glutathione levels.

Healthy levels of glutathione are tremendously important for maintaining health. Glutathione deficiency has been linked to cancer, arthritis, and autoimmune disease. It's easy to administer transdermally, and our best friends with cancer need all the help they can get.

Essiac Tea: In 1922, a Canadian nurse named Rene Caisse learned of a Native American tea from the Ojibwe tribe that could cure cancer. It was made from burdock root, sheep sorrel, slippery elm, and rhubarb root. Caisse made this tea for her aunt, who had been diagnosed with incurable cancer, and the cancer completely resolved.

Caisse continued to use this tea to treat people with cancer. Because of this, she was persecuted for nearly forty years. When she was threatened with arrest, doctors and patients always came to her rescue. Caisse never claimed that the tea was a cancer cure; rather, she said that it does relieve pain and improves a person's odds of overcoming the disease.

In 1959, Caisse introduced her Essiac ("Caisse" spelled backward) formula to Dr. Charles Brusch, physician to President John F. Kennedy. She started a study, supervised by eighteen doctors, on both human terminal cancer patients and laboratory mice with cancer. In the humans and the mice, the Essiac formula reduced the size of their masses. Human patients also reported a reduction in pain and discomfort.

In 1990, Dr. Brusch commented that tumors were easier to remove surgically and there was less bleeding after patients had been on a course of Essiac. In fact, he had cured his own bowel cancer with Essiac.

Most health food stores carry packets of the mixed herbs, which you brew on your own, or a prepared mix. It is convenient and inexpensive to use. Dosages for dogs are available along with preparation guidelines on the instructions that come with the tea. It should be used three times a day for twelve consecutive weeks.

Hoxsey Herbs: Harry Hoxsey was an herbal folk healer who developed an herbal therapy that he learned from his great-grandfather. In the 1840s, the elder Hoxsey, a veterinarian, put a horse with leg cancer out to pasture to die. He observed as the horse grazed on certain plants, and the cancer diminished. He formulated a salve from these plants and used it to treat cancer in other horses.

Today, the Hoxsey therapy consists of herbal preparations for internal and external use. The formula is made up of red clover, buckthorn bark, burdock root, stillingia root, barberry bark, chaparral, licorice root, prickly ash bark, and cascara amarga. The external formula also contains bloodroot, an old Native American herb used to treat cancer. Humans with lymphoma, melanoma, and skin cancer seem to respond most favorably to this treatment.

Polysaccharides: Polysaccharides are becoming very important molecules in preventing and fighting cancer. Polysaccharide peptide (PSP) in particular has a very promising role in cancer prevention because it creates an exceptionally healthy cellular environment in which the cells can repair their damaged DNA. Damaged DNA is the single most important element that contributes to cancer-cell formation. PSP supplement comes as a powder that you can add to your dog's food, and it works in the body at the cellular level, feeding the DNA, RNA, and mitochondria and thus supporting glucose energy metabolism. This special kind of nutrition is necessary to create and maintain healthy cells, healthy communication structures, and strong immune responses.

A proprietary processing technique produces unique functional characteristics of alpha-glycan PSP that are easily recognized by DNA, RNA, and genes. The extremely small molecular size of this product allows for 100 percent assimilation into the cell for maximum benefit. This is in contrast to the other known glycan supplements, known as beta-glycans, which consist of very large molecules and thus are limited in their ability to be assimilated into cells. Consequently, the alpha-glycan PSP is exponentially more effective than is the beta-glycan PSP.

The alpha-glycan PSP provides the perfect fuel for the mitochondria in cells. As mentioned, mitochondria act as a cell's power source, and the better the fuel, the healthier the cell can become. The healthier the cell, the better its ability to repair and correct itself. Alpha-glycan PSP acts within the cell to cause the elimination of toxins and the formation of an alkaline environment. In this incredible cellular environment, cellular repair is enhanced.

PSP has been made from both mushrooms and special strains of rice. Furthermore, the *Coriolus versicolor* mushroom, known commonly as the Yun Zhi mushroom, has been used in traditional Chinese medicine for more than 2,000 years and contains PSP. Some recent studies have suggested that PSP has a tumor-fighting effect in addition to its immune-boosting properties.

At the University of Pennsylvania School of Veterinary Medicine, two faculty members, Dorothy Cimino Brown and Jennifer Reetz, conducted a cancer study in 2012 that yielded very promising results. The specific type of cancer that they studied, hemangiosarcoma, is becoming more and

Cancer-Fighting Foods

- Garlic
- Parsley
- Tomatoes
- Garbanzo beans
- Plain yogurt (with no sugar or artificial sweeteners)
- Fish
- Olive oil
- Butter
- Herbs
- Apples
- Whole grains
- Wheat bran
- Lentils
- Brown rice
- Organic chicken and turkey
- All vegetables, especially carrots, broccoli, cauliflower, red and yellow peppers, and leeks
- Seeds and nuts, especially sesame seeds and almonds

Foods That Cancer Patients Should Avoid

- Beef
- Pork
- All organ meats, such as liver, heart, brain
- Sugar
- White flour
- Unsaturated fatty acids (corn oil, sunflower oil)
- Margarine
- Sausages, bacon, cold cuts, tuna (a 6-ounce can of tuna contains an average of 17 mg of mercury)
- Beef jerky
- Bonemeal
- Dog treats
- Processed commercial dog foods

more common, particularly in certain breeds, such as the Golden Retriever.

They found that dogs with hemangiosarcoma who were treated with a compound derived from the *C. versicolor* mushroom had the longest survival times ever reported for dogs with the disease. "We were shocked," Cimino Brown said in an article for *PennNews* on the University of Pennsylvania's website. "Prior to this, the longest reported median survival time of dogs with hemangiosarcoma of the spleen that underwent no further treatment was 86 days. We had dogs that lived beyond a year with nothing other than this mushroom as treatment." The product used in the study was an extract called I'm-Yunity,® which effectively delivers PSP isolated from the COV-1® strain of the *C. versicolor* mushroom.

Vitamin D₃: Vitamin D_3 is needed to facilitate the intestinal absorption of calcium as well as for other important body functions. *Scientific American* stated that 75 percent of young adults and adults are deficient in vitamin D_3. Often called the "sunshine vitamin," it's created when enzymes in our skin use sunlight to make vitamin D_3. Our dogs are covered with fur, and their

Cleaning Up

Damage to the DNA is always the first step toward cancer. Of course, there are numerous ways in which our DNA can be damaged, thereby later initiating fatal disease. Once the DNA is altered, the cell's genome changes, and it has the potential, in the right environment, to become a cancer cell. The antioxidants mentioned in this chapter act to clean up the free-radical debris in the cells and help them function as well as possible.

ancestors got their D_3 mostly from eating raw liver. Nowadays, processed pet foods add synthetic vitamin D to the mix, and it's the last thing you want to count on if your dog has cancer. In our case, milk is supplemented with D_2, and that's not the real McCoy, either. The bottom line is that you want to find an excellent manufacturer of D_3, and D_3 only. It's often available in an oil-based liquid, and dogs don't mind the taste of it in their food.

D_3 is actually a hormone, not a vitamin, but we won't get into semantics because the most important thing to understand is that it has many important functions in our dogs' bodies. Vitamin D_3 affects mood and, more importantly, is an integral immune-system booster. In fact, one of the reasons people get fewer colds and flu in the summer is thought to be the increased levels of this essential vitamin in their systems due to more sunlight.

More to the point, the Department of International Health, Immunology, and Microbiology at the University of Copenhagen found that D_3 activates the important immune-system killer cells and helper cells that play a major role in immune-system function. These cells can't even mobilize without adequate vitamin D.

Vitamin D has been getting a lot of press, and scientists are duly impressed with how important D_3 is to health. So, if you want to get all of the gears going in your dog's body so he can fight his cancer, you want to make sure that he gets from 1,000 to 2,000 IU of vitamin D each day, depending on his size. Vitamin D overdoses are very rare, and this level of supplementation is very safe. Remember, we are fighting cancer.

Veterinary Immune Tabs, Professional Formula: Dr. Joe Ramaeker began his work with nutrition in the 1970s. His philosophy is that nature has most of the answers if we don't get lost in the forest. His research, along with the number of clinical cases he has tested, is quite extensive. It all started with the hair analysis of tens of thousands of patients in order to learn what minerals were deficient in their systems.

With many years of hands-on clinical experience behind him, he began working on a specific formulation for cancer treatment, resulting in the professional-strength formula of his Veterinary Immune Tabs, which is available only through veterinarians. He has given this special nutritional immune-modulator compound to more than 50,000 animals. Many of his patients, including those with different types of cancer, Cushing's disease, and hypothyroidism, have experienced excellent results.

PA10: I stated previously that once cancer is established, there are a number of ways that it can

Homeopathy for Cancer

The choice of homeopathic cancer remedies listed here will depend on the type of cancer. The potencies of the remedies and the dosage schedules are suggested ones. When I treat a cancer case, I decide on the remedy, potency, and dosage rate according to the unique presentation of each patient's illness. Consult with a professional who uses homeopathy for the duration of your pet's cancer treatment.

Cancer, general
Carcinocin 30c—three times a day for two days only
Thuja 200c—twice a day for thirty days
Tuberculinum 100c—three times a day
Viscum album 30c—twice a day

Cancer, abdominal
Conium 200c—for hard tumors and abdominal masses; give once a day

Cancer, bladder
Berberis vulg 6c—three times a day
Taraxacum 6c—three times a day

Cancer, bone
Silicea 1m—once a day
Phosphorus 30c—twice a day
Symphytum 200c—twice a day
Arsenicum album 200c—twice a day

Cancer, fibrosarcoma
Calcarea fluorica 200c—once a day

Cancer, liver
Hydrastis 3x—three times a day
Chelidonium 3x—three times a day
Cadmium sulph 30c—twice a day

Cancer, lung
Arsenicum album 200c—once a day
Conium 200c—once a day

Cancer, lymph
Carbo animalis 30x—twice a day
Aurum met 6c—three times a day
Conium 200c—twice a day

Cancer, mammary
Asterias rubens 6x—twice a day
Phytolacca 30c—twice a day

Cancer, melanoma
Carduus mar 30c—three times a day
Lachesis 200c—once a day
Thuja 30c—three times a day
Argentum nit 6c—three times a day

Cancer, prostate
Conium 200c—three times a day
Sabal serrulata 6c—three times a day
Crotalis horr 200c—once a day for three days

Cancer, tonsil
Nux muschata 10m—two to three times a week

My Ideal Scenario for Fighting Cancer

It's not easy to come up with the perfect individual regimen for each cancer patient. The following products, some of which must be obtained through a veterinarian, may be effective with many cancers because some promote healthy cells in the body while some destroy cancer cells.

1. Healthy home-cooked low-protein anticancer diet, including cancer-fighting foods

2. Double Helix Water, given several times a day

3. Generous doses of Vitamin D_3

4. Quality multivitamin/multimineral/superfood supplement, such as Canine Everyday Essentials

5. Glutathione, administered transdermally

6. Polysaccharide polypeptide (PSP) product made from specific strains of rice or mushrooms

7. Raw garlic, chopped and allowed to sit for ten minutes before serving, added to one meal each day

8. Veterinary Immune Tabs, Professional Formula

9. Depending on the type of cancer, perhaps herbs, Chinese herbs, homeopathic remedies, PA10 anticancer vaccine

avoid being destroyed by the immune system. One way is to form a capsule around itself. Another is to secrete and release a substance that tells the immune system, in effect, to "go away and leave it alone." In nature, such substances are very useful. For instance, if a human fetus did not secrete a hormone called human chorionic gonadotropin (HCG), it would be destroyed by the mother's immune system. The HCG protects it just as it protects the sperm from destruction so it can go on its merry way.

It turns out that most tumors produce a choriogonadotropic hormone. HCG has been found on the cells of every type of cancer studied. It is produced by cancer cells and found in greater quantities on metastatic cancer cells than on other types of tumors. Again, cells use HCG to avoid being attacked by the immune system. The tumor makes itself immunologically inert.

PA10 is a natural product, created by a pharmaceutical company, containing an antihuman HCG. It is very similar to a hormone produced by dogs, so it is effective in dogs. It works to control the HCG on cancer cells, thus allowing the immune system to get to the tumor and attack it.

Years ago, I did a preliminary study for the pharmaceutical company in my practice in Pennsylvania. The results were very promising. Today, the daily regime of intramuscular injections that I use is very successful. You see, this choriogonadotropic hormone is also a growth-stimulating hormone, and the tumors use it to stimulate their own growth.

It's believed that PA10 has its initial effect by causing white blood cells to produce antibodies that seek out the HCG made by cancer cells. If the protective effect of the HCG is neutralized, the tumor is now at the mercy of the immune components from which it was previously sheltered. PA10 also kills tumor cells by directly lysing them and/or attracting immune components. Slowing tumor growth, killing tumor cells, controlling and limiting metastasis, improving the quality of life, and increasing survival time with no side effects create an excellent win-win situation for a canine patient with cancer.

Choosing the Right Course

When loving dog owners are confronted with cancer in their dogs, reason may fly out the window. A sense of urgency combined with shock and fear could impair the formation of a well-considered and educated decision. Never be afraid to ask questions and ask for documentation. If chemotherapy is offered, request the statistics for that type of cancer treated with the proposed drug. Don't rush into therapy that doesn't work because you are too worried and frightened to do anything else.

When choosing holistic alternatives to conventional cancer treatment, don't forget that you don't have to choose just one therapy. You can create a program for your dog by combining conventional treatments with natural therapies or by combining a few indicated natural and nontoxic programs. Remember that many of these treatments slow the growth of the cancer and do not kill the malignant cells outright.

Protocols that boost the immune system and activate the cancer-killing cells can be combined with those that slow the growth of the cancer. Large tumors that can be easily removed should be taken out because your dog's body will, as a result, have less of a cancer load to deal with.

12. When It Comes Time to Say Good-bye

There are no feelings quite so pure, so selfless and devoted, as those of dogs for their owners. The extent to which a dog's focus revolves completely around the members of his human family is so strong as to transcend either peril or pain. An older dog will readily disregard the stiffness and aching joints of arthritis to enjoy the pleasure of walking with his beloved master or mistress or to check out any unusual noise in the house. From my years of experience, I can assure you that dogs' concerns about the safety of their human companions far outweigh any concerns they might have for their own well-being. And when they feel themselves slipping away, I'm firmly convinced that their greatest anxiety is about how their owners will manage without the presence of their physical and emotional support.

Many years ago, I was asked to examine a German Shepherd named Gretchen whose owners lived in Maryland, some distance away from my practice. Gretchen had been seen by several specialists, and none of the medications they prescribed could put a stop to her continual seizures, the frequency of which had increased to about one every twenty minutes. Her owners

"It's only a dog," some will say to console you
when your loyal companion is gone
It's hard not to let this memory control you
That's all that is left from now on.

Yes, it's only a dog—giving love and affection
when all daily tasks are complete
Always alert for his master's protection
and closely curled at his feet

When death's at his doorstep he'll look up toward you
while licking your trembling hand
A final gesture of love to reward you
and tell you, "I understand."

Yes, it's only a dog, devoted and caring
on whom you can always depend
Lucky are those who choose to be sharing
the love of a four-legged friend.

—Ben Shulman

did not have an air-conditioned car, and it was a hot summer's day. I evaluated the situation and concluded that there was nothing I could do to help her condition—something I explained to the owners as Gretchen listened. They were very worried about taking her home in the hot car, as her temperature was already quite elevated due to the seizures.

As Gretchen looked at me, we seemed to make a telepathic connection as the images of three young children suddenly flashed across my mind. I asked the owners if they had any children at home. "Yes," they replied, "we have three small children, and she behaves like a nanny to them." Tears came to my eyes as I conveyed to them what it was that Gretchen seemed to be saying—that she wanted to see the children just one more time. I explained to Gretchen that she might not make it through the hot ride home. She seemed to understand and accept that her time had come, her only concern being how the children might react and whether her loved ones would be all right without her watchful eye and constant devotion.

The Gift of a Golden Twilight

As with all veterinarians, there have been times when people have brought their pets to me, convinced that it is time to end their suffering. Often, the whole family will show up, emotionally distraught. I know that they have gone through hours, perhaps days or even weeks, of heart-wrenching decision-making and have finally prepared themselves to face this difficult and dispiriting decision. But sometimes, when I have looked at the dog whose fate seemed to have been decided, I will notice a certain brightness still residing in his eyes, reflecting the tenacity to hang on to life despite the distress and pain of the affliction.

While I know it would be much easier for the family at that point to simply end the ordeal, as a healer of animals I feel obligated to convey to them what I sense to be the dog's viewpoint. In such instances, I will quietly tell them, "It is not yet his time. He is not ready to go now." Their eyes will brighten up as well, and they will look at the dog as if to say, "OK then, you continue to hang in there with us, buddy, and you tell us when your time has come." The special kind of love that they have had between them for years becomes even more powerful as they respect their pet's desire to have perhaps just a few more cherished days with them.

Many people, upon learning that their pets have only a short time left to live, find a new perspective on life and love. So many of the things that they had long taken for granted suddenly begin to take on a precious and beautiful glow. Whether it be a sunrise or a special gift received from a loved one years ago, each experience becomes savored and remembered with a heartfelt reverence. Arguments and disagreements suddenly seem petty, and sharing love becomes all important.

Just as that love proves to be the eternal aspect of our lives, so it is with the lives of our pets. If anything, their depth of feeling for the families with whom they live is even purer (and more forbearing and forgiving) than that of most people. And because their time on earth is so much shorter than that of other loved ones, every day they spend with us is that much more meaningful. That's why, even when a dog has been discovered to have a terminal illness, it shouldn't necessarily be viewed as a cause to cut short his remaining days simply to "put him out of his misery." What may seem like a painful existence to us is likely to be mitigated for the dog by the chance to spend additional precious time with the people to whom he is so devoted—a kind of golden twilight that you can give your companion as a parting gift.

Such was the case with KC, a wonderful black Cocker Spaniel I had treated for many years. I had pulled KC through a number of serious health crises. Finally, it came time for her owners to make a painful decision. She was suffering from severe heart failure, her abdomen was filled like a tight drum with fluid, and she was breathing with difficulty. I looked into her eyes, and she looked back at me. "Not now," she seemed to be saying.

"It's not yet her time," I told her owners. But they were clearly worried because they would be leaving shortly for their son's wedding, which was to be held high atop a mountain in New Hampshire. How could they take her in such a condition? Who could they possibly leave her with? "We'll do whatever it takes," I said. I proceeded to manually drain a good deal of the fluid from her abdomen, making her breathing somewhat easier, and altered the schedule of her herbs and medications. KC not only attended the wedding on that mountain, she became the guest of honor, traveling in high style in a baby carriage. She knew how excited her family was over this event, and she got to be an important part of it. The quality of her life, in fact, remained good for several more months. And when the time finally came that nothing more could be done to make her comfortable, and she was obviously failing fast, I explained it to her and sensed that she agreed.

But euthanasia is not something that should simply be dictated by convenience or by the understandable desire to prevent a dog's quality of life from diminishing as an illness progresses. Far too often, people are influenced by people who tell them that the dog should be put to sleep simply because he does not walk as well as he used to, or that it's better to simply get a new dog rather than to prolong the health problems of their current dog. Offensive though it may seem to some people's sensibilities, I feel compelled to share with you a hypothetical example I often give to clients who are torn over what to do with a dog who has been given only a short time to live. Imagine that a close relative—say, an aunt who has always been a kind, gentle, and loving person, asking little for herself—has just been diagnosed with liver cancer. Can you imagine the rest of the family coming to the hospital to tell her they have decided that she should be "put to sleep" because she has only six months to a year remaining and it would be just too painful for everyone to see her through the ordeal?

The Afterlife of a Dog, as Reflected in Eternal Love

While Western theology has perpetrated the belief that only human beings are blessed with a divine spark and a spiritual existence beyond death (based on the idea that man is created in God's image), anyone who has shared a relationship with a dog is likely to find that hard to accept. Dog owners know that the unconditional love exhibited toward us by our canine companions can be one of the most precious things in the universe—a sublime and powerful flow of energy that is about as close to divine love as any experienced on earth. And they know that a dog has a soul as pure as that of the most noble of humans. That's why I strongly believe a dog's affection for his master to be a form of spiritual energy that transcends earthly existence—an energy that we can call upon any time we need it, even long after our four-legged best friends have departed this life.

There is another spiritual aspect of a dog's passing that should be a source of great comfort to those left behind. Some of my own experiences have firmly convinced me that dogs and their masters can be reunited after death; this is a theme that has been reflected in both song and story throughout the ages. Many years ago, I treated an English Setter named Morgan who was suffering from a terminal illness. His owners preferred that he go naturally rather than be put to sleep. His condition was not particularly painful, so I concurred. They needed to work during the day, so they left him at my practice so he could be with us. When they called to see how he was doing, I told them that they needed to communicate with him mentally and tell him it was OK for him to go.

The Rites of Passage for Dog Owners

Talk to your dog. Let him know that you understand that he is suffering and that you will help him heal in any way you can. The effectiveness of this holistic approach cannot be underestimated.

If it is clearly obvious that the dog's condition is terminal and nothing can be done to save him, let him know that you are there to support whatever decision he makes about how much longer he wants to hang on.

If his eyes and attitude indicate that he still cherishes life, try to keep him as comfortable as possible and provide him as often as you can with those things that he finds most enjoyable.

If he gives you signals that he's ready to go, as pets often do, allow him to say good-bye to any other animal companions, and let them all know what is happening. If you need to have the veterinarian put him to sleep, allow all those who knew and loved him to pay their final respects before he goes.

Stay with him during the procedure, and surround him with loving and caring thoughts. Focus on things like wonderful walks or games of catch, along with the protection he gave you and your family and how special he was and always will be to you.

Have a mild sedative given to him and, if you can, hold his head and stroke it comfortingly.

After the final injection has been administered, say a special silent prayer for him and envision the love between you as a unique and special gift that you will never misplace. If you are among those who believe in such things, tell him that he would be welcome to rejoin your family in a new body, if he desires. Take whatever time you need to feel that your personal farewell is complete.

If you choose to bury your dog at home or in a pet cemetery, make sure that it is done with a proper ritual in his honor, much like a funeral for a person. If you have him cremated, do the same when his ashes are returned.

Upon your return home, tell the other animals in your house what happened both by talking to them and mentally conveying the image of the passing to them.

Mourning for a pet requires a period of time. But following the above steps can help mitigate the grief with a sense of serenity, comfort, and spiritual elevation that stems from a recognition of the eternal bond of love between you and your special companion.

A while later, I returned to the kennel area, where Morgan was lying on a soft comforter. In between the stainless steel cages, I saw an elderly man with white hair and a closely cropped beard holding Morgan's head gently in his lap and stroking him. When I got to his cage, however, the stranger was gone. Then Morgan let out a small sigh and peacefully passed away. I called the owners to tell them that Morgan had passed, and I described the apparent apparition I had seen. They said little in response to my story.

Two weeks later, the owners came to the clinic to pick up Morgan's ashes. They took me aside and produced a picture of an elderly gentleman, asking, "Was this the man you saw?" Taken aback, I told them that it was indeed. "He was my father," one of the owners said. "Morgan and he were the best of friends until my father passed away three months ago."

My experience with families grieving over the loss of beloved pets has also convinced me that there are times when animals attempt to communicate with us from the other side, to reassure us in their own way that they are happy and at peace. One such case involved Torro, a German Shepherd who came to be my good friend. He came to my clinic once a week for acupuncture to alleviate the effects of a spinal disease that made his back legs weak, and he seemed to especially enjoy the visits. After Torro died, his owner related to me a strange tale told to her by a friend. The friend said he had seen Torro in a dream, jumping and playing and running so as to convey to him that he was happy and just fine. She added that if anyone else had told her that, she would have thought it was just an attempt to make her feel better—but this was an extremely down-to-earth sort of individual, and it would be completely unlike him to say anything like that unless it had actually happened.

A Final Display of Affection and Admiration

Just as it is for a person, the most desirable way for a dog to leave this life is in the comfort of familiar surroundings and in the company of loved ones. Many dogs are able to pass away in such

a beautiful manner, sometimes in the arms of a beloved master or mistress. Whenever they seem to be reasonably comfortable and able to cope with their condition, it is usually best to allow them to choose their own time. When the time that a pet needs help to pass on does come, and I can't emphasize this enough, animals need to be treated with the greatest of love and respect. It helps them to be surrounded by the family members they love so much, who will let them know that they will be eased out of their pain. This is the time for them to be shown admiration and appreciation for the protection, comfort, healing, and love they have provided and to be properly honored with a ritual of recognition. Such a ceremony is equally important for any other animals in the house, who should be given the message about what's become of their friend. Often, pets will wander the house for days or weeks in search of companions who have left and never returned.

Animals do not fear death, having never been exposed to ideas that would predispose them to worry about what awaits them. I believe they know when their bodies are no longer serving them and in their own way are aware that their spirits will continue to exist in another realm. When they have reached this stage, what concerns them most, I am convinced, is leaving behind their loved ones. That's why it is so important to euthanize a pet only when the animal is ready.

There must be a preparation period in which loving communication transpires between the dog and the rest of the family. The owners should sense that the dog has given his consent to the procedure. In my practice, I talk to the dog, reassuring him that we will be gentle and loving, and I often administer a sedative. As it takes effect, the owners and family members are asked to surround their pet with loving thoughts and to recall the special times they had together. I suggest that they focus on the emotional bond they have shared with their companion all these years so that it fills the space around their pet. I ask that they concentrate on their admiration and appreciation for

all that this animal has taught them and for all the love and loyalty he has brought into their lives. And if they cannot hold back the tears, I explain to the dog that this is only because he is so special to them and will so be missed. The better this is communicated and the more harmonious the environment, the easier it is for the pet.

When a pet departs this life surrounded by love and respect, it can be a beautiful and peaceful experience for those to whom the pet was closest. If the weather permits and the animal and the family seem to like the idea, we often perform the procedure outside, on the serene and picturesque grounds that surround my clinic. As the dog ascends into the spirit world, his last impression of the earth is at its most ideal, with the sound of chirping birds and the scents of flowers and pine trees.

Giving a dog such a farewell ceremony is no more silly or frivolous than a funeral for a person. In fact, if there are any clients in the waiting room at the time, we often find them in an emotional state and extending their condolences, although typically they knew neither the dog nor the people involved.

Several years ago, a most unusual-looking dog named Nicholas started coming to my clinic for treatment of severe arthritis in his hips and multiple disk problems in his back. At first, he was frightened and in a great deal of pain, but as the treatments gradually relieved some of his discomfort, he began to genuinely enjoy his visits. As I reflected on his distinctive appearance, it occurred to me that he looked like a sort of cross between a herding dog and a wildebeest, and I laughed as I told his owner that Nicholas must have been a rare "great wildebeest herding dog." From then on, it became our personal joke, and the owner began to describe him as such to anyone who wanted to know his breed. She also began putting a different bow tie on him each time he came to visit the clinic.

My heart warmed whenever Nicholas entered the door, at which point I would exclaim, "Look who's here!" He, in turn, seemed to revel in the attention.

Nicholas grew to be very old, and when he had reached the point at which it was no longer possible to alleviate his suffering, he waited outside, lying on a blanket on a warm sunny day. He looked at me with trust and love and seemed to understand that it was his time. Afterward, I received a letter of gratitude from Nicholas's owner, who after recalling how her dog had showed his happiness at visiting my office by becoming its "self-appointed social director, greeting all two- and four-legged creatures as they came to the door," went on to tell me the following:

> Nicholas' spirit was released where he wanted to be. He was surrounded by love and filled with joy and trust. To ease him along that final step was your loving gift to him. I know as he gazed at you at that final moment, he was at peace and felt all the love you had for him. I too am finding peace in remembering that last day.

It's fitting that I began this chapter with a poem by my cherished departed friend Ben Shulman. Ben, my son's piano teacher's father, was my friend for many years. My two boys began their piano lessons when they were three years old, so I had many years of piano recitals to attend. Ben and I spent years together, standing in the back of these piano recitals, joking around and generally exhibiting behavior unbecoming of a mother and an elderly gentleman. We laughed at each other's terrible jokes (retold in all their glory twice a year at the recitals), huddled together and chortling at the back of the room. On some occasions, we even broke into the food that all of the parents had brought for the end of the recital.

As the years went by, Ben began to tell me of his aches and pains. He was a wise and happy man who had always enjoyed living. He came to be in chronic pain, with a heart condition and all sorts of aches. One day, he was rushed to the emergency room and placed in intensive care. Without the injections and monitoring that he could receive only in intensive care, he would not live more than a few days. Ben took a good look at what his life had become and made his decision. He was ready to go. He wanted to leave with all of his friends and family around him.

I rushed to his house to be with him. His daughter and I fell into each other's arms, crying, thinking of how much we would both miss his loving wisdom. Oddly, the atmosphere in the house was ethereal and beautiful. Ben had made his decision and was at peace. He laughed at my same old tired jokes and listened to stories and music. Within a few days, as predicted, he serenely passed on. His poems were read at his funeral, and his music was played. Just as he wanted.

That's the way it should be, and that is what, among many other things, Ben taught me. Being surrounded by your loved ones, listening to stories that elucidate how much you were loved, and hearing about the favorite moments of a wonderful life work to heal and comfort both the dying and the ones who loved them most.

Part III

Holistic Fixes
A to Z

A Guide for Taking Homeopathic Remedies

Homeopathic remedies come in both pellet and liquid form.

- The liquid form is usually preserved with alcohol and can have from 20 to 87 percent alcohol. Dogs will not like the taste of the higher alcohol preparations, but you can easily dilute it in water and then administer it. Add several drops of the remedy's liquid preparation to a 1- or 2-ounce amber dropper bottle that contains distilled or spring water. Administer the diluted remedy with the dropper according to your veterinarian's instructions on the amount and frequency of the dosage.

- When homeopathic remedies appear in pellet form, the size of the pellets varies. Dogs often spit out the larger pellets. In my practice, I use the very tiny #15-sized pellets, which are so small that they stick to a dog's gum; because the dog can't spit them out, they melt in the dog's mouth. If you have larger pellets, you can crush them in a small folded piece of paper and then use the folded paper to slide the powder into the dog's mouth, or you can add several pellets to a 1- or 2-ounce amber dropper bottle with water (as with the liquid preparation) and shake until the pellets have dissolved and mixed with the water to make a liquid preparation. Make up a new, fresh preparation of the liquid remedies every week or two because there are no preservatives in the mixture.

Twelve Handy Remedies

You may want to purchase these commonly used remedies to have on hand in case the need arises. They are small and make a great travel kit, too.

Remedy	Great for...	Dosage
Apis mellifica	Bee and other insect bites that appear hot and red	Give every twenty minutes for a few doses after a bee sting
Arnica	Soft tissue damage, general pain, stiffness due to overexertion, soreness, and musculoskeletal injuries	Give a few doses the day of and day after overexertion or after any surgery
Arsenicum album	Gastrointestinal upsets from eating spoiled food where there is both vomiting and diarrhea	Give twice an hour for a few hours
Borax (not the cleaning powder!)	Fear of thunderstorms and fireworks	Give the 6c potency twice a day for a month during the season
Calendula	Any kind of external infections, scrapes, or wounds	Apply in ointment form a few times a day until healed
Hepar sulphur	Painful abscesses anywhere on the body and painful infected anal glands	Give three times a day for three days
Hypericum	Any pain due to nerve damage or injuries to nerve-rich areas; injuries from nail clipping	Give every thirty minutes for a few doses after the injury occurs
Ledum	Any type of puncture wound, including insect-bite wounds that are cool to the touch and appear bruised	Give three times a day for a few days
Myristica	Anal-sac infections and chronic anal-sac problems	Give three times a day for two weeks
Rhus tox	Stiffness/pain from arthritis that improves after moving around, general musculoskeletal injuries, red swollen eyes, skin infections, and skin itching	For arthritis, give two or three times a day for a month
Ruta	Injuries to tendons or ligaments, especially knee or cruciate injuries	Give three times a day for a month
Silicea	Splinters or foxtails (to push them out of the skin)	Give twice a day for a month

How do I handle the remedies?

Many sources warn that you cannot handle homeopathic remedies, which, in fact, is not true. *As long as your hands are clean*, you can handle the pellets without a problem. I have been doing this for more than thirty years, and I can assure you that it works just fine.

Should I give homeopathic remedies with food?

To allow optimal assimilation of homeopathic remedies, it is best to wait about twenty minutes after your dog finishes eating to administer the remedies. If you are giving remedies before a meal, wait at least ten minutes after administering the remedies to feed your dog. Do not mix the remedies into your dog's food.

How much should I give each time?

The most important thing to remember is that the number of tablets or drops of liquid is not critical. In fact, it's not at all important. You can give 1 drop to an elephant and 10 drops to a mouse. The size of the pellets is also not important because you are administering the "energy" of the medicine rather than the actual "material substance" of that medicine.

How often should I adminster the remedy?

Follow the directions from your practitioner or the dosage information on the bottle.

How do I store homeopathic remedies?

Keep pellets at room temperature and refrigerate homemade liquid preparations. If you spill the remedy, do not put it back in the bottle to avoid contamination. Keep remedies away from computers and microwaves.

What do the numbers and the "c" or "x" on the bottle mean?

The strength of a homeopathic remedy is actually proportional to the number of times it is diluted and shaken. A 6 means that it has been diluted and shaken six times; a 30 means thirty times. The "c" potency is diluted 1:100 times each time, while an "x" potency is deleted 1:10 times each time.

In closing, it is more important to select the right remedy than to worry about how many pills to give and what strength. The weight of the animal is not important.

196 *Dr. Khalsa's Natural Dog*

A

Anal Glands

Your dog's anal sacs are located on either side of his anal area. They routinely empty during a bowel movement. They can become obstructed or infected.

Signs and symptoms of anal sac problems include:

- Scooting and sliding the rear end on the floor
- Frequent licking under the tail
- A pungent, foul smell coming from the rectal area
- Red and inflamed rectal area
- Painful bowel movements or ceasing to have bowel movements

Treatment

Check with your veterinarian or groomer to see if your dog's anal glands need to be expressed. Epsom-salt soaks are an absolute must when anal glands are occluded or infected. Purchase Epsom salt from the pharmacy and prepare a bath according to the directions on the container. Soak the dog's anal area for five minutes, two to three times a day. Make sure that the water is at a warm, comfortable temperature. If your dog won't sit in the bath, soak large cotton balls or washcloths in the salt and warm water and use these as compresses on the dog's anal area. Treat with Epsom-salt baths or compresses for three days to one week, depending on the severity of the condition; this treatment will drain the anal sacs and help the tissues heal.

The best homeopathic remedy for chronic anal sac problems is Myristica 30x. Give one dose four times a day for one week. Follow this with one dose twice a day for one more week. Hepar sulph 30x is an excellent remedy for painful abscesses anywhere on the body and thus works well for anal abscesses. Often, dogs with anal abscesses are very uncomfortable and in pain. Hepar sulph 30x will help reduce the pain and inflammation, promote drainage of the area, and handle the infection. Give this remedy four times a day for three or four days. Silicea 6c is another good remedy, but it should not be given at the same time as Hepar sulph. Give Silicea 6c once a day for one to two weeks once the anal sacs are no longer inflamed to complete the drainage and healing of the anal sacs.

Anemia

Anemia is a condition in which the number of red blood cells in the body is insufficient to oxygenate cells. Anemia can be caused when the body loses blood or when the body's bone marrow cannot produce enough red blood cells. Anemia can also be caused when the body destroys its own red cells; such is the case with autoimmune disease. It's important to schedule a visit with your veterinarian if you think your dog might be suffering from anemia.

Signs and symptoms of anemia include:
- Tiredness and lethargy
- Pale gums and/or inner eyelids
- Labored breathing

Treatment

Certain vitamins and minerals, such as vitamin B$_{12}$, folic acid, copper, and iron are important in creating new red blood cells. Liver contains blood-building nutrients, and I recommend organic liver. Leafy greens are filled with chlorophyll, which provides important elements necessary for new blood production. Lightly steam leafy greens such as kale and mix into a tasty food. In the Canine Café section, there are recipes for omelets that can contain leafy greens. Alternatively, you can purchase chlorophyll tablets or liquid at a health food store. Super blue-green algae, barley grass, and wheatgrass powders and tablets are also high in chlorophyll.

There are several homeopathic remedies that are beneficial to anemic dogs. I recommend China 30c in cases where the dog has experienced sudden blood loss. Give one dose three times a day. Ferrum metallicum (iron) 6c, twice a day, is an excellent remedy to help promote the formation of new red blood cells. Phosphorus 30c, twice a day, is excellent for the blood, liver, and bone marrow. Arsenicum album 6c, two or three times a day, helps resolve anemia and acts as a tonic for the entire body. You can also give a combination of the aforementioned remedies.

Check for the Signs

If you press down on your dog's gums and then release, the gums will momentarily look pale but should return to normal color before you can count to three. If your dog seems very tired, and his gums look pale, not returning to normal color a few seconds after you place pressure on them, go to your veterinarian and have him or her give your dog a blood test. Another way to check for anemia is to look at the inside of your dog's eyelid by stretching the lower lid down gently. Look into the tissue on the inside of the eyelid and see if it is pink or if it looks pale or white. If you look in a mirror and stretch down your own lower eyelid, you'll see the pink part of the inner lid that I'm talking about.

Arthritis

Just like people, dogs can get arthritis as they age. Arthritis can occur in the hips, elbows, knees, or other joints of the body. The marketplace is chock full of natural products for arthritis. It would be impossible to cover them all. The good news is that my years of experience allows me to share with you the most effective remedies for this problem to help your dog have a full, happy, and pain-free life.

Signs and symptoms of arthritis include:
- Changes in gait; motion becomes short and choppy
- Difficulty going up or down the stairs

- Pausing while walking
- Exhibiting discomfort when hips are touched
- Hesitation in getting up from lying-down position
- Groaning or whining when trying to get up
- Decreased interest in playing

Treatment

Gold bead implants are very effective in young dogs who exhibit hip dysplasia early in life. Go to the AHMVA website and look for practitioners in your area who perform the gold bead implant procedure. Acupuncture also provides real relief for arthritis in many patients. You can also find acupuncture practitioners on the AHVMA site.

Cetyl myristoleate (CMO; brand name Myristin), for dogs is by far the most effective product for dogs with arthritis. I've always found the results to be exceptional. It is a safe, natural alternative to nonsteroidal anti-inflammatory drugs (NSAIDs), working quickly with excellent results. CMO promotes recovery of the joint, helps create synovial fluid, and reduces pain and inflammation while regulating the immune response for optimal joint recovery. It comes in a chewable tablet.

I've been using the human form of this product for more than twenty years, and I used to save it for the worst cases. Now, a chewable veterinary tablet is available, so I go right to prescribing CMO for my arthritic canine patients. At least 90 percent of the dogs I have treated with CMO have had phenomenal results.

Deserving Pets vitamins contain alfalfa and vitamin C along with many other ingredients that help with arthritis. Many older animals come off their arthritis medication after a few weeks on the Deserving Pets vitamin mixture and start acting much younger.

Homeopathic remedies for arthritis include Rhus toxidendron 30x. This remedy is good for dogs who are sore and stiff after resting and better after they've moved around a bit; this type of patient is also affected by damp and cold and feels better in warm weather. The remedy Bryonia alba 30x is indicated in dogs who are sore after exercising and more limber once they've exercised. Causticum 30c is good for the older dog with arthritis. Many arthritic senior dogs experience severe pain along with deformities of the joints, such as bony swellings at or near the joint, and possibly weakness in the hindquarters.

Bladder Infections (Cystitis)

A simple bacterial infection of the urinary bladder is called cystitis. Most of the time, straining and discomfort while urinating is caused by cystitis. Other reasons for bladder discomfort are

stones in the bladder and tumors of the bladder. Male dogs can develop an infected or enlarged prostate, resulting in a urinary tract problem. In some cases, bladder infections can become chronic. Additionally, if resistant bacteria are causing the problem, antibiotic therapy must be relentless and thorough.

Signs and symptoms of cystitis include:

- Urinating more than usual and needing to go out more
- Having accidents in the house
- Dribbling of urine or starting and stopping of the urine stream.
- Discolored, dark, red-tinged, or cloudy urine

A urine analysis is important to ascertain if your dog has a urinary tract infection. If your dog does have a bona fide urinary tract infection, I recommend getting a culture and sensitivity to find the best antibiotic. You must treat such an infection with the full recommended course of antibiotics. I also recommend another urine analysis one week or so after the antibiotics are finished to make sure that the infection has cleared up completely. A bacterial infection in the bladder could move up into the kidneys and cause a secondary infection of the kidneys.

Many bacteria cannot grow well in an acidic pH. Certain foods and supplements help maintain a healthy acidic urine and can fight off infections in the bladder.

The cranberry is a powerfully healing food for cystitis. First, it lowers the pH to a healthy acidic pH and keeps it there for about twelve hours. Bacteria cannot survive when the pH becomes acidic. Cranberries fight urinary tract infections in another way, too: cranberries contain a polysaccharide called mannose, which decreases the bacteria's ability to adhere to the cells lining the urinary tract. The bacteria will adhere to the mannose in the cranberries rather than to the surface of the cells and then get flushed out in the urine. Give cranberry capsules or tincture at least twice a day for two weeks.

Vitamin C can also help normalize the pH, but its effects do not last as long as those of cranberry. Be aware, though: too much vitamin C all at once can cause diarrhea, so you shouldn't treat with both cranberry and vitamin C. If using vitamin C, give your dog from 100–300 mg three times a day with food to acidify the urine.

Cherry juice is good for chronic bladder infections. I have seen patients' chronic bladder infections resolve with cherry juice after no other type of treatment worked. A small dog gets ¼ teaspoon three times a day, while a very large dog gets ½–1 teaspoon three times a day.

Homeopathic remedies are not a substitute for antibiotics in cases of cystitis. One particular Chinese herb called Huang Lian Jie Du Wan (Mayway Herbs) has an excellent antibiotic effect and can be used, in addition to homeopathic remedies, along with veterinary care and oversight.

Cantharis 30c is an important remedy when your dog has an inflamed urethra and is experiencing pain; it resolves the burning discomfort in the urethra. Give this remedy three or four times a day until your dog appears relieved. Uvi ursi 30 is, in general, another good remedy to use for bladder infections. Give this remedy three times a day. Causticum 200c, once a day for ten to fourteen days, can help with chronic bladder infections.

Bladder Stones

Stones in the bladder can present some of the same symptoms as cystitis, making it easy to confuse the diagnosis. Often, with stones, the problem will occur repeatedly, necessitating an X-ray or ultrasound to confirm the presence of stones. If the stones are large enough, sometimes they can be found in routine abdominal palpation. Although there are many herbs and remedies that help dissolve stones, surgery may be necessary depending on the size and number of the stones. Holistic therapies and prescription veterinary diets have effectively eliminated stones, but you do need veterinary supervision if you go this route.

It's important to work to prevent stones from recurring by changing the conditions in the bladder through diet and nutrition. Certain vitamins have a profound effect on the potential for minerals to enter the bladder; for example, vitamins K_2 and D_3 work together to help metabolize and process minerals. Importantly, K_2 prevents calcium from washing into the bladder while D_3 creates efficient mineral metabolism. Vitamin D_3 also significantly improves immune function. Research indicates that vitamins K_2 and D_3 may be very important in preventing urinary crystal and stone formation.

In my clinical opinion, the formation of stones is caused by faulty urinary pH combined with poor-quality, incorrectly proportioned minerals in the diet along with insufficient amounts of high-quality K_2 and D_3.

The following remedies will help with stones: In general, Lycopodium 6x, given twice a day, is an excellent remedy for helping eliminate/prevent stones. Hydrangea 6x, given three times a day, is effective in dissolving stones. Again, when implementing dietary changes and using holistic regimes to handle bladder stones, it is important to work closely with your veterinarian and have your dog checked routinely.

C

Cough

Chronic coughing can be due to allergies, bronchitis, heart disease, a collapsed trachea, heartworms, lung cancer, or pneumonia, to name some of the most probable causes. Chronic coughing requires a complete veterinary examination and medical workup.

Acute onset of coughing, especially with a fever, may be due to infection. Kennel cough is a respiratory infection that dogs commonly contract in boarding kennels, thus the name "kennel cough." Pneumonia is a very serious respiratory infection.

Treatment

Homeopathic remedies can be excellent in helping resolving kennel cough quickly. Drosera 30c, four times a day, is effective in relieving the spasmodic coughing that is characteristic of kennel cough. Antimonium tartaricum 30c, three times a day, helps prevent the infection from going deeper into the lungs and causing secondary pneumonia. Ferrum phosphoricum 30c, three times a day, reduces general inflammation and prevents the infection from worsening. Bryonia 30c, three times a day, has a special affinity for the tissues that line the chest cavity. If your dog seems hesitant to move, he may benefit from this remedy. Spongia tosta 30c, three times a day, is indicated for the hoarse dog with a harsh, dry cough. If more than one remedy is indicated for your dog, you can combine them and dose three times a day. A Chinese herbal combination called Clear Mountain Air comes in pill form and is also helpful in cases of kennel cough.

If your dog contracts pneumonia, he should be under veterinary care. Holistic remedies recommended for pneumonia should be used in conjunction with antibiotics and any other treatments prescribed by your veterinarian. Two homeopathic remedies are especially effective with pneumonia: Bryonia 30c and Phosphorus 30c. Bryonia is excellent for left-sided pneumonia, and phosphorus is an excellent general remedy for pneumonia. You can give both four to six times a day.

D

Dental Problems

If tartar buildup has formed on your dog's teeth, try one or more of the reliable natural products available to remove tartar. These products do not require brushing and can minimize or eliminate the need for expensive dental cleanings under anesthesia. Of course, if your dog has a tooth that needs to be removed or more complicated dental problems, the veterinarian needs to use anesthesia for the procedure.

VetzLife Oral Care Spray or Gel softens and eliminates tartar and can reverse oral disease. You just apply it with a toothbrush or warm washcloth, ideally before bedtime. After a few applications, remove the softened tartar with a washcloth. In addition, a product called LEBA III is also very effective in removing and preventing tartar. Both products contain safe herbal extracts. If your

dog seems to accumulate tartar like nobody's business, there's a homeopathic remedy called Fragaria 6x that may solve the problem when administered twice a day for a month.

Bones not only taste good and are fun to chew, but the process of chewing them stimulates the gums, exercises the jawbone, and—yes—cleans the teeth! A good bone will provide your dog with hours of pleasure and help ensure his dental health. However, you need to make sure it's the right kind of bone. I'm talking about the large femur or leg bones and knucklebones from a cow, which are practically impossible to swallow or chip. Nonetheless, you have to watch to make sure that it doesn't get too small and, if it does, be sure and exchange it for a new one. When you find that your dog is enjoying his bones, relax and enjoy the fact that his teeth and gums will be all the healthier for it.

Diabetes

When your dog eats food, he digests the complex food molecules, which turn into simple sugars, much of which is glucose. Glucose then enters the blood, where insulin from the pancreas manages the distribution and uptake of these simple sugars. Insulin opens the cellular "door" to allow glucose to enter and be used for energy.

In cases of diabetes, the cells cannot absorb the sugars that they need. The sugars keep circulating in the blood and are finally secreted by the kidneys into the urine. Glucose gives the cells the energy they need to survive. When the cells are starved of the sugar necessary to run their metabolism, a trigger in the brain for hunger goes on. Therefore, diabetic dogs exhibit both excessive thirst and hunger.

Signs and symptoms of diabetes include:
- Noticeable intake of more water
- More frequent urination
- Weight loss
- Increased appetite
- Unusual- or sweet-smelling breath and urine, or both
- Secondary bladder infection

Designing a Diabetes Diet

Feeding several small meals a day, with a larger portion given before an insulin injection, works well for diabetic dogs. Vegetables such as green beans, squash, kale, dandelion greens, and parsley are recommended, grated and served either raw or lightly cooked. Garlic should be used generously in these meals. Meats, which should be lean, can be served cooked or raw. Grains should be well cooked; excellent grain choices are millet, brown rice, barley, and oatmeal. Olive oil is the best oil for diabetic dogs.

You may wonder why this diet calls for you to serve lean meats but add olive oil. The answer is that not all fats are alike. Animal fat, particularly cooked animal fat, is very unhealthy and has been shown to predispose a person or animal to diabetes. Olive oil, fish oils, and omega-3 oils, such as flaxseed oil, are very healthy and help prevent and control diabetes.

In the Canine Café recipe section, you'll find several recipes for diabetic dogs. The recipes can be adjusted easily to incorporate combinations of the aforementioned suggested grains and vegetables. Recipes serve as a basic template that can change along with your dog's preferences or the best buys at the supermarket.

Treatments

There are several types of treatments for dogs with diabetes, including vitamins and minerals, botanical medicines, and homeopathic remedies. If glucose levels in the blood are only mildly elevated, diet, vitamins and minerals, herbs, and homeopathy may control or eliminate the diabetes. Pharmaceutical insulin will be needed in more severe cases of diabetes.

Vitamins and Minerals

Chromium: This mineral improves the action of insulin and helps move nutrients, such as glucose, into the cells. Research proved a certain type of chromium to be so beneficial for improving the cells' uptake of insulin that researchers named it glucose tolerance factor (GTF) chromium. Give 100–300 micrograms twice a day.

Vanadium or vanadyl sulphate: This unique trace mineral lowers blood sugar by mimicking insulin. It also helps improve the cell's sensitivity to insulin. This mineral plays a role in blood sugar balance and cardiovascular function and may help your dog's body with sugar metabolism. You can find vanadium in cabbage, mushrooms, parsley, and grains. The therapeutic level of vanadium is from 15–25 milligrams daily. To treat diabetes, give 50–75 milligrams a day. Vanadium is very safe; it appears to be nontoxic, and the consequences of deficiency are unknown. Vanadium is available in liquid, tablet, or capsule form and is sold in health food stores. It is often found in human multivitamins.

Vitamin E and fish oils: These oils are very important for diabetes, along with being excellent antioxidants, and they can be given twice a day. The dose of vitamin E can range from 100–400 IU a day, depending on the size of the dog. You simply add fish oils to the food.

Multivitamin/multimineral supplement: I recommend Canine Everyday Essentials by Deserving Pets.

Botanical Medicine

Gymnema sylvestre: From a plant native to India, this herb appears to have the ability to regenerate the insulin-producing beta cells in the pancreas. The recommended dose is 200 milligrams a day for a small dog, 300 milligrams a day for a medium dog, and 400 milligrams daily for a large dog.

Lagerstroemia speciosa or **banaba leaf:** This plant from Asia contains a compound called colosolic acid, which activates glucose transport into the cells. The suggested dose is 5–15 milligrams a day, depending on the size of your dog.

Fenugreek seeds: These seeds, taken as a tea, can help lower blood sugar. Make tea by adding 1 cup of boiling water to 1 teaspoon of seeds and give ½–1 teaspoon two or three times a day, or add a few teaspoons to the dog's food. Store in the refrigerator.

Polygonum multiflorum: This is a Chinese herb that is specific for controlling blood sugar levels; you may be able to find it in a Chinese pharmacy. It can be given as a powder, tea, or capsule twice a day. To figure out the correct dose, use a quarter of the suggested human dose (divided into two daily doses) for a small dog or half of the suggested human dose (divided into two daily doses) for a large dog.

Mabel's Story

Mabel was drinking lots of water and wanting more and more to eat, yet she was losing weight and her coat appeared lackluster and shabby. At first, her owner thought that the summer heat was the reason for her thirst, but she was now drinking several bowls of water a day. After examining Mabel, I took a blood and urine sample from her. The urine was positive for glucose, and the glucose level in her blood was very high. Mabel began taking insulin that was appropriate for her weight. We started with a dose on the low side, and I instructed her owner on how to monitor Mabel's urine with test strips to check its glucose level. About every other day, Mabel's owner was to bring her in to the clinic a specific number of hours after giving the insulin shot so we could check the glucose level in Mabel's blood.

Within a few days, Mabel was feeling much better. Her sugar levels were moving toward normal, and her thirst was decreasing. We started her on 250 micrograms of GTF chromium and 50 milligrams of vanadyl sulfate twice a day. Her owner began cooking for her and added parsley, garlic, and some green beans to her food every day. Her meals consisted of basic low-glycemic-index grains and lean meat, poultry, or fish with some vegetables. Mabel got two tablespoons of olive oil mixed into her food each day and a multivitamin/multimineral supplement. Mabel was also given a combination homeopathic remedy formulated for diabetes and 300 milligrams of gymnena sylvestre once a day.

It often takes a bit of work to find just the right insulin dose for a diabetic dog. It was no different for Mabel. A month after diagnosis, she was stable and needed a much lower dose of insulin than expected. This may have been due to the holistic supplements. Mabel will need to stay on her insulin and the holistic supplements for the rest of her life unless her pancreas regenerates and recovers fully from the diabetes. Her homeopathic remedies may be adjusted over time, but she will continue to take supplements, such as the GTF chromium and vanadyl sulfate, to keep her at optimal health. Diabetics require routine veterinary examinations and blood sugar evaluations. A well-thought-out diet with proper supplements helps to regulate the body and control diabetes.

Diabetes Diet: The Basics

The following is a basic guideline for a diet for a diabetic dog; specific recipes can be found in the Canine Café.

$\frac{1}{3}$ lean protein: fish, chicken, turkey, or very lean beef (cooked or raw), or cooked egg whites
$\frac{1}{3}$ low-starch vegetables and some fruits: string beans, broccoli, cauliflower, blueberries, apples
$\frac{1}{3}$ slow-cooked oatmeal or slow-cooked barley
Olive oil
Cinnamon, garlic, parsley as healing herbs

Note: Kitchen favorites such as basil and garlic may also have beneficial effects for diabetic dogs when added to the diet.

Cinnamon: This spice comes from the inner bark of the shoots of a tree (*Cinnamomum zeylanicum*) that grows predominantly in India, China, and Ceylon. The inner rind, when dried and rolled into cylinders, forms the cinnamon of commerce. The fruit and coarser pieces of bark, when boiled, yield a fragrant oil. Cinnamon is aromatic and one of the best-tasting spices. Researchers have long speculated that foods, especially spices, could help treat diabetes. In lab studies, cinnamon, cloves, bay leaves, and turmeric have all shown promise in enhancing insulin's action. There has been a lot of talk these days about cinnamon because scientists have discovered that cinnamon extract has strong antioxidant activity and has the potential to help maintain healthy blood sugar.

Homeopathy

Iris vers 6c: Given twice a day, this remedy has a specific beneficial effect on the pancreas. It can be given twice a day.

Syzigium 6c: This remedy, given two or three times a day, helps relieve a dog's increased thirst.

Phosphoric acid 6c: This remedy has been helpful in improving the condition of diabetic dogs and can be given once a day.

Natrum muriaticum 6c: This remedy has also been shown to improve the condition of diabetic dogs and can be given twice a day.

Homeopathic remedies may help reduce symptoms and help stabilize diabetic patients on insulin by assisting in controlling insulin levels. With diabetes, the appropriate remedy often needs to be given to the dog for the long term.

If your animal is diabetic, watch the sugar in his urine and blood carefully as you begin these supplements and homeopathic remedies. Your veterinarian will show you how to monitor the urine and blood for sugar levels. Your dog may need less insulin after taking these remedies for while, and you want to know when it's time to lower the insulin dose.

The pancreas is a pinkish, semioblong-shaped organ that is a few inches in length. It helps digest food by producing digestive enzymes. The pancreas also produces insulin, which, as previously mentioned, allows sugar carried in the blood to transfer into the cells.

Digestive Problems

Digestive problems in dogs include diarrhea, vomiting, and constipation. Some dogs may have occasional digestive upset after getting into the garbage, whereas others may have such sensitive digestive tracts that any alteration of their diets results in days or weeks of discomfort. By knowing the basic facts about your dog's problem and learning some quick, easy, and workable solutions, you may be able to save yourself a lot of extra cleanup and trips out to the yard.

Diarrhea

Diarrhea is one of the most common medical problems that occurs in dogs. If your dog goes to a remote area of your yard to make his deposits, the problem may elude you. Otherwise, it's pretty obvious, especially when there are accidents in the house. Dogs with diarrhea have soft, often watery, stool. The stool can have mucus and sometimes a little bit of blood in it. Your dog may have accidents in the house or ask to go out more often. Diarrhea can come on quickly and go away quickly, but it can also persist and worsen.

The common denominator in just about all cases of diarrhea is an imbalance in the flora of the intestine. The environment of the intestine is filled with good bacteria that help digest food and produce vitamins. Bacteria, protozoa, and other organisms exist in the intestinal tract in delicate balance. When that balance is tipped, diarrhea may result. Anything that upsets the digestive tract can cause diarrhea in your dog.

Imbalance in the intestine can come about because your dog ate something he shouldn't have, drank water that was foul, had a marrowbone or another type of very rich treat, got into the garbage, or ingested something else that upset the balance of his GI tract. In these cases, rebalancing the intestinal tract with probiotics along with a bland diet can often correct the problem. The good bugs will begin to overrun the bad bugs, correct balance will return, and the problem will disappear. Uncomplicated diarrhea is not hard to correct.

If it is not a simple case of the dog's having ingested the wrong thing, the cause of the problem must be isolated and corrected. Diarrhea can be caused by food allergies, irritable bowel disease, and parasitic infections such as worms or *Giardia*. Diarrhea accompanied by a fever may require an emergency trip to the veterinarian because serious diseases such as parvovirus and distemper can cause diarrhea (that may or may not be bloody). Diarrhea along with repeated vomiting may also be due to a serious medical condition, such as intestinal cancer.

For recipes that can help dogs suffering from diarrhea, see the special-needs section in The Canine Café. Many foods can be beneficial. For example, sweet potatoes and yams have a natural substance in them that decreases inflammation in the intestine and can work even better than the typically recommended chicken and rice dishes. There are also various types of treatment; the treatments discussed here are for uncomplicated diarrhea. If your dog's diarrhea persists, take him to a veterinarian.

Rice and Egg Drop Soup

This recipe is an excellent one for a dog with diarrhea.
- 2 cups basmati rice
- 6 cups water
- 3 eggs, beaten

Cook 2 cups basmati rice in 6 cups water for fifteen minutes. The mixture that results should be a little soupy; if not, add more water. Rapidly mix in beaten eggs and allow to cool to room temperature. It should firm up as it cools. Serve when cool.

Conventional Treatments

Kaopectate is an over-the-counter drug available in drugstores and supermarkets. It contains a special mineral that absorbs the diarrhea-causing bacteria along with the toxins in the intestine. Give your dog from 1 teaspoon to 1 tablespoon of Kaopectate every hour or two for several hours. It works best if given often on the first day or two.

Metronidazole (Flagyl) must be dispensed or prescribed by your veterinarian. Often, one pill in the very beginning of the problem will nip it in the bud. After the one tablet is given, add some extra probiotics to your dog's food for added benefit.

Homeopathic Remedies

Homeopathic remedies are ideal for problems such as diarrhea and vomiting. Because they melt in the mucous membranes and do not have to be swallowed, they are easy to administer, allowing you to rest the digestive tract and treat your dog with some very effective medicine at the same time. It's a win-win situation. The following homeopathic remedies are helpful for treating dogs with diarrhea.

Podophyllum 30c: This is a very good remedy for just about all diarrhea, especially light brown or yellow diarrhea, which is very common in young nursing puppies. Give this remedy four times a day. After the stool becomes firm, reduce the frequency of dosage to twice a day for two to three days to make sure that the problem has completely cleared up.

Aloe 30c: This remedy is good for diarrhea that has a jelly-like mucus. With this type of diarrhea, you may hear rumbling in the dog's bowel, and he will have a great urgency to relieve himself. This remedy may be given four times a day until the diarrhea clears up. You also may mix podophyllum 30c and aloe 30c; giving the mixture four times a day will help quickly alleviate most cases of uncomplicated diarrhea.

Mercurius corrosivus (Merc corr) 30c: This remedy is for diarrhea in which there is much straining. Your dog may stay in the arched position and go several times, producing diarrhea with mucus and a slimy appearance. There also may be spots of blood in the stool. This remedy can be given three times a day. If your dog displays these symptoms and does not begin to respond to the treatment within twenty-four hours, take your dog's temperature, get a stool sample to take to your vet to be checked for worms, and schedule a veterinary exam.

Arsenicum album 30c: This remedy is especially useful for cases of diarrhea accompanied by vomiting. The stool may have a very rank odor, and the dog may be restless. This is also a good remedy for dehydration. Administer the remedy every hour or two, and reduce the dosing in frequency as improvement occurs. Keep dosing at least twice a day until the condition is well under control. Again, see your vet if your dog does not respond to treatment.

China 30c: This remedy is effective when your dog has lost a great deal of fluid because it will help restore strength and maintain electrolyte balance. Give this remedy three times on the first day only.

Nux vomica 30x: This remedy helps alleviate the discomfort your dog may feel. Give once in the evening before bedtime.

Probiotics and Prebiotics

You can help restore the natural balance of the intestine by adding beneficial bacteria such as lactobacillus acidophilus to your dog's meals. Look for yogurt from the health food store that contains a desirable mix of cultures and the needed probiotics. Several tablespoons, or even a whole container, of beneficial yogurt, depending on your dog's size, can be added to your dog's food as part of a meal.

Probiotic bacteria in powder form, liquid preparations, tablets, and capsules are also widely available over the counter at health food stores. Good intestinal bacteria should be part of your dog's routine diet, so I recommend that you continue giving probiotics even after the diarrhea clears up.

Prebiotics are foods that allow specific healthy changes in both the composition and activity within the community of friendly bacteria. Prebiotics also confer benefits to the host's well-being and health. Prebiotics are nondigestible food ingredients that promote the growth and proliferation of "good" gut bacteria. In other words, prebiotics are the health food for probiotics. Prebiotics have been shown to work faster than probiotics in restoring healthy intestinal balance by giving the friendly bacteria the materials they need to grow and multiply.

Kale, dandelion greens, and chard are good examples of healthy prebiotics that can be added to any dog's diet. Perhaps dogs have retained a primal knowledge of the positive effects that certain nondigestible fibers have on the gastrointestinal tract. Because our dogs can't get into the refrigerator and pull out a bunch of kale, they are forced to choose grass, which is a poor substitute for a prebiotic.

Chinese Herbs

Po chai is a pill made of common Chinese herbs that you can find in the Chinatown section of most large cities or through online retailers. It is usually sold in sets of ten or twelve small vials filled with tiny pellets. This herb works wonderfully in dogs with diarrhea. The dosage for a large dog is usually one vial three times a day. A small dog can get one half of a vial three times a day. Administer this herb until the diarrhea has fully cleared up, at which point you should discontinue use.

Botanical Medicine

Two substances that can be used for diarrhea are slippery elm and carob powder. A small amount of powdered slippery elm bark in water forms a jellylike substance that can be administered to your dog to help slow the diarrhea. Typical dosage is 1–2 teaspoons three times a day, depending on the size of your dog.

Carob powder is also mixed with water. The recommended dosage is ½–1 teaspoon three times a day, depending on the size of the dog. You also can mix 1 teaspoon of slippery elm with a teaspoon of carob powder and administer the two remedies together.

Vomiting

Many dogs occasionally eat grass and vomit. Dogs can also regurgitate their food once in a while, particularly if they have eaten quickly. This type of intermittent vomiting is not serious, but repeated episodes of vomiting, in which a dog cannot keep his food down, is a serious situation and requires a full veterinary examination. If the vomiting is spasmodic and continual, it is considered an emergency.

First Steps

The first step in treating acute vomiting (that which comes on suddenly) is to stop feeding your dog and fast him for twelve to twenty-four hours to rest his digestive tract. Start by removing both food and water. If your dog doesn't vomit over the next few hours, reinstate the water, but only in small amounts. Don't put down a large bowl of water and let him drink most of it because he will probably vomit again. Instead, offer about ½ cup of water to your dog every half hour for a medium-sized dog; adjust the amount accordingly for a large or small dog.

After all is well for twelve to twenty-four hours, feed him a light homemade meal of cooked yams, scrambled eggs or chicken, and rice. If the vomiting continues, you must call your veterinarian. Additionally, if your dog has a temperature above 102.5°F, bring him to see your veterinarian. Severe problems, such as pancreatitis, can cause vomiting.

Homeopathic Remedies

Arsenicum album 30c: This is very useful in a case where the dog is both vomiting and has diarrhea. Give the remedy every few hours until the condition improves, and reduce the frequency of dosing as the problem starts to clear up. For example, it can be given every hour for three doses, then every two hours for two doses, and then three times total on the next day. Once the problem is resolved, stop the dosing altogether. It should begin to work within three hours after the initial once-an-hour dosing starts. Of course, your dog should also be resting his digestive tract as previously mentioned.

Nux vomica 30c: This has a beneficial effect on the entire intestinal tract. It is best used for the dog who routinely has the occasional vomiting with grass and has regurgitated his food. In cases in which this remedy is indicated, the dog is ready to eat again almost immediately after he throws up. It can be given three times a day for three days.

Ipecac 30c: This homeopathic remedy can relieve the symptoms of vomiting. Ipecac is an excellent example of "like treats like"—if given as the straight compound, it induces vomiting, but as a homeopathic remedy, it treats and relieves vomiting. This remedy is helpful for the dog who has no interest in food after vomiting; it can be given three times over a period of a day.

Constipation

If your dog is in good health, he will have one or two (sometimes more) bowel movements every day. But if a day or more goes by without bowel activity, it means that he's constipated. Other symptoms of constipation are the dog's straining to move his bowels, producing small or very hard feces, or producing a very small amount of feces.

It's not difficult to prevent or relieve simple constipation. In fact, many of the same things that work for people will also help your dog keep regular. If, however, the situation doesn't respond to initial treatment and becomes chronic, it can be a signal of a larger problem.

Prevention and Care

Canned pumpkin is an excellent addition to a dog's regular diet to help with constipation. Add from ¼ to 1 cup of canned pumpkin to the dog's food every day. It is an excellent source of fiber, and it works extremely well to prevent, correct, and counteract constipation.

Additionally, be sure to:

- Keep your dog's water bowl full.

- Take your dog for walks; the activity of a longer walk helps encourage the bowels to move.

- Make sure that his food has enough fiber and roughage. Dietary fiber absorbs water in the intestines, making the stools larger, softer, and easier to pass. A sprinkle of bran cereal on his food will add a healthy dose of dietary fiber. Psyllium husks and flax seeds are also very high in fiber and good for the bowels. Make sure that your dog is drinking plenty of water when you add fiber.

- Add cooked vegetables and fresh fruit to your dog's diet.

- Try some home cooking. as suggested in the recipes in The Canine Café section.

- Add probiotics (acidophilus and other beneficial bacteria) to your dog's food. About ½ teaspoon in each meal is an adequate amount. Probiotics that contain acidophilus and other beneficial bacteria help build the stool and create the normal passage of stool.

- Add digestive enzymes to your dog's food. This is especially important for the older dog whose system does not make as many digestive enzymes as it once did. Adding digestive enzymes will help him digest and utilize his food better and will promote better stools. Digestive enzymes are available in powdered form at pet supply stores.

- Add raw garlic, which is good to counteract constipation, to the dog's food.

- Add olive oil to the dog's food. The suggested amount ranges from 1 teaspoon to 2 tablespoons, depending on the size of the dog.

Do not use laxatives made for humans unless your veterinarian recommends it because these products may give your dog diarrhea and upset the bowel further.

Causes of Constipation

One of the two basic causes of constipation in dogs is problems with food. Most commercial foods, even those of the poorest quality, are designed to produce normal, firm, and easy-to-pick-up stools in most dogs. Manufacturers have long known that people look at their dogs' excrement as a reflection of food quality.

Lack of roughage in the diet is the most common cause of simple constipation. This is particularly true of a diet very high in fat and meat and very low in roughage. Scan dog-food labels for things such as blueberries, apples, beets, and herbs—all elements of good roughage—and purchase foods that have roughage. You won't find these ingredients in most of the low-end dog foods available at supermarkets.

The other basic cause of a dog's constipation is metabolic or organic problems. The dog's colon is the part of the intestinal system that absorbs water. When the colon absorbs an abnormally high amount of water, stools become hard, dry, and difficult for your dog to pass. A few of the conditions affecting the colon, generating constipation through high absorption of water, are kidney failure, heart failure, and diabetes.

Constipation is far less common in dogs than is diarrhea, and it is more likely to occur in older and less active dogs. Homeopathic remedies and herbs can be used in mild cases of constipation that are of short duration. If your dog seems uncomfortable, go right to your veterinarian and get your dog an examination. You should also see your veterinarian in cases in which constipation occurs for a period of time or even for short durations with severity and straining.

Homeopathic Remedies

Nux vomica 6x or 30x: This remedy is good for acute constipation. It tones and detoxifies the digestive organs. It is the first remedy to consider for constipation or sluggish bowels. Give this remedy three or four times a day for a few days and then reduce the dose to twice a day for a week.

Lycopodium 6c: This remedy is good to give to a dog with chronic digestive problems. He may have a poor appetite and may be the kind of dog who could be described as a "worrier." Give this remedy twice a day for ten days to benefit the digestive tract.

Ear Infections

Ear infections are a common problem that veterinarians frequently see in their practices. Allergies and ear infections go hand in hand. Many dogs with allergic skin conditions, mild or severe, also have recurring ear infections, but any dog can contract an ear infection. These infections can become painful and uncomfortable. The conventional ear ointments typically resolve the symptoms, yet the infections come back over and over again. To really cure a deep and chronic ear infection, it is usually necessary to treat the allergies holistically in addition to treating the ear infection aggressively with conventional medications.

Both yeast and bacteria inhabit a healthy dog's ear. They live in a delicate balance and keep each other in check. When one overgrows, an infection occurs. Typically, the yeasty-smelling dark-brown infection comes first. This yeast infection can go on for a long time and can commonly recur. After some time, the yeast infection develops into a bacterial infection. Further down the line, the bacteria that colonize the ear become those that are resistant to most antibiotics. *Proteus* and *Pseudomonas* are the two most common bacteria that become antibiotic-resistant, and these two bacteria have a very foul odor that is easy to recognize.

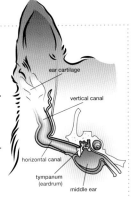

Inside the Ear

The dog's ear canal is made up of a long vertical canal and a short horizontal canal. It resembles the letter "L." Typically, we can only see about one-third of the way down the vertical section of the ear canal. The top part of the ear canal may look healthy and clean when the conventional ear medication is finished. However, deep in the bottom part of the ear, the infection still festers. Give it a little time and it will reappear—this time with a vengeance.

ear cartilage

vertical canal

horizontal canal

tympanum (eardrum)

middle ear

It is important for you to know that this scenario of frequent reinfection occurs because each infection is never completely cleared up. The yeast or bacteria remain in the lower part of the ear canal, so the infection that "came back" never really went away.

Look for the following signs and symptoms of ear infections:

- Head shaking and whining
- Scratching in and around the ear
- Brown waxy discharge with a sweet, musty, yeasty odor, which is typically itchy although not painful
- Purulent foul-smelling yellow- or green-tinged discharge, which typically indicates a bacterial infection

Yeast Infection Treatments

A yeast infection is the simplest type of ear infection to treat. Clean your dog's ears with a simple solution of one part hydroxide peroxide and one part water. Warm water will be more comfortable in your dog's ear. Clean the ears with this solution twice a week. This will help bubble up the debris deep in the ear.

You can also try using undiluted hydrogen peroxide in the ear. Place the liquid in the ear with a dropper (use about 1 teaspoon) and then massage the base of the ear to work the liquid into the ear. Now, let your dog shake his head to dislodge the debris (do this outside or in an area where the walls or furniture will not get splattered). Clean out the rest with cotton balls. This will only clean the ears; you need to treat the ears religiously for a while to handle the yeast. Zymox makes enzymatic ear solutions (one without steroids and one with dexamethasone) that work well for yeast infections in the ear. If your dog is very uncomfortable, start with the dexamethasone formula and then switch to the steroid-free formula for maintenance. There is also a formula that you can make (see sidebar).

Yeast Infection Miracle Solution

4 ounces rubbing alcohol
1 tablespoon boric acid
4 drops Gentian violet (1 percent solution)

Mix all ingredients in a dropper bottle and shake well. Do not use if your dog's ears are inflamed or ulcerated. If your dog exhibits discomfort after application, discontinue use immediately. Use a half dropperful in the ear twice a day for one week. After the first week, use one dropperful once a day in the ear for one or two more weeks. Continue to use the solution twice a week for two or three months to handle the infection that persists deep down in the ear.

Bacterial Infection Treatments

Bacterial infections often come along later, as the result of chronic reinfection. Conventional antibiotics, both oral and those applied within the ear, are often necessary to control the infection and to alleviate the severe pain that a dog can experience with a bacterial ear infection. Your veterinarian may have to do a test called a "culture and sensitivity" to find out which type of bacteria is growing and what antibiotic will work best. Many Chinese herbs and herbal combinations are available to assist in building the immune system, thus strengthening your dog's ability to fight off this problem.

Homeopathic Remedies

Hepar sulphuris 30c: This is a good remedy to give a dog whose ears are painful and infected with pus. Give this remedy three times a day.

Kali muriaticum 6c: This remedy helps calm the inflammation and should be given three times a day.

Belladonna 6c: This will help decrease redness and inflammation in the ear. Give this remedy three times a day.

Note: These three aforementioned remedies can be combined and used in cases of painful, infected, and inflamed ears.

Mercurius solubilis 30c: This remedy is good for infections that have a green-colored discharge and musty smell. Give this remedy twice a day.

Mercurius corrosivus 6x: This remedy may be useful for treating ear infections that have bloody ulcerations. Give this remedy twice a day.

Hypoallergenic Antiyeast Meal

Here's a good meal to prepare for a dog with yeast problems:

3 cups diced potatoes
1 cup beef, chicken, fish, or lamb (for dogs who also have allergies, use tilapia or another bland white fish)
1 cup mixed vegetables (cauliflower, string beans, broccoli)
2 cloves garlic
1 tablespoon apple cider vinegar
1/3 cup olive oil

Chop garlic and let it sit while the meal is prepared. Place potatoes in saucepan with just enough water to cover and cook until tender. Add diced meat, vegetables, and olive oil. Heat until meat is done, about ten minutes. Let cool. Mix in garlic and apple cider vinegar.

Emotional Problems

Dog owners have all observed the wide range of emotions that dogs can exhibit. Because I spend so much of my time in the world of dogs, it is a fairly easy task for me to gauge how a dog is feeling. For example, a Golden Retriever can jump onto my chest, emanating love and trust. His mood is obvious. The wonderful thing about dogs is that their emotions tend toward the positive, with lots of love and playfulness. Perhaps that's why they are such a tonic to us.

Dogs can also feel afraid and insecure, just as we can. Dogs who have had bad experiences can display mistrust, probably with good reason. Dogs can get upset and concerned, just as we can. Sometimes a dog can become anxious or worried when left alone. It can be difficult for even the most loving dog owner to understand why his dog is experiencing unwanted or unpleasant emotions. It can also be frustrating because we cannot simply sit down and have an open chat with our dogs as we could with a human friend who is afraid or worried.

When pets are left alone for the majority of the day, they may get bored, lonely, or anxious. It is important to understand that they need love and quality time. All of us, including myself, can get so wrapped up in our work and projects that we sometimes forget that our furry friends, who give us so much love, also need love, along with some attention and playtime.

The following information suggests remedies for separation anxiety and some other common fear problems in dogs. Additionally, a calming diet is listed in the special-needs section of the Canine Café recipes.

Separation Anxiety

Many families who own pets are out of the house for the majority of the day, leaving their animals at home for extended periods of time. Dogs can become anxious and sometimes destructive when left at home alone. In addition to the suggested remedies, there are practical steps you can take to help a dog who is suffering from separation anxiety.

- Have more than one pet. Two dogs who are compatible with each other will provide each other with company. A compatible cat can also provide your dog with company.
- Tell your dog that you are leaving and when you will be back. Picture your return in your mind and send that picture to your dog with your words.
- Leave soothing music, such as Mozart, playing softly in the background.
- Leave your dog with safe toys to chew on and play with.
- Hire a professional dog walker or a trustworthy neighbor to take your dog for an afternoon walk and break up his day.
- Stuff almond butter or treats into a durable hollow chew toy to keep your dog challenged and busy during the day.
- Take your dog for a run or long walk in the morning before you leave to burn up some of his excess energy.
- Set up a recording device to record video or audio during the day. Listen to the recording to discover if any particular events, such as the mailman's arrival, triggers unwanted behavior.
- Set aside a specific time every day to spend quality time interacting with your dog.

Homeopathic Remedies and Botanical Medicine

Ignatia 30x: This is one of the best remedies to use for separation anxiety. If the lower potencies do not produce the desired effect, move up to the higher potencies. Give this remedy three times a day for two to four weeks.

Pulsatilla 30c: This remedy is suitable for gentle, loving dogs who tend to be clingy. These dogs typically have sweet expressions and devotedly follow their owners all over the house. It is a remedy predominantly used with females. Give this remedy twice a day for two to four weeks.

Lycopodium 6c or 30c: The dog who needs this remedy does not like solitude. He will not cling, but he will stay in the same area that you do. He will move from room to room with you. He may also be the type who worries. Give this remedy once a day for one month.

Phosphorus 6c or 30c: This remedy is good for the dog who loves people and company. He will push for attention and often be the star of the moment. A sense of fun predominates this dog's personality. The dog who needs this remedy may be fearful of loud noises, such as gunshots and thunder. Give this remedy once a day for one month.

St. John's wort: This herb is used to treat anxiety and calm the emotions, and it is readily available at health food stores. It can be given in conjunction with any of the aforementioned indicated homeopathic remedies. Give one or two tablets, depending on the dog's size, twice a day.

Fear of Thunderstorms

Fear of thunderstorms has become more and more common in recent years, and a number of homeopathic remedies have proved helpful. One of the problems with treating this condition is that it is often difficult to know when a thunderstorm is coming. Therefore, the indicated remedies may be given during storm season. Beginning the remedy at least one week before thunderstorm season or giving the remedy before a storm is predicted is advantageous. After the remedies start to work, the dosing can be reduced and then stopped. In many cases, dogs have been cured of their fear with the appropriate remedies.

Homeopathic Remedies and Botanical Medicine

Borax 6x: This refers to a homeopathic remedy, not the cleaning product! This remedy is specific for fear of thunderstorms and can be given twice a day for one or two months.

Phosphorus 30x: This remedy is good for animals who are afraid of thunder and the sound of gunshots. Give this remedy once every other day for twenty days. Increase the frequency to twice a day if you think it is helping but not doing the whole trick.

Natrum muriaticum 6c: This is a good remedy for the quiet dog who tends not to look people directly in the eye. Give this remedy twice a day for one month.

Aconite 30c: This is a specific remedy for fear and can be given every fifteen minutes for one hour during a thunderstorm.

Rescue Remedy: This is a Bach flower remedy that soothes troubled nerves. Give this remedy every fifteen minutes until noticeable calming occurs.

Nervousness
Homeopathic Remedies and Botanical Medicine
Gelsemium 6c or 30c: This is an excellent remedy for nervousness. It is particularly beneficial when given before a particular event that causes nervousness. For example, it may help animals who are nervous in the show ring. Give this remedy every half an hour for a few doses before the event.

Argentum nitricum 30c: This remedy is excellent for dogs who become so nervous that they have diarrhea as a result.

Arsenicum album 6c or 30c: Dogs who need this remedy can appear to be fidgety and meticulous, often making frequent trips to the water bowl for a drink. Give this remedy once or twice a day for two weeks.

Phosphorus 6c: This remedy can be used for the nervous dog who seeks affection and is afraid of sudden loud noises. Give this remedy twice a day for a few weeks.

Eye Problems
Corneal Ulcers
Certain breeds, such as the Pug, have bulging eyes that can be more prone to corneal ulcers. A common cause of a corneal ulcer is a scratch or puncture to the outer surface (cornea) of the eye. Your veterinarian will stain the cornea with a fluorescent dye to identify the ulcer.

Symptoms include:
- Squinting and/or keeping the eye closed
- Redness of the white part of the eye
- Excessive tearing of the eye

Treatment
Your veterinarian may want to use a topical antibiotic to prevent infection, and many holistic products are available to assist in rapid and uneventful recovery. Fresh aloe is a miracle in treating many eye problems and can easily be used topically. You must use the fresh plant and not the bottled gel because the plant has ingredients that disintegrate after a few days and thus are no longer available in the packaged product.

Calendula: The Wonder Herb
In my practice, I routinely flush a dog's mouth with calendula after dental surgery. It quickly stops any bleeding, and the dog wakes up without pain and rapidly heals. Calendula can often stop bleeding where nothing else works. I also apply calendula to wounds in their initial stages, because I'm confident that the calendula will prevent infection. The more frequently you apply calendula to an injured area, the faster it will heal. It's quite a special herb.

To use fresh aloe, cut the aloe plant leaf so the gel in the middle is exposed and then put the gel on the eyelid. It will soak into the eye through the eyelid and help the cornea heal quickly. Apply this three to four times a day for two or three days.

Tincture of calendula, diluted in boiled, cooled water, can be applied three or four times a day. Calendula tincture must be diluted before using—one part calendula to nine parts water—and it promotes rapid healing. It is usually available at health food stores. Extra vitamin A in the form of beta carotene can be given for a few weeks.

Entropion

Entropion is a medical problem of the eye that occurs when the lower lid of the eye turns inward, often causing the eyelashes to rub against and irritate the cornea. Surgery is often recommended to correct the problem.

Treatment

One particular homeopathic remedy should be tried in all cases. I have found the success rate of this remedy to be very high; I have used it with many patients in which the problem totally resolved, avoiding surgery. Borax 6c or 6x (the homeopathic remedy, not the cleaning powder!) should be given twice a day for three months.

$$\mathcal{F}$$

First Aid At Home

The following are some of the common problems that almost every dog owner experiences at some point, along with simple first-aid fixes.

Hives

Hives appear as discolored reddish or purple welts on your dog's skin. They can occur within minutes and are triggered by many different things. Allergic reactions to foods, pollens, and insect bites are common causes of hives. A dog with hives is very itchy and uncomfortable. Hives usually aren't serious, and they usually disappear within twenty-four hours. However, if, after your dog breaks out in hives, you notice that his face is swelling or he is having trouble breathing, then you have an emergency on your hands and should get your dog to the veterinarian immediately.

Treatment

The usual conventional treatment is to administer antihistamines, such as Benadryl, which is readily available in pharmacies. A small dog can take 25 mg orally, and a large dog can take 50 mg orally.

Homeopathic remedies have consistently proven very helpful in cases of hives. Apis 30c can be given every half hour for up to ten doses. The remedy Urtica urens 30c should be administered if the dog has hives that worsen when touched, scratched, or bathed. If you suspect poison ivy, use Rhus tox 30c for several doses.

If the hives are localized, apply the gel from inside your aloe vera plant to the area. For generalized hives, soak your dog in a colloidal oatmeal bath. Splashing witch hazel on the areas can also be soothing to the dog.

Insect Bites and Stings

First, remove the stinger if you can see it. To look for the stinger, gently push on either side of the reddened area; if you see the stinger, remove it with tweezers. If the sting is inside the mouth, rinse the area with ice water to discourage swelling.

Treatment

To treat the sting topically, put some aloe vera gel from inside of the plant on the area of the bite. The enzymes in the plant will help stop the swelling and ease the pain. Another remedy is to moisten a tea bag in warm water and hold it on the area for five minutes or soak a gauze pad in apple cider vinegar and place it on the area. A product by BHI/Heel called Traumeel comes in a cream form and will immediately stop the pain and swelling (this product is excellent for relieving the pain of almost any injury).

Homeopathic remedies can prove very helpful in reducing pain and rapidly resolving the symptoms of an insect bite. Apis 30c can be used every fifteen minutes for six doses. Other remedies, such as Ledum 30c and Hypericum 30c, can be used every half hour for six doses.

When a dog experiences a very severe allergic reaction to an insect bite or sting, his face and muzzle may begin to swell. If this happens, give Benadryl (25 mg for a small dog or 50 mg for a large dog) and administer Apis 30c every five to ten minutes. If the swelling stops, continue to watch your dog carefully until the swelling goes down. If your dog's muzzle continues to swell, get him to your veterinarian.

Sprains and Strains

Leaping, jumping, bounding, and playing hard are common activities for dogs, thus sprains and strains are common injuries in dogs. Most of the time, the dog's regular activity is harmless. A dog can run and jump and catch Frisbees for an hour every day, but then one day he lands a little "off" and sprains his knee.

The ligaments and tendons bind the joints together. Overstretching or tearing a ligament causes a sprain. Ligaments heal slowly, so the dog must rest the affected joint along with treatment.

Overstretching or tearing muscle tissue causes a strain. The symptoms of a strain are similar to those of a sprain: swelling, stiffness, and pain.

Treatment

Several homeopathic remedies are indicated for sprains and strains. They can be used alone or in conjunction with one another. Ruta 30c is specific for ligament injuries and should be given four times a day for the first week and three times a day for the second week. It should be continued once or twice a day until the injury is fully healed. Arnica 30c is beneficial in the initial stages of the injury when given four times a day for the first several days. Boswellamine is an herbal remedy that acts as an anti-inflammatory. Use the full human dose for a large dog, half of the human dose for a medium dog, and one-quarter of the human dose for a small or tiny dog.

Painkillers are the last thing I recommend for injured ligaments. Although I do not want your dog to be in pain, I also do not want him to run on the damaged leg, thinking that it has healed because the pain has disappeared. The aforementioned homeopathic remedies help alleviate pain and promote rapid healing, but resting the injured area is one of the most important aspects of recovering from ligament injuries. Keep your dog restricted for at least two weeks after the injury appears to be healed. Of course, simple muscle injuries heal much more rapidly than ligament injuries.

Wounds

Simple surface wounds heal rapidly with holistic treatments. If the wound is very large or deep, your veterinarian should examine it because such a wound may need sutures. Your dog should also be seen by the veterinarian if his temperature is above 102.5°F because he may have an infection.

Treatment

Flush simple skin scrapes with a solution of one part calendula and one part saline. Let the area dry and then apply calendula ointment topically. Repeat the application two or times a day until the wound has completely healed.

Puncture wounds require additional remedies to prevent infection. Ledum 30c and Hypericum 30c should be given four times a day for the first week. If the puncture was caused by a splinter, remove it carefully with tweezers. The remedy Silicea 30c can be given three times a day for two weeks if you suspect that some material remained in the wound; Silicea will push the foreign material out of the wound. Porcupine quills are another source of puncture wounds. After removing the quills, follow the protocol for puncture wounds.

If bruising accompanies a wound, administer Arnica 30c four times a day for a few days after the injury. Arnica is a wonderful remedy to rapidly heal injuries of the soft tissues.

Treating a Wound

Many years ago, a good friend came to my clinic with her dog. He had been racing around outside when their street was being paved, and the gravel truck had run over his front paw. Chunks of gravel and dirt were embedded into the tissues. An area of skin, approximately 2 inches by 4 inches, had been completely stripped from the surface of the leg. I could see all of the ligaments and muscles, laid out just like in anatomy class.

I picked out all of the gravel and dirt and used a solution of one part calendula and one part saline to clean the area. I then soaked several gauze sponges in the solution and made a moist bandage around the entire area.

I instructed my friend to change the bandage two to three times a day, each time using clean gauze pads soaked with the calendula and saline. The wound healed rapidly. When the wound had healed and decreased to one-half of its original size, we began to use calendula ointment and dry bandages. When I initially examined the injury, I was sure that this dog would need skin grafting because the area was so large. Calendula is bacteriostatic and helps cells regenerate rapidly. The wound healed completely with no need for skin grafts or any surgery.

Fungal Infections

Fungal infections also go hand in hand with allergies. Fungi do not grow well in laboratory conditions, so they are often not identified. Certain breeds, such as the West Highland White Terrier, Basset Hound, Cocker Spaniel, English Springer Spaniel, and Chinese Shar-Pei, have a propensity for allergies with concurrent fungal infections. Fungi grow slowly yet tenaciously. A fungal infection can be difficult to get rid of because once it is established, it is slow to recede.

Malassezia

When a dog has thick, dark, elephant-like skin on the underarms, belly, or feet, he may be infected with a fungus on his skin called malassezia. This complicates a skin allergy because the fungus causes its own set of symptoms and problems. The presence of the malassezia alone would make a dog very itchy.

Signs and symptoms of malassezia infection include:

- Elephantlike, hairless, thickened, darkened skin
- Off-white, grayish crust that flakes off the skin
- Symptoms more prevalent in underarm areas and under the neck
- Musty, sweet, yeasty odor
- Itchiness
- Budding yeast organisms found in skin cytology
- Possible persistent itchiness even after allergies begin to improve
- Possibly accompanied by brown, sweet-smelling ear infection

Treatment

Although the bacterial infections of the skin are typically recognized and treated, fungal and yeast infections can often go undetected. Antibiotics actually do have some antifungal activity, and dogs who have a yeast or fungal infection can appear better while taking the antibiotic. A few weeks after the antibiotic is stopped, however, the whole problem returns.

Special shampoos with antifungal ingredients are available at most veterinary offices. Drugs such as Nizoral (ketoconazole) and Sporanox (itraconazole) can be prescribed by your veterinarian to help resolve a fungus problem. Zymox makes an excellent enzymatic shampoo and creme rinse that can be very effective with malassezia. There are natural products that also work as an antiseptic for the skin, as well as some suggestions for natural rinses and sprays in this book.

Ringworm

Ringworm is a fungal infection, so named for its appearance. A round area of fur is denuded as the fungus grows in a circular pattern. The far edge of the circle can have a red edge; often, the fur in the very middle of the circle is growing in, so the pattern appears as a ring. This distinct appearance makes ringworm one of the easier fungi to identify.

Signs and symptoms of ringworm include:
- Moth-eaten appearance to the fur
- Circular lesions, predominantly on the underside of the dog (the side that gets little sun exposure)
- Possibly accompanied by secondary bacterial infections within the circular area of the fungus

Treatment

One homeopathic remedy for ringworm consists of Bacillinum 30c, Chrysarobinum 30c, and Psorinum 30c. Mix all three of these remedies together and give twice a day for two weeks.

Plants as Diuretics

Plants can act as natural diuretics and help remove excess fluid from the body, which can help dogs with congestive heart failure. Parsley and asparagus are both effective diuretics.

Parsley: Fresh parsley can be chopped up and put in your pet's food or made into a tea. To make a tea, put 1 teaspoon of chopped parsley in 1 cup of boiling water. Let this steep for half an hour. Add 1–3 tablespoons of this tea to your dog's food twice a day. Parsley has more vitamin C than oranges, high levels of vitamin A, and a very high iron content. It also helps with liver detoxification. Parsley is also available in tablet form at health food stores.

Asparagus: I often dispense tablets containing asparagus and parsley in cases of pulmonary congestion. Purchase asparagus at the supermarket and steam several stalks for your dog. A little salt-free butter or olive oil mixed with garlic will make the asparagus tastier.

Dandelion: It has been shown that a 4-percent dandelion extract is a more effective diuretic than the conventional drug commonly known as Lasix. Lasix can cause serious potassium depletion and liver and kidney toxicity, but if your veterinarian feels that Lasix is necessary to prevent or relieve fluid in the lungs, you should use it as directed. Natural diuretics such as dandelion can be used in conjunction with Lasix, and, with your veterinarian's approval, you may be able to reduce or stop the Lasix. Dandelion detoxifies the kidneys and liver and does not cause any depletion of minerals in the body because it actually supplies potassium. Dandelion has no toxic side effects.

The fresh juice of the plant is the most powerful way to use this herb. Capsules containing dandelion are often available from health food stores, as are herbal tinctures or extracts. You can also make an infusion by placing several dandelion plants or 2 full tablespoons of dandelion powder into 2 cups of boiling water. Steep this infusion for about twenty minutes, refrigerate, and give your dog 2 tablespoons a day.

Capsules containing 200–500 milligrams of dandelion powder can be taken by medium-sized and large dogs three times a day. A small dog takes 200 milligrams two times a day. Dandelion can have a powerful effect on the digestive system, particularly the gall bladder, and this may cause your dog to have diarrhea. Therefore, start with a quarter of the recommended dose and increase the dose slowly. If the bowels are affected, lower the dose. The appropriate dose is one that prevents your dog from coughing and retaining fluid without causing diarrhea. If one tablet a day does the job, you do not need to give a higher dose.

It is important that you work together with your veterinarian because a dog in advanced congestive heart failure is already functioning at a lower capacity.

Heart Problems

Dogs can develop a variety of heart problems. Just as in humans, a dog's heart can become weak and enlarged, but dogs do not experience hardening and thickening of the arteries as people do. Dogs also do not suffer the same kind of heart attacks that people do.

Your dog's heart is made up of four chambers, separated by heart valves. The valves open and close in rapid sequence, allowing each chamber to fill and then sealing each chamber so that a rhythmic muscular contraction will drive the blood on to the following chamber.

The most common heart condition in dogs is a heart murmur. A murmur is detected when your veterinarian listens to your dog's heart with a stethoscope. When a valve is "leaky," the sound that the leaky valve makes is called a murmur. When your veterinarian hears your dog's heart murmur, he assigns the murmur a grade. The grade of a heart murmur tells us the degree of severity, or how badly the valve is leaking.

A valve typically becomes leaky due to scarring. A chronic low-grade infection, such as that which occurs with chronically infected teeth, can become systemic. The immune system quickly clears up the infection, but sometimes the bacteria settle on the delicate, paper-thin valve. The infection is resolved, but the valve scars and thus contracts. The scarred valve does not shut tightly like it used to, and blood backflows when the heart contracts; this is heard as a murmur.

Because of the leaky valve, the heart has to work harder to get the blood out to the body, and the heart muscles begin to tire and stretch as time passes. When the heart is so stretched that it cannot do its job, the kidneys sense that the blood pressure is getting low and try to help by retaining fluid. Finally, as the kidneys desperately hold fluid in the body in an attempt to compensate, this fluid begins to pool in the lungs, and the result is congestive heart failure.

A mild heart murmur can and should be treated holistically. Very advanced murmurs benefit from holistic treatments, but often some conventional treatment may be necessary to maintain homeostasis in the body. It is important to incorporate holistic medicine in the beginning as well as in more advanced states because holistic medicine works very well in supporting the heart's ability to function. Even if you need to use conventional medications, it is also necessary to support the heart with nutrition, remedies, and herbs.

The symptoms of congestive heart failure include:

- Heart murmur, audible through a stethoscope
- Exercise intolerance
- Coughing, especially in the morning or after sleeping and resting
- Increased thirst

If you understand why a heart fails, you won't be surprised to know that the best time to treat your dog for a heart condition is at the onset, before the heart stretches and becomes enlarged. Regular examinations allow your veterinarian to listen for a murmur; this is another reason why annual veterinary examinations are important.

Nowadays, we are fortunate enough to have specialists in veterinary cardiology. Because of this, your dog's heart can be evaluated in detail and its condition ascertained. The echocardiogram that a cardiologist performs is an ultrasound of the heart, and it can reveal the condition of the heart's valves and walls.

Remember, the grade of a heart murmur indicates how severe it is; the higher grades indicate louder murmurs. The time to begin treating a heart problem is when a heart murmur is found. Congestive heart failure, in which the lungs are congested with fluid that the heart cannot eliminate from the body, occurs in later stages. Nutritional supplements, herbs, and homeopathy effectively strengthen the heart tissue and assist in maintaining health. And make sure that you put your dog on a no-salt diet. There are recipes for dogs with heart conditions in the special-needs section of The Canine Café.

Treatments for Heart Conditions

In my practice, I have found holistic products to be immeasurably helpful in prolonging the life of the heart. I've treated many dogs who have enjoyed extended and fuller lives because healthy natural supplements and homeopathic remedies were added to her heart regimen.

Treatments for Murmurs and Congestive Heart Failure

No-salt diet: Salt (sodium) is linked to water retention, which will worsen the fluid retention already associated with congestive heart failure.

Coenzyme Q10: This wonderful antioxidant helps produce the energy molecule of the body, called adenosine triphosphate (ATP). The heart works all the time and needs energy molecules to run efficiently. CoQ10 helps keep the heart healthier and improves the function of its muscle tissue. A small dog can take 30 milligrams once a day; a large dog can take 30–100 milligrams once a day. The dose should be doubled in cases of very advanced heart failure.

Omega-3 fatty acids: Omega-3 fatty acids, fish oils, and flaxseed oil are readily available at health food stores. Omega-3 fats act as tissue stabilizers.

Hawthorn berry (genus *Crataegus*): This very important herb improves myocardial function and is beneficial to the heart muscle. Give 500 milligrams twice a day orally to a medium-sized dog. This herb has incredible benefits for dogs with heart conditions.

Multivitamin/multimineral supplement: Combination supplements from a good source contain the minerals and vitamins needed for heart function.

Vitamin E: Give your dog 400 IU once a day.

Treatments for Pulmonary Congestion

When the heart has weakened to the point of congestive heart failure, fluid begins to pool in the lungs or extremities. If fluid is pooling in the lungs, your dog may cough during the night or in the early morning after he has been lying still for some time.

Here are two remedies that help reduce fluid in the lungs:

Apis mellifica 6x: This remedy helps drain the fluid out of the lungs and can be given three times a day. This remedy is specifically used for the fluid, not for a cough that is not caused by fluid.

Hydrastis 6x: This remedy helps drain the lymphatic system and can be given along with Apis mellifica to help the fluid move out of the body. It is given twice a day.

Other Homeopathic Remedies for the Heart

These remedies do not interfere with the use or effect of conventional drugs. Whichever remedies are indicated for your dog's condition, they can be given in pellet form or can be combined with a small amount of liquid, stirred, and administered a few drops at a time. Whether given in individual pellets or in liquid, the frequency of dosage is twice a day unless otherwise specified.

Crataegus 3c: This is the homeopathic form of the hawthorn berry. It is a remedy that should be given for all heart conditions.

Convallaria 3c: This remedy is good when there is an arrhythmia, or uneven heartbeat.

Digitalis 6c: This is a wonderful remedy for the heart without the side effects of the conventional drug of the same name.

Cactus grandiflorus 6c: This is recommended if your dog seems uncomfortable and is not improving with the other remedies.

Calcarea fluorica 6c: This remedy helps strengthen the tissues of the heart and should be given once a day.

Heartworm

Heartworm preventive is available in forms that are administered daily or monthly. I prefer to give the monthly form and prescribe it during the time that the animal is likely to be exposed to mosquitoes. Most of the dogs in my practice take it from May to December because it gets cold where I live, and there are no mosquitoes in the Northeast in the winter. The southeastern and Gulf Coast states experience the highest prevalence of heartworm disease.

The monthly heartworm preventive kills the larvae that may have infected the dog over the previous month, but it does not prevent future infection. Therefore, a dose taken on May 1 covers the month of April and even some of March. Heartworm preventive can be given once every forty-five days and still provide adequate protection. In this way, exposure to the drug is limited, but the infection is prevented. Heartworm-preventive medication has resulted in some drug-related deaths. I do not recommend the once-a-month preventives that treat everything under the sun because these compounds contain an even more concentrated concoction of toxic ingredients. In order to further reduce the risk of any drug reactions, I prescribe the monthly medication on a forty-five-day basis.

Dogs with liver failure, cancer, or other serious diseases can have even more pronounced problems when given their monthly heartworm pills, and I encourage owners of these dogs to use more natural methods to prevent heartworms. Furthermore, if there is any possibility that your dog may have contracted heartworms, he will need to be tested before he begins the preventive to avoid any adverse reactions. Symptoms typically surface after the infection is well established and has already done some damage.

Signs and symptoms include:

- Coughing
- Lethargy
- Weight loss
- Exercise intolerance

Conventional Treatment

One of the reasons that veterinarians are so intent on preventing heartworms is because the treatment for heartworm infestation is dangerous and toxic. The compound used can be damaging to the internal organs, such as the kidneys and liver, and the dead heartworms that are released from the heart into the lungs can cause clots and damage to various organs.

The product that kills mature heartworms in dogs contains the active ingredient melarsomine dihydrochloride (brand name Immiticide). This medication is injected in either two or three doses. A three-dose treatment works best because it prevents too many adult worms from dying at once and causing circulatory shock. In a three-dose treatment, the dog is injected once, followed by two more injections a month later.

While undergoing treatment, dogs should be kept indoors for a month and avoid any physical activity that will increase the heart rate to minimize the risk of circulatory embolism.

If you choose to give your dog conventional heartworm treatment, I recommend a supplement that supports cells and detoxifies, such as Canine Everyday Essentials from Deserving Pets.

After this, consider using milk thistle seed to cleanse and tone the liver. Dandelion also reduces congestion in the liver and can even help with jaundice. The leaves work as a liver tonic, and the root will cleanse and detoxify the liver. Dandelion is also an excellent herb for kidney health. You can make dandelion tea by following the instructions given in the "Plants as Diuretics" section.

Alternative Treatment

Many years ago, I came upon a combination alternative heartworm treatment using the herb black walnut along with the homeopathic remedy Arsenicum album 6c twice a day for a few months. This combination sometimes worked and sometimes didn't. In my experience, the combination of the following homeopathic remedies, all mixed together and given twice a day over a period of a few months, has proved to be much more successful: Croton tiglium 9x, 20x, 30x, and 200x; Lycopersicum esculentum 9x, 20x, and 30x; Tanacetum 9x, 20x, and 30x; Allium cepa 9x, 20x, 30x, and 200x; and Allium sativum 9x, 20x, 30x, and 200x.

Mix all of these remedies together, in the indicated various potencies, and give a few drops orally, twice a day for three months. Combining these different potencies of the same remedy produces what is called a *potency chord*. These work on a number of different healing levels in the body at the same time and can be faster acting and more effective than other methods.

After two months on this remedy, ask your vet to run an occult heartworm test twice a month to monitor your dog's progress. It may take two to five months for tests to come back negative, but I've had great success with it.

If Your Dog Is Very Ill

If the heartworms have caused serious damage to your dog's heart, or if he is older or has a kidney or liver problem, you may want to use the homeopathic treatment concurrently with *Crataegus* (hawthorn) tincture to strengthen the heart. Give a few drops, three or four times a day, along with CoQ10 (30–100 mg twice a day) to boost the metabolism in the heart muscle and detoxify the body.

Homeopathy and herbs can be used to safely treat heartworm in dogs or to protect and detoxify the liver and kidneys after conventional treatment. If you opt for conventional treatment, remedies and herbs to help with existing kidney or liver problems can also be used before and after treatment if needed. Please remember that heartworm is a serious disease, and it is very important to find a holistic veterinarian who will work with you if you decide to use alternative treatment options. Heartworm can be treated with less collateral damage to the other organs.

Hypoestrogenism (Urinary Leakage in Females)

After a female dog is spayed, she can be susceptible to a problem called urinary incontinence or leakage, also known as hypoestrogenism. When a female dog is spayed, the ovaries are removed. The ovaries make estrogen, and this hormone gives strength to the sphincter muscle that controls urination. This problem can occur at any age after a dog is spayed, although it is more common in older dogs. With this particular problem, the female dog drips or leaks urine, most typically when she's sleeping or in a relaxed state. You may find a wet or damp area on the bedding.

Treatment

A commonly used medicine is called Proin (phenylpropanolamine hydrochloride [PPA]), given twice a day. This drug was actually an over-the-counter diet medication for people until the FDA took it off the market. The FDA issued a public health advisory against this use of the drug in November 2000. In this advisory, the FDA requested that all drug companies discontinue marketing products containing PPA. The agency estimated that PPA caused between 200 and 500 strokes per year among 18- to 49-year-old users. In 2005, the FDA removed PPA from over-the-counter sale. It is still available for veterinary use in dogs, however, as a treatment for urinary incontinence. The FDA deems it safe for dogs, although the safety studies make for interesting reading.

Before starting treatment, check with your veterinarian to make sure that your dog does not have a urinary tract infection. To treat the incontinence, the old-fashioned remedy of a ½ teaspoon of sea salt along with a ½ teaspoon of Epsom salts in at least 2 cups of drinking water is worth trying. Health food stores have glandular concentrates or glandular dietary supplements that help the body produce more natural estrogen, which will also help. Some of these are combination products with ovaries, adrenal glands, and pituitary gland, or you can use the formula with just the ovaries.

The homeopathic remedies Causticum 30x, Equisetum 30x, and Gelsemium 30x can be given as a combination twice a day for a few weeks, often with success.

K

Kidney Failure

The kidneys are very important organs because they are responsible for concentrating and removing waste from your dog's body and excreting it in the urine. They are very efficient organs and are excellent at their job. People can lose a kidney in an accident or donate a kidney to a relative and maintain excellent kidney function with only one remaining kidney. With one kidney, or 50 percent kidney function, the body is cleaned and maintained perfectly. The kidneys have to be at least 75 percent destroyed to just begin to show elevations of wastes (called the blood urea nitrogen and creatinine) in blood tests. The elevations reflect the inability of the kidney to concentrate and therefore dispose of the body's wastes. By the time a blood test registers any damage to the kidneys, they have already become severely damaged.

Your dog will drink more water in an effort to compensate for the reduced kidney function. If the kidneys can concentrate wastes at only 50 percent of what they used to, your dog will want to drink twice the water he normally does in order to correct the situation. Your dog may start drinking more water to compensate even before the blood tests show any sign of kidney failure.

Signs of kidney disease include:

- Increased water intake
- Bad breath
- Increased urination

- Picky eating or poor appetite due to the increased waste level in his system, making him feel ill
- Vomiting and diarrhea (in the last stages)

Annual blood and urine tests are important for dogs over six years of age so that kidney failure can be detected as early as possible.

Designing a Kidney Diet

The protein content and the type of protein are important when designing a kidney diet. Typically, pet foods that are low in protein are recommended for animals in kidney failure. However, many of the commonly used commercial pet foods have very poor-quality protein. This protein cannot be digested well or easily utilized in the body, and it therefore becomes a burden to the kidneys. The protein content of a diet for a dog in kidney failure should be low, and the proteins chosen should be those that burden the kidney the least.

A high-quality digestible protein will be utilized well and will cause less stress on the kidneys. Proteins from dairy and legumes have a different structure and cause much less stress on the kidneys than do meat proteins.

The kidneys are responsible for a lot more than just filtering out waste products. They also are linked to the heart and circulatory systems, where they maintain a mineral and pH balance in the body. An alkaline pH is important for the health of the whole body, particularly the kidneys. In the case of impaired kidneys, an alkaline pH helps them function at their optimal level. In an acidic environment, the kidneys are much less efficient. The kidney diet should help keep the kidneys in their healthiest state.

Proteins in the diet are acid-forming. Parsley is an alkaline-forming food and is therefore healthy for the kidneys. Other common foods that help maintain the alkaline balance of the body are sweet potatoes, yams, daikon radishes, miso, pineapples, watermelons, broccoli, and lentils. Foods such as garlic, asparagus, parsnips, and molasses also help promote an alkaline balance. For specific kidney-friendly recipes, see the special-needs section in The Canine Café.

Treatment

Treatments for dogs suffering from kidney problems include acupuncture, botanical medicines, homeopathy, and intravenous fluids.

Acupuncture

Acupuncture can be very helpful to promote blood flow and Qi to the kidneys. I have found acupuncture and Chinese herbs very helpful. Nowadays, there are many certified veterinary acupuncturists who administer acupuncture to balance and strengthen the kidneys.

Hepatitis and Fibrosis

Two common liver problems are hepatitis, which causes inflammation of the liver, and fibrosis, which is scarring of the liver.

Botanical Medicine

Dandelion is an excellent herb for kidney health. Make dandelion tea by placing 2 tablespoons of dandelion powder or several dandelion plants into 2 cups of boiling water and steep for fifteen to twenty minutes. Serve 2 tablespoons to your dog and refrigerate the remaining portion. Give 2 tablespoons of the tea to your dog each day. Other beneficial teas can be made in the same way, substituting the dandelion with parsley or dried cornsilk.

Homeopathic Remedies

Homeopathic remedies for kidney problems can be difficult to choose because the symptoms are not very differentiated. There are homeopathic remedies, however, that specialize in draining and treating particular organs, such as the kidneys.

Berberis vulgaris 6x, 6c, 30x, or 30c: This is a remedy that drains and cleans the kidneys. It also detoxifies the liver. Because the liver becomes more taxed when the kidneys cannot do their job, this is an excellent remedy. It can be given three or four times a day.

Helonias 6x or 6c: 6x is very good for kidney failure in which there is protein in the urine, and it is also good for the anemia that can occur with chronic kidney failure.

Lycopodium 6c: This remedy works to drain and tone the kidneys. It also helps with digestion and with liver function. Give this remedy two times a day.

Solidago 6c: This can be a useful remedy for draining the kidneys and promoting the excretion of toxins. Give this remedy once a day.

Arsenicum album 6c: This remedy is indicated for the patient who craves warmth and drinks small amounts of water frequently. The dog's coat may be dry with some white flakes. This remedy can be given twice a day.

Intravenous Fluids

Intravenous fluids at the veterinary hospital or subcutaneous fluids at home are necessary in severe cases of kidney failure. These fluids flush the toxins out of the body, which is necessary to allow treatments such as acupuncture and homeopathy to gain a hold. In my practice, I put vitamin C into the fluids to help the pH balance of the body and promote detoxification. While the intravenous fluids flush the toxins out, acupuncture increases the blood flow to the kidneys; I recommend daily acupuncture for hospitalized patients in my practice.

Knee Injuries

Your dog's knee is a complex joint. Strong ligaments, the anterior and posterior cruciate ligaments, are attached in a crosswise fashion to add stability to this joint. These ligaments act together with two outer bands of fibrous ligaments, the lateral collateral ligaments, and the kneecap to maintain your dog's knee stability through a wide range of motion.

Xylitol poisoning can happen to even the most observant of dog owners. Here's how a little protein called glutathione can save a life.

Oscar is a hefty dog, weighing well over 100 pounds. He's a shepherd mix, and, like most dogs, he loves his walks. He also likes to get into the garbage when he can. So, when Oscar found three delicious cupcakes in the trash, he gulped them right down. Unfortunately, the three cupcakes Oscar snarfed up were baked with xylitol.

Xylitol is a naturally occurring substance that's widely used as a sugar substitute. Chemically, it's a sugar alcohol, and, in nature, it's found in berries, plums, corn, oats, mushrooms, lettuce, trees, and fruits. Although it's been used as a sugar substitute for decades, its popularity has increased dramatically in the last few years. Xylitol is manufactured into a white powder that looks and tastes similar to sugar.

Although xylitol is OK for humans, it's extremely toxic to dogs. Even small amounts of xylitol can cause hypoglycemia (low blood sugar), seizures, liver failure, or even death in dogs. The most common source of xylitol poisoning reported to the Pet Poison Helpline is sugar-free gum that contains xylitol. As xylitol is becoming more popular and is included in more and more foods, we've got to be on alert because our dogs will also find these foods appetizing—and a decent percentage of our best friends practice the art of stealth food burglary.

When a dog eats something containing xylitol, it's quickly absorbed into the bloodstream, resulting in a potent release of insulin from the pancreas. Xylitol can kill a dog. If liver failure or a bleeding disorder develops, the prognosis is generally poor. Most dogs who develop severe liver problems do not survive.

Oscar's owner, Meredith, managed to get Oscar to the emergency center in no time at all. He was placed in intensive care. In spite of all of this, his liver enzymes skyrocketed. An ultrasound showed liver necrosis. Soon afterward, his kidneys began to fail. There was no doubt that Oscar's days were numbered. He didn't have the strength to stand up or eat. Meredith contacted me for a phone consult, and we went to work.

The most important thing we did was to begin giving Oscar glutathione—*quickly*. Glutathione exists in every cell. It protects the cell's tiny but important engines, the mitochondria. Glutathione is the most important, abundant, active, and powerful of the antioxidants. The highest level of glutathione in the body is in the liver. It's no accident that the liver (the major organ of detoxification) desperately needs its glutathione to stay healthy. Oscar's liver was in a double bind because its cells were rotting and dying and needed glutathione to repair themselves, and it could not create its own glutathione.

The thing about glutathione is that it's very poorly absorbed when taken orally. The oral route doesn't really work at all. So we found a local pharmacist who made up a form of glutathione that could be administered intramuscularly.

The change was immediate and dramatic. Oscar perked up, and his liver enzymes normalized within hours. I'd also put him on several homeopathic remedies. The good news is that Oscar made it, and he is a big, strong, and healthy dog again. I've known Meredith for many, many years and I am—to this day—so very glad that she called me. It saved Oscar's life.

It was once thought that cruciate ligament problems appeared after a sudden twisting or jumping movement, but it is now known that inflammation and weakness of the ligament often precedes and contributes to the injury. The fact that it's very common for a dog to have a problem with his second knee at some point in his life supports this new theory that the damage is more than just the result of a simple accident. A very small group of dogs with cruciate injuries do get them from true sports injuries, and these are typically dogs who test the physical limits of their bodies through vigorous exertion in extreme sports.

Cruciate ligament damage occurs much more frequently in overweight, neutered, middle-aged dogs. Dogs older than four years who are spayed or neutered are considerably more likely to suffer cruciate tears than are dogs who remain sexually intact. It's been found that spaying and neutering dogs early will increase their tendency to experience cruciate problems because sex-related hormones are involved in the development of bone, tendon, and muscle. Dogs receiving corticosteroid medications for long periods of time are also likely to suffer from cruciate problems. It is uncertain if these pets develop the problem because they gain weight or because corticosteroids decrease the strength of the ligaments.

It's important to learn how to recognize this problem. Some dogs hold the affected hind leg in the air, while most use the leg tentatively, tiptoeing after getting up and then moving with a slight to severe limp.

Ligaments are white because they get very little direct blood supply, and their limited circulation causes them to heal very slowly. It's important to remove strain from the knee area as it heals. nonsteroidal anti-inflammatory drugs (NSAIDs) and painkillers defeat this purpose because many dogs will overuse an injured knee as a result of feeling less pain after being given these medications. NSAIDs and steroids also retard healing.

Homeopathic Remedies

Ruta graveolens 30x: This is the main homeopathic remedy used for cruciate ligament injury. This remedy is specific for ligament injuries, and it is also specific for the knee joint. When a knee injury first occurs, give ruta grav 30x together with arnica 30x, dosing several times a day.

Bryonia 30x: If your dog is stiff after a walk or exercise, you can also give this remedy three times a day.

Rhus toxicodendron 30x: If your dog is still after resting and when first getting up, give the remedy Rhus tox 30x.

Note: You can combine all or some of the remedies, but always give the remedy Ruta graveolens.

Prolotherapy

Webster's New Collegiate Dictionary defines prolotherapy as "the rehabilitation of an incompetent structure, such as a ligament or tendon, by the induced proliferation of new cells."

A specific natural mixture is injected into the ligaments around the joint, which stimulates the ligaments to regenerate. Ligaments typically only regain a small percentage of their tensile strength after severe injuries, but it's not unusual for full tensile strength to be recovered as the result of prolotherapy.

This therapy is key to stimulating the growth and repair of collagen, ligaments, and connective tissue. I myself have treated hundreds of patients with greater than 95 percent success. Prolotherapy accelerates healing, and one or two treatments usually handles the problem. Pain often resolves following the first treatment. The owner does not have to restrict the dog's walking and exercise for a long period of time.

L

Liver Problems

After years of practicing veterinary medicine, I'm still amazed when I consider the importance of the liver and its many critical functions. Its job description is intimidating:

Wanted: An organ to fulfill a multitude of functions. Must be able to:

- Detoxify the body (filter out chemicals, poisons, and excess hormones)
- Produce bile (to help digest, store, and convert fats to starch)
- Control and eliminate allergic reactions
- Screen food that leaves the stomach before it goes into the bloodstream
- Perform about 190 other essential tasks

It's the liver's job to clean leftover poisons from the body. When your dog runs through lawns that have been treated with herbicides and insecticides, the liver is the organ that must protect his system from the chemicals received via contact and inhalation. After an application of one of the more noxious tick and flea preventatives, its the liver's job to clean those chemicals from your dog's body.

Because of all the toxins your dog is often exposed to, the liver is one of the most frequently insulted organs in his body. And the problem does not stop with toxins. Pathogens, such as bacteria, viruses, and mycoplasma, can invade the liver and chronically infect it.

Until a problem with the liver becomes severe, it can easily go undiagnosed. It's important to check the liver with a routine blood test because sometimes that's the only way that the problem can be caught nice and early. This is why I favor a yearly routine blood test for all dogs, and this becomes extremely important after the age of six.

It's also a good idea to cleanse and detoxify your dog's liver on a routine basis using herbs and homeopathic remedies. At my clinic, we like to reduce the number of toxins to which dog is exposed and flush and tone the liver to promote optimal health. It's that important.

Symptoms

In many cases, we find out about a liver problem only by doing a blood test. In the early stages, your dog may be tired or may be drinking more water. When the problem is caused by an invading pathogen, he may run a fever.

In later stages, an affected dog may drink and urinate excessively, lose weight, show a loss of appetite, run a fever, experience digestive upset, and possibly have pain in the area of the liver. In very late stages, your dog's eyes may even develop a yellow tint because of jaundice.

Preventing Liver Problems

- Feed your dog a natural, healthy, toxin-free diet.

- Give Deserving Pets Canine Everyday Essentials vitamins every day along with dandelion and other liver-preserving homeopathic remedies.

- Use filtered water, without fluoride if possible, for your dog's drinking water.

- Put your dog on a liver detoxification regime one to two times a year.

- Sparingly use products that can harm the liver. As mentioned in the section on heartworm, I prescribe either a homeopathic heartworm preventive or the conventional monthly heartworm every forty-five days and only during the warm months when mosquitoes are present.

- Have your veterinarian perform a yearly blood chemistry panel, especially once your dog reaches six years of age.

Treatment

Vitamins and Supplements

Antioxidants: Antioxidants are very important for liver function. Metabolizing toxins in the body produces undesirable products called *free radicals*.

SAMe: Pronounced "sammy," this is made of a substance called S-adenosylmethionine. This supplement protects the liver from toxins and is a precursor for glutathione, one of the most important liver antioxidants. SAMe can be given in a daily dose of 400 mg to a small dog and 800 mg to a large dog.

Glutathione: Glutathione is excellent for the liver, but it cannot be taken orally because it is made up of three amino acids and is digested before it can do any good. You can obtain transdermal glutathione sprays and gels with a prescription, and injectable glutathione is available to veterinarians to treat severe liver problems.

Vitamin C: This is an important vitamin because it helps detoxify the entire body. It also promotes a good general pH of the body and boosts the immune system. Vitamin C can cause diarrhea if a very high dose is used initially, so start at a low dose and slowly increase the dose to prevent diarrhea. A small dog can get 250 milligrams of vitamin C twice a day. A medium-sized dog can get 500 milligrams twice a day. A large dog can get 1,000 milligrams twice a day. Again, no matter your dog's size, start small; for example, 50 mg twice a day for a small dog, then increase the dose a little more each day. A medium dog should start at 100 milligrams twice a day, and a large dog can start on 200 milligrams twice a day.

Deserving Pets: The Deserving Pets Canine Everyday Essentials vitamin formulation has lots of leafy greens, vitamin C, dandelion, and antioxidants. Giving this vitamin every day protects the liver.

Botanical Medicine

Chlorophyll: The green compound that occurs in plants and algae is very good for the liver. It also helps flush and clean the cells and can improve your dog's bad breath. Typically, dogs get very little chlorophyll because the average dog gets no green vegetables in his diet. Chopped organic greens are good to add to your dog's diet, or give him chlorophyll drops or pills, which are available at health food stores.

Dandelion: This is a phenomenal herb that cleanses and detoxifies the liver. You can buy fresh dandelions or use dandelions from your lawn if it is not treated with any chemicals. Try cutting up dandelions and mixing them with your dog's food to disguise the plant's bitter taste. Dandelion also comes in a tincture and in capsules, which are available at many health food stores. As with vitamin C, dandelion can jump-start the intestinal tract, so start with a lower dose and increase it slowly. Work up to one capsule a day for a small dog, two capsules a day for a medium-sized dog, and three capsules a day for a large dog.

Milk thistle (*Silybum marianum*): This herb protects the liver and comes in tablet form. A small dog can get half of a tablet twice a day, a medium-sized dog can get one full tablet twice a day, and a large dog can get two tablets twice a day.

Homeopathic Remedies

Ptelia 30c: This remedy can be a remarkable remedy for the liver. It can also help stimulate the appetite. It is a good remedy to use for most liver problems and should be given twice a day.

Aesculus hoppocastanum 30c: This remedy drains the liver and portal system and is excellent in cases of fibrosis and cirrhosis of the liver. Sometimes liver failure is so extreme that there is fluid is present in the abdomen, and this remedy will help drain some of the fluid. It can also help ease accompanying constipation. Dosage is twice a day.

Taraxacum 30c: This is the homeopathic remedy made from the dandelion. It can be given three times a day to help drain the liver.

Carduus marianus 30c: This remedy is made from milk thistle and should be given twice a day. This is a drainage remedy that acts powerfully on a single organ. It is an excellent remedy for gallstones as well as a very good remedy for liver problems.

Chelidonium majus 30c: This is a prominent remedy for the liver and is an excellent digestive remedy. This remedy may also be used when there is jaundice. It is beneficial for just about any liver problem and should be given three times a day.

Berberis vulgarus 30c: This remedy drains both the kidney and liver and promotes the flow of bile in the liver. It is good to use with jaundice and should be given twice a day.

Gentiana 30c: This remedy, given twice a day, promotes healthy liver function and drains the liver. Often, animals with liver problems do not want to eat, and this remedy also works to promote the appetite.

Nux vomica 30c: Given once in the evening before bed, this remedy detoxifies the body, drains the liver, and stimulates digestion. It is an excellent remedy for general drainage and is a wonderful remedy for constipation.

Phosphorus 6c, 30c, or 200c: This is one of the most important remedies for cirrhosis of the liver. Give this remedy twice a day for several weeks.

Lyme Disease

Lyme disease is one of the world's most common infectious diseases and is the leading tick-borne disease in the United States. Lyme disease came to the forefront in the late 1970s with an outbreak of puzzling proportions in the wooded areas in and around Lyme, Connecticut, a sleepy town on the coast of Long Island Sound. It's transmitted to both animals and people by tiny deer ticks. Today, there are few areas in the country that are still considered to be free of these ticks, and it's believed that they've been dispersed throughout the country by clinging to birds making their seasonal commutes.

Lyme disease is a difficult illness to pinpoint because initial symptoms, in a variety of combinations, are often read as symptoms for a number of other conditions. The early symptoms of lethargy, stiffness, diminished appetite, and rising temperature are fairly common and can also be attributed to many other ailments in dogs.

I routinely see dogs who have been vaccinated for Lyme disease contract it post-vaccination, so vaccinated dogs should also be checked for Lyme disease if indicated. The IDEXX in-house SNAP test will come back be positive *only* if your dog has been infected naturally.

I recommend following up on a positive IDEXX in-house SNAP test with the C6 antibody test by IDEXX (this one must be sent out to the laboratory) because it gives you a quantitative result. You see, there is no way to determine the extent of the infection from the SNAP test because the darkness of the spot does not indicate the degree of infection; the spot simply indicates a positive result. However, if your dog tests high on the C6 antibody test, you will need to start treatment for Lyme disease right away.

Another important use of the C6 antibody test is for monitoring your dog's response to treatment. You monitor the progress of therapy by looking for at least a 50 percent reduction in the result. Testing a few months after completion of treatment will often let you know how successful the treatment has been. Additionally, it's important to know if your dog has a new infection or if the SNAP test is simply registering the old infection. Not all dogs will stay positive forever, but some retain an immune response, so the C6 antibody test is more effective in testing for re-exposure to the infection than is the in-house SNAP test.

The microorganism that causes Lyme disease is *Borrelia burgdorferi*. This is a spirochete (spiral-shaped) bacterium. Spirochete bacteria also cause diseases such as syphilis. Spirochetes can remain hidden in the tendons, muscle tissue, lymph nodes, brain, heart, joint fluid, nervous system tissue, and other parts of the body, where they remain dormant for years. This is part of the reason that these diseases are sometimes so very difficult to clear completely.

Lyme nephritis (sometimes called protein-losing-nephropathy) is an autoimmune disease that can occur in a dog after he is infected with Lyme disease. It usually progresses slowly, enabling the dog to compensate for the kidney damage. Because of this compensation, symptoms are not noticed until it's too late, so by the time the dog sees the veterinarian, the disease is already well established. Every dog who has contracted Lyme disease should have a routine urine analysis done every year to check for elevated protein in the urine.

Treatment

I treat dogs with Lyme disease with doxycycline for two full months. I choose to do this for two reasons: (1) because I am using antibiotics anyway, I want to make totally sure that I have handled as many of these stealth pathogens as I can; and (2) the kidney problem that can occur as an aftermath of Lyme disease is so dangerous that I want to do all I can to prevent it. Dogs can be given some cooked sweet potato with the doxycycline to prevent any upset stomach.

Extra magnesium at the very beginning of treatment will lure the bacteria out of the tissues so the antibiotic can get to it. You can purchase a magnesium supplement called Natural Calm. Use the recommended human dose for a dog the size of a Golden Retriever and increase or decrease the dose accordingly for larger or smaller dogs.

Give Nux vomica 30x once in the evening during the last two weeks of the antibiotic treatment and for one week after you stop the antibiotic, for a total of three weeks. Nux vomica helps detoxify your dog's body from the antibiotic. Give Ledum 200c or 1m twice a day for five days at the very beginning of antibiotic treatment, and give Lyme disease nosode 30c or 200c three times a week for four weeks.

A probiotic and prebiotic will maintain healthy gut flora during and for two months after the antibiotic treatment, and you should give your dog a complete and balanced supplement every day.

O

Obesity

If far too many people tend to be overweight these days, so, too, do their pets. Dogs who have been eating commercial dog food all their lives, however, probably have a better excuse for putting on those extra pounds. Although the stuff isn't all that nutritious, its heavy fat content and combined ingredients are likely to contribute considerable girth to your canine companion. In addition, most dogs don't get nearly as much exercise as they should, given their owners' busy schedules. All told, it's an unhealthy situation that can lead to a variety of medical problems, just as with humans.

If you're worried about your dog's weight, especially if he eats relatively little and is also relatively chubby, the first thing I'd suggest is having his thyroid tested. Hypothyroidism, an underactive thyroid gland, can contribute to obesity in dogs.

Barring any thyroid problems, my next recommendation is that you start your dog on a weight-reduction diet. The recipe for chubby dogs in the special-needs section of The Canine Café is a healthy regimen I've prescribed for many overweight dogs. It's one I've rarely known to fail because it consists of foods that dogs love and helps them lose weight naturally.

On this diet, your dog may have as many steamed or grated vegetables as he wants. Cook the veggies in meat broth or flavor them with garlic and a little olive oil or a small amount of butter if vegetables are not his favorite. Frozen mixed vegetables are a great time-saving alternative to fresh.

The amount of food recommended depends on the size of the dog; a smaller dog gets less, and a larger dog gets more. Provide plenty of fresh, clean water for your dog at all times. Don't forget that a superior multivitamin/multimineral supplement, such as the one produced by Deserving Pets, is also very important.

Watch your dog. In addition to losing weight, he should have more energy, and his skin and coat should continue to improve on this diet. If he seems listless, go to your veterinarian for an exam and appropriate testing.

S

Sarcoptic Mange (Scabies)

The beginning stages of sarcoptic mange (scabies) may look just like an allergy. Mange is caused by mites, and scabies (*Sarcoptes scabiei*) mites are very difficult to find in skin scrapings. If your dog starts scratching suddenly and very intensely, and he plays with other dogs who may carry the mite, scabies is a possible culprit. If you are getting small clusters of itchy red bumps on your body at the same time, it's a good indicator that the culprit could be scabies.

The mites that cause scabies resemble microscopic crabs, and they tunnel deep into a dog's skin, causing allergic reactions and irritation. This contagious mange travels easily from dog to dog. Foxes also can carry this mite and transmit it to dogs. When the mites jump on people, they can cause the aforementioned clusters of red, itchy bumps on the skin. These bumps can be very itchy, especially during and after a hot bath or shower.

Detecting Scabies

Scabies mites are very hard to detect in the typical skin scrapings done by veterinarians because they live deep down in the skin. It's important to know that the beginning stages of scabies can look just like a skin allergy. When I'm considering scabies in a dog, I know that the chances of isolating the mite under a microscope are fairly low, so I look for bumps on the owners and ask whether there are any other dogs in the family who are also itching. If it's only one dog out of four who's itching, the possibility of scabies decreases. I also check out how intensely the dog is scratching. Most dogs with skin allergies scratch most intensely when they're bored, but a dog with scabies will stop in the middle of playing or chasing a squirrel and just go at it. A dog with scabies may have very dry, flaky, itchy areas on the tips of his ears, and this is also an important finding.

Being a good detective is a necessary part of diagnosing scabies. Late-stage scabies has a particular pattern of white, thick crust on the tips of the ears. Many dogs do not have this crust in the initial stages because it takes quite a while to develop. Loving dog owners can take such good care of their pooch that the typical signs of scabies never surface.

Quite often, a veterinary dermatologist will start the canine patient on a course of treatment for sarcoptic mange in order to make sure it is not being missed. Patient improvement from the treatment indicates that the mange was present.

Signs and symptoms of scabies include:
- Ferocious scratching, especially if the dog will stop whatever he's doing to scratch
- Other scratching dogs in the household
- Contact with unknown dogs or a fox

- Red bumps on humans in the household
- Dry crusty areas on tips of ears
- Appearance of something that resembles a skin allergy (allergic dermatitis)

Treating Scabies

Your veterinarian will help you choose which of the following treatments is best for your dog:

Several oral doses of ivermectin: This is prescribed by your veterinarian and has the advantages of being quick acting and easy to give. With a healthy animal, it is relatively nontoxic unless it is contraindicated for your breed of dog (as it is for some herding breeds), so it is best to check with your vet.

Lymdyp: This is a lime-and-sulphur solution that smells like rotten eggs. It is used as a rinse on your dog and left on his coat to dry once a week for several treatments. It is very safe and can be used on a dog of any age, but the odor results in less owner compliance in the winter months.

Selsun Blue shampoo: For very mild cases only, this can be used to shampoo your dog twice a week for two weeks.

Monthly parasite preventive: Administer a monthly preventive, such as Revolution, that protects dogs from sarcoptic mange.

Note: No matter what treatment you use, all bedding should be washed and areas thoroughly vacuumed after each treatment. All dogs who have scabies should be treated simultaneously.

V

Vaccine Reactions
Post-Vaccination Homeopathic Remedies

Hypericum 30x: This remedy is used if there is pain and swelling at the site of the vaccination.

Ledum 30x: Like hypericum, this remedy is good to use if there is discomfort after puncture wounds, including injections. They can be used together.

Belladonna 30x: If there is fever, or even a mildly elevated temperature after the vaccination, this remedy can be used three times a day for a day to two after the vaccination.

Ferrum phosphoricum 30x: This can be used for a week after the vaccination if your pet seems "off" in any way. It is a good remedy to use with any mild inflammation because it balances the body.

Apis 30x: Use this remedy with any swelling or puffiness, either around the site of the vaccination or around the face. With swelling at the site, give three doses for just one day. With swelling around the face, jowls, or eyes, use it every half hour and watch your dog carefully. If the swelling does not subside, give over-the-counter Benadryl. If the swelling still persists, go immediately to a veterinary clinic.

Thuja 30x: This is one of the most valued remedies in veterinary medicine. It is given twice daily for one month to resolve issues related to chronic vaccine reactions and overvaccination.

Look into your dog's loving eyes around, say, 6 p.m., and you know what's on his mind: "What's for dinner?" The Canine Café will help you give your dog an answer to that question. Many of the dishes described here can be prepared and frozen for up to six weeks, so you can prepare them on more leisurely days to have meals ready for a busy work week. If you're like most people, you won't always be able to prepare a homemade meal for your best friend, no matter how much tail wagging goes on, but that's OK. Try shortcuts, such as those described in the Quick Meals section, which enable you to throw together nutritious meal s in minutes.

The point of this book is to enhance both your dog's health and your relationship with your best friend—not to make you feel guilty if you are short on time. I have only one request: that you *enjoy* the time you spend with your dog. Have the wisdom to know when you can relax and when you want to be a-cookin' for the canine. And if you have a picky eater, every meal may not be a hit, but you will surely find several recipes that are real winners with your dog.

Part IV

The
Canine Café

*T*here are many wonderful meal options available in The Canine Café. The recipes in the Toppers section give you many choices for healthy, yummy additions that are sure to please many a canine when added to healthful kibble. Toppers add diversity and healthy, fresh ingredients to routine fare, and they store easily in the refrigerator or freezer. The "meals in a muffin" can also be crumbled and used as toppers. A muffin meal may serve as a whole meal for a small dog and may also be made in mini-muffin tins and given as snacks to a large dog.

Unknowingly, I invented my first topper as a young veterinary student. I lived in a big old Philadelphia house with seven bedrooms that I shared with six other students. Every week, I baked a nutritional oatmeal dish that, when cooked, had the look of bread. I would store it in the refrigerator, which I also shared with six other people, and treat my dog to some of it every day. It smelled good, and it looked good, and until I began leaving notes in the refrigerator that said "Please don't eat my dog's food," my fellow tenants would eat it nearly as fast as I could bake it!

Be forewarned that most of these recipes will have you smacking your lips along with your dog. They just smell *so good* as they cook. My husband tells me that the eggshells we add to the "hearty man stews" are the only thing that keeps him at bay!

Gluten- and Grain-Free

You can make wheat-free, gluten-free, and grain-free meals for your dog by simply substituting the following productsf or wheat and grain products in the recipes. We combine different flours to simulate the baking properties and texture of white or wheat flour as closely as possible. You can also use rice noodles in place of regular noodles to make a recipe gluten-free (but not grain-free).

For Gluten-Free : 1 Cup of Wheat Flour =
    ½ cup chickpea (garbanzo bean) flour + ½ cup almond flour
    ½ cup chickpea flour + ½ cup tapioca flour
    ½ cup fava bean flour + ½ cup tapioca flour
    ½ cup coconut flour + ½ cup tapioca flour
    1 cup almond flour
    ½ cup almond flour + ½ cup tapioca flour
    Potato flour or potato starch can be used as a substitute for tapioca.
    Brown rice flour, white rice flour, buckwheat flour, or quinoa (in flake form) can be substituted to make a recipe gluten-free but not grain-free. For example, instead of 1 cup of wheat flour:
    ½ cup brown rice flour +1/4 cup tapioca flour + ¼ cup white rice flour
    ½ cup brown rice flour + ¼ cup buckwheat flour + ¼ cup white rice flour

Vet School Oatmeal Bread

5 cups uncooked oatmeal
½ cup olive oil
¼ cup powdered milk
1 teaspoon kelp powder

1 teaspoon garlic powder
½ teaspoon ground rosemary
½ cup nutritional yeast

Preheat oven to 375°F. Mix all dry ingredients in a bowl. Add the oil and then the water, blending until it reaches the consistency of thick mush. Spread mixture in a single layer in an oiled rectangular cake pan. Bake for one hour. Let cool and then break it into chunks to feed as a reward or as a supplement to a meal.

Toppers

Veggie Toppers

Raleigh's Favorite Healthy and Fresh Topper

2 cups diced carrots
2 tablespoons chopped parsley
2 cups chopped broccoli stems (one broccoli stem makes about one cup)
3 eggs (with shells)
3 cups of chicken or beef broth or water
4 cups whole-wheat bread squares (substitute 4 cups cooked diced potatoes for grain-free)
4 diced garlic cloves
½ cup olive oil

Heat the garlic in the olive oil in a large skillet. Add the diced carrots, broccoli stems, and parsley to the pan and sauté for about 5 minutes. Add the chicken or beef broth and simmer for 15 minutes. Blend the eggs and eggshells in the blender. Add the bread squares (or potatoes) to the vegetables in the skillet and stir. Lower the heat, add the beaten eggs, and stir again for about 3 minutes. Cool, serve, and/or store.

Cauliflower and Cheese Topper

3 cups diced cauliflower
¼ cup ground walnuts (optional)
3 tablespoons nutritional yeast (optional)
½ cup toasted wheat germ (optional) (delete wheat germ for grain-free)
½ cup grated Parmesan cheese
3 tablespoons butter

Steam the cauliflower until tender but not soft. Strain and coat in butter. Add the rest of the ingredients and toss. Cool, serve, and/or store.

Squash Porridge Topper

3 butternut or acorn squashes
⅔ cup olive oil
½ cup chicken broth
6 eggs, beaten
1 teaspoon garlic powder

Preheat oven to 350°F. Cut the squashes in half and bake them until soft (about 40 minutes). Let them cool and then scoop out and mash the insides. The squash seeds are very healthy, and you can place the inner seeds in the blender and chop them up to add to the mix. Blend the eggs (shells optional), chicken broth, and garlic powder in a blender. Mix blended liquid with mashed squash (with or without chopped seeds). Pour the mixture into an oiled casserole dish and bake at 350°F for 45–50 minutes or until a knife inserted in the center comes out clean. Cool and serve as a topper.

Crunchy Toppers

Oatmeal and Garlic Crunch

8 cups rolled oats
4 cloves garlic
1 cup olive oil

Preheat oven to 250°F. Dice the garlic. Warm the oil in a large frying pan. Add the garlic and cook lightly, stirring for 1–2 minutes. Stir the oats into the hot oil and immediately remove the pan from heat. Spread the mixture onto two greased cookie sheets and bake at for 20–30 minutes, stirring occasionally. Cool completely. Store in an airtight container.

Coat-Nourishing Topper

6 cups rolled oats
2 cups shredded coconut
1 cup wheat germ (delete wheat germ
    for grain-free)
2 teaspoons rosemary
1¼ cup olive oil

Preheat oven to 250°F. Heat the olive oil with the rosemary in it in a large pan. Stir in the rolled oats, coconut, and wheat germ and remove the pan from heat immediately. Spread mixture onto two greased cookie sheets and bake for 20–30 minutes, stirring occasionally. Cool completely and store in an airtight container.

Whole-Wheat Crunchy Bread Topper

2 loaves whole-grain or whole-wheat bread (replace with 6 cups of
    cooked brown rice for gluten-free)
1 tablespoon garlic powder
½ teaspoon dried rosemary
1 tablespoon dried parsley
½–1 cup Parmesan cheese
1 large plastic bag

Preheat oven to 300°F. Place the bread slices on an oven rack for 30 minutes. Place the toasted slices in the plastic bag and roll with a rolling pin to make crumbs. When all of the bread has been made into crumbs, add the garlic powder, parsley, rosemary, and Parmesan cheese and shake. Serve as a topper. Store the rest in an airtight container in the refrigerator or freezer, as it defrosts quickly when needed.

Stale bread is fine to use with these recipes.

Pancake Topper

Buy whole-wheat or buckwheat pancake mix. Add the recommended amount of water and stir the batter until smooth. Add 2 tablespoons of fresh chopped parsley or 2 teaspoons of dry parsley. Butter a large frying pan well and preheat it. Pour in the pancake batter and let it heat for just a few minutes. Then begin to stir the mix just as you would scrambled eggs until the batter is cooked through.

Chewy Toppers

Lentil Surprise

1 cup lentils
3 cups water or chicken stock (or one salt-free chicken bouillon cube)
1 cup carrot, finely chopped
2 tablespoons parsley
3 cups bread cubes (either use gluten-free bread or replace with 3 cups cooked
    brown rice or 3 cups cooked oatmeal for gluten-free)
3 eggs (with shells), blended in blender
4 tablespoons olive oil
2 cloves garlic

Add the lentils to the water or stock and bring it to a boil. Lower the heat and simmer until soft (about 20 minutes, but there many types of lentils, and they cook at different rates). Add the carrot and parsley and cook for 15 more minutes. Place the olive oil in a large frying pan and heat the garlic lightly. Add the lentil mixture to the pan and stir well.

    Add the bread cubes to the pan and mix in. Pour in the beaten eggs and mix well over medium heat. Cool, serve and/or store. You can use this to top kibble or as the main meal.

One cup of lentils has 7.8 grams/100 calories of protein.

Millet Mix Topper

1 cup millet
4½ cups water
1 no-salt beef bouillon cube
½ cup blended sunflower or pumpkin seeds
1 tablespoon olive oil
½ teaspoon sage
½ teaspoon rosemary
½ teaspoon thyme
1 teaspoon garlic powder
3 tablespoons olive oil
1–2 cups of leftover cooked vegetable bits, such as broccoli stems, green beans, carrots, parsnips, and kale

Bring water and bouillon cube to a boil. Add the millet, stirring as you add, and then simmer, covered, on low heat for about 40 minutes or until all of the water is absorbed. Add the olive oil, blended seeds, and herbs/spices and stir. Add in the cooked vegetables and mix well.

Pumpkin Nut Loaf Topper

2 cups whole-wheat flour (replace with 1 cup coconut flour
   and 1 cup tapioca flour for grain-free)
2½ teaspoons baking powder
½ teaspoon baking soda
1½ teaspoons cinnamon
2 cups pumpkin pulp (canned or fresh)
½ cup molasses
½ cup milk
3 eggs
¼ olive oil
1 cup pumpkin seeds, finely chopped (easy to do in food processor)

If you use fresh pumpkin, first bake it in the oven with the seeds and then place the seeds and pumpkin in the blender instead of using dried pumpkin seeds.

Preheat oven to 350°F. Mix or sift together the flour, baking powder, baking soda, salt, and cinnamon. Combine the pumpkin, molasses, milk, olive oil, and eggs in a mixing bowl or blend in a blender. Add the dry ingredients to the wet ingredients and stir in the chopped pumpkin seeds. Spread the mixture in a well-greased standard loaf pan and bake for 45–55 minutes or until a toothpick comes out clean. Cool and crumble on top of kibble.

Meals in a Muffin

This is a wonderful way to prepare and store meals, particularly for a small-breed dog, or you may choose to use mini-muffin tins and use these recipes for snacks. Dogs are pack animals and like to eat when we eat, so some of these recipes are wonderful for breakfast and some for dinner. Make a few baker's dozens and freeze them, defrosting what you need before each meal. I give my dogs a large breakfast, and they each get one or two muffins for a snack at dinnertime. They just love them!

Oat and Chicken Muffins

Muffins can be made into loaves or loaves into muffins. The recipes are interchangeable.

2½ cups whole-wheat flour (replace with 1¼ cups chickpea flour)
  and 1¼ cups almond flour for gluten-free)
2 cups oats
1½ teaspoons baking soda
½ cup olive oil
3 beaten eggs (shells optional; you can blend the eggs
  and shells in a blender)
2½ cups yogurt or buttermilk
1 cup grated chicken

Preheat oven to 300°F. Mix together the oats, flour, and baking soda. Blend the olive oil, yogurt, and eggs. Add the wet ingredients to the dry ingredients and stir in the grated chicken. Pour the mixture into oiled muffin tins and bake for 30 minutes or until a toothpick comes out dry. Extra muffins can be frozen for up to 6 weeks.

Apple, Banana, and Turkey Breast Muffins

1 cup yogurt
1 cup turkey breast lunchmeat, chopped
3 medium bananas, very ripe
2 teaspoons baking powder
4 cups unbleached flour (use 4 cups chickpea, coconut, or
  almond flour for grain-free)
⅔ cup olive oil
2 teaspoons cinnamon
½ teaspoon powdered sage (optional)
1 cup chicken broth
4 eggs, with shells
3 medium apples, peeled and grated

Preheat oven to 350°F. Place the yogurt, bananas, chicken broth, olive oil, and whole eggs in a blender and blend until smooth. Combine the unbleached flour, baking powder, sage, and cinnamon. Mix the liquid mixture with the flour mixture. Mix in the turkey breast and grated apples. Bake for 30 minutes or until the top is brown and a toothpick inserted into the center comes out clean.

Muffin Meat Loaf

1 pound ground round or chuck
½ cup milk
2 eggs
¾ cup whole-wheat bread crumbs (replace with ¾ cup brown rice flour or cooked brown rice for gluten-free or replace with almond flour for grain-free)
1 cup frozen carrots and peas
1 tablespoon Italian spices

Preheat oven to 350°F. Beat eggs and milk together. Mix in seasonings and bread crumbs. Fold in the meat and the frozen vegetables. Bake for 20–25 minutes.

Healthy Bran Muffins

1 cup whole-wheat flour
1 cup All-Bran cereal
2½ teaspoons baking powder
½ teaspoon baking soda
½ cup honey
¾ cup yogurt or buttermilk
1 egg
¼ cup butter or olive oil

Preheat oven to 375°F. Combine the flour, baking powder, and baking soda in a large bowl. Mix in the cereal. Beat the egg and add in the yogurt (or buttermilk) and the butter (or olive oil) along with the honey. Mix the wet and dry ingredients together. Grease muffin tins and pour the mixture into muffin molds. Bake for about 20 minutes.

Thanksgiving Muffins

2 cups whole-wheat flour (replace with 1 cup almond flour and 1 cup tapioca flour for grain-free)
2½ teaspoons baking powder
½ teaspoon ground cinnamon
4 teaspoons ground nutmeg
⅓ cup olive oil
2 large eggs
1¼ cups canned pumpkin puree
½ cup milk
1 cup turkey breast, coarsely chopped
1½ cups cranberries, fresh or frozen, coarsely chopped

Preheat oven to 400°F. Mix the flour, baking powder, cinnamon, and nutmeg. In a separate bowl, mix together the oil, eggs, pumpkin, and milk. Combine wet and dry ingredients. Fold in the turkey and cranberries. Fill oiled muffin tins and bake for 20–25 minutes.

White Fish, Oat, and Blueberry Muffins

1½ cups whole-wheat flour (replace with 1 cup almond flour and
    ½ cup tapioca flour for grain-free)
6 tablespoons honey
1 tablespoon baking powder
1½ cups rolled oats
1 cup milk
1 large egg
1 tablespoons olive oil
1 cup blueberries, fresh or frozen
1 cup tilapia or other mild white fish, cooked and coarsely chopped or flaked

Preheat oven to 400°F. Mix the flour and baking powder together and then add the oats and mix. Mix the milk and eggs, lightly beating the eggs, and then add the honey and melted butter. Combine the dry and wet ingredients Fold in the tilapia and blueberries. Bake for 12–15 minutes.

You can substitute 1 cup of any type of frozen or fresh veggies for the blueberries.

Carrot and Liver Muffins

2 cups whole-wheat pastry flour (replace with 1 cup coconut flour and 1¼ cup tapioca flour for
    grain-free)
¼ cup wheat germ (omit for grain-free)
1 tablespoon baking powder
½ teaspoon powdered nutmeg
½ teaspoon grated fresh ginger
½ teaspoon cinnamon
½ cup milk
½ cup olive oil
½ cup honey
3 eggs
1½ cups carrots, grated
½ cup sautéed cold liver bits, diced

Preheat oven to 400°F. Combine the ginger and cinnamon. Combine the milk, olive oil, honey, and eggs in a separate bowl. Mix these two mixtures together and then add the carrots and liver. Spoon batter into oiled muffin tins. Bake for 15 minutes for regular-sized muffins or 8 minutes for mini-muffins.

Allergy-Free Muffins

1 cup rice flour
1 teaspoon baking soda
½ cup oat bran
1 cup millet flour
1 cup goat's milk
½ cup water

Preheat oven to 400°F. Mix dry ingredients. Mix wet ingredients in a separate bowl. Mix wet and dry ingredients together. Spoon batter into oiled muffin tins. Bake for 40 minutes.

High-Protein Vegetarian Muffins #1

1½ cup whole-wheat flour
½ cup powdered whey
1 cup wheat germ
4 teaspoons baking powder
3 eggs
¼ cup olive or walnut oil
1 cup yogurt
2 cups pumpkin seeds, chopped

Preheat oven to 350°F. Mix together the flour, whey, wheat germ, and baking powder. Combine the eggs, yogurt, and oil and add to the flour mixture. Stir in the pumpkin seeds and mix. Pour into muffin tins and bake for 30 minutes.

High-Protein Vegetarian Muffins #2

1 cup whole-wheat flour (replace with 1 cup almond flour for grain-free)
1 tablespoon molasses
¼ cup sunflower seeds, ground in a blender
2 tablespoons dry milk powder
1 cup milk
2 tablespoons olive oil

Preheat oven to 350°F. Combine all ingredients and pour into oiled and floured muffin tins. Bake for 30 minutes until lightly browned.

Casseroles and Loaves

These recipes smell so good in the oven, and they keep smelling good after I take them out to cool. My dogs seem to know when we are cooking for them, and the looks on their faces seem to say to me, "I know I am loved *soooo* much."

Carrot, Pea, and Turkey Loaf

4 cups frozen mixed carrots and peas
4 cups brown rice, cooked
2 cups raw turkey, chopped (can substitute chicken or ground beef)
1 cup whole-wheat bread crumbs
4 eggs
3 tablespoons parsley, minced

Preheat oven to 350°F. Combine all ingredients and pour into in a loaf pan that has been greased with olive oil. Bake for 45–50 minutes.

Broccoli and Beef Casserole

2 cups ground beef
1 cup buttermilk or yogurt
2 cups bread crumbs (replace with 2 cups cooked brown rice for gluten-free)
1 cup instant oatmeal
1½ cups broccoli stems, chopped and very lightly steamed
3 eggs, beaten
3 tablespoons olive oil

Preheat oven to 350°F. Combine all ingredients and pour into in a loaf pan that has been greased with olive oil. Bake for 45 minutes.

Three Ps and Carrot Loaf

2 cups potatoes, diced
1 cup parsnips, diced
1 cup carrots, diced
3 tablespoons fresh parsley, chopped
6 eggs, beaten
1 cup yogurt
3 tablespoons flour
½ cup olive oil

Preheat oven to 350°F. Steam the potatoes, parsnips, parsley, and carrots for 20 minutes. Blend the eggs, yogurt, olive oil, and flour in blender. Mix the cooled vegetables and blended liquid together. Pour the mixture into a well-oiled loaf pan and bake for 45 minutes. Cool and divide into portions to serve.

Macaroni Custard

1 cup whole-wheat macaroni, cooked (replace with 1 cup brown-rice macaroni for gluten-free)
1 cup whole-grain bread crumbs (replace with 1 cup cooked brown rice for gluten-free)
1½ cups milk
3 eggs, beaten
1 cup cheddar cheese, grated
pinch cayenne
2 tablespoons mixed fresh herbs or 1 tablespoon dried Italian herbs

Preheat oven to 325°F. Soak the bread crumbs in the milk and stir in the eggs and seasonings. Place the macaroni in an oiled casserole dish and crumble the cheese on top. Pour the bread crumb mixture on top of the pasta and cheese without stirring in. Set the casserole dish in a pan of hot water and bake for 1 hour.

Potatoes au Canine

3 cups potatoes, boiled and sliced
¼ cup cheese of your choice, grated
½ cup cottage cheese
2 tablespoons vegetables of your choice, grated
1 tablespoon nutritional yeast
¼ cup whole milk

Preheat oven to 350°F. Place a layer of potato slices at the bottom of a buttered square casserole dish. Spread half of the cottage cheese over the layer of potatoes and then add another layer of potatoes. Spread the rest of the cottage cheese over the top layer of potatoes. Pour the milk over the layered mixture and top with grated cheese and grated vegetables. Bake until the cheese is melted and slightly browned, which usually takes 15–20 minutes at 350°F. Serve when cool. Will keep in the refrigerator, covered, for up to five days.

Liver Lover's Loaf

2 cups broccoli florets and stems, chopped
2 cups string beans, chopped
1½–2 pounds beef liver
1 cup olive oil
4 cloves garlic, chopped
3 fresh sage leaves, minced, or ½ teaspoon powdered sage
2 fresh thyme sprigs or ½ teaspoon powdered thyme
12 cups (1 large loaf) whole-grain bread, torn into smaller
    pieces (replace with 12 cups cooked brown rice for gluten-free
    or 12 cups of cooked white organic potatoes with skin for grain-free)
6 whole eggs, beaten

Preheat oven to 350°F. Combine the chopped vegetables and add the herbs and garlic to the vegetable mix. Chop the liver into smaller pieces. Place the bread chunks (or rice or potatoes) in a large bowl and mix in the olive oil and liver pieces. Mix in the vegetables and eggs. Add enough water (1–2 cups) to moisten the bread. Pour into two loaf pans or a square casserole dish and bake for 1 hour.

Salmon Loaf

2½ cups whole-wheat flour (replace with 2½ cups chickpea or tapioca flour for grain-free)
2 cups rolled oats (replace with 2 cups almonds, toasted and crushed, for grain-free)
1½ teaspoons baking soda
3 cups yogurt, kefir, or buttermilk
1 teaspoon dried rosemary
2 tablespoons fresh parsley, chopped
2 garlic cloves, chopped
16-ounce can salmon

Preheat oven to 300°F. Combine the flour and baking soda and add in the oats (or almonds). Add the yogurt, kefir, or buttermilk and mix. Mix in the herbs and garlic and then mix in the canned salmon. Pour into an oiled loaf pan and bake for 45 minutes.

Herb and Chicken Loaf

2 cups whole-grain bread, cubed (replace with 2 cups sweet
   potatoes, cubed, for grain-free)
1 tablespoon parsley
2 cloves garlic, chopped
1 teaspoon dried tarragon
2 cups cooked chicken, chopped
½ cup yogurt
3 eggs, beaten
⅓ cup olive oil

Preheat oven to 350°F. Mix the bread, chicken, and herbs together in a large bowl. Beat the eggs and add the yogurt and olive oil to the eggs. Pour the egg mixture over the bread and chicken and mix in. Pour into a greased loaf pan and bake for 35–40 minutes.

Sweet Potatoes and Eggs*

4 cups sweet potatoes or yams
½ cup cream
4 eggs, beaten
1 cup whole milk

Preheat oven to 350°F. Skin sweet potatoes or yams and bake at 400°F for 60–90 minutes or until thoroughly cooked and then dice. Put all ingredients in a blender and puree to the consistency of pancake batter, adding more cream and milk if necessary. Pour pureed mixture into a 13- by 9-inch pan. Bake for 40 minutes. Cool and serve. Refrigerate leftovers, covered, for up to five days.

*highly recommended for dogs with diarrhea

Old-Fashioned Meat Loaf

2 cups broccoli stems, chopped fine
2 pounds ground chuck
½ cup Italian parsley, minced
1 teaspoon garlic powder
3 large eggs
½ cup milk
2 cups rolled oats (replace with 2 cups cooked brown rice for gluten-free or 2 cups almond flour for grain-free)

Preheat oven to 350°F. Mix meat, broccoli stems, garlic powder, and Italian parsley together in a large bowl. Beat the eggs and milk together and add to the meat mixture; mix well. Add the rolled oats and continue mixing. Place in a 10- by 13-inch baking dish. Bake for about 50 minutes. Cool and slice into portions.

Potato and Cheese Pudding

5 medium potatoes, skin on, cooked and mashed
2 eggs
1 cup cottage cheese
¾ cup milk

Preheat oven to 350°F. Blend the eggs and milk together in a blender. Add the cottage cheese to the mixture in the blender and blend until smooth. Stir the blender mixture into the mashed potatoes. Pour mixture into an oiled 2-quart casserole dish. Bake for 1 hour or until the top is brown and a toothpick inserted into the center comes out clean.

Pasta, Lentil, and Veggie Loaf

1⅓ cups brown lentils
2 cups whole-wheat pasta in a small shape (replace with 2 cups cooked brown rice for gluten-free)
½ cup olive oil
3 garlic cloves, chopped
1 large carrot, chopped
1 stick celery, chopped
1 egg, beaten
2 tablespoons fresh parsley, chopped

Preheat oven to 350°F. Boil water in a large saucepan and stir in the lentils. Simmer, uncovered, for about 40 minutes or until the lentils are soft. Cook pasta until tender. Heat olive oil in another saucepan; add garlic, celery and carrot; and lightly sauté until vegetables are soft. Add cooked lentils, pasta, parsley, and beaten egg to the vegetable mixture. Pour into a loaf pan and bake for 40 minutes. Cool and serve.

Yummy Stews and Soups

There is no need to preheat the oven for these recipes because they are all done on the stovetop. Even better, these yummy stews are one-pot preparations. Cleanup consists of a knife and a cutting board. Remember to not have the flame on too high and to stir and watch the mixture during the cooking process. I often let these stews cool and then store them in their stainless-steel pots in the refrigerator.

Everyday Stews and Soups

In the Middle Ages, a large cooking pot over the fire was continually filled with leftovers and cooked and recooked. We're not going quite that far, but stews and soups are wide open for all kinds of leftovers. Dogs do not think that you ruined the recipe when you add more yummy things to it.

Nuit's Favorite Stew

bones, such as chicken wings, chicken thighs, or soup bones
2 pounds ground beef, turkey, or chicken
1½ cups brown basmati rice
½ cup barley
garlic (fresh or granulated)
1 cup chopped parsley
16-ounce package frozen chopped veggies of your choice, thawed

Make meat broth by cooking the bones in 2 quarts of water. Remove the bones from the broth, pull any meat from the bones, and put the meat back into the broth. Add the ground meat, basmati rice, barley, garlic, and parsley and simmer until everything is cooked and tender, adding water if needed (it should be moist but not runny). Add the thawed veggies and stir in. The heat from the mixture will be enough to cook the vegetables. Remove from heat and serve in portions based on your dog's size and needs.

Chicken and Root Vegetable Stew (Grain-Free and Gluten-Free)

3 cups chicken parts (boneless)
2 tablespoons olive oil
4 large boiling potatoes
4 large carrots
¼ cup fresh marjoram, chopped
3 large parsnips
6 cups low-salt chicken broth
3 medium turnips
¾ cup heavy whipping cream

Place chicken in a large pot. Wash the potatoes well and cut into pieces. Wash the carrots well and slice. Peel the parsnips and slice. Peel the turnips and dice. Add the vegetables to the pot with the chicken. Add the olive oil, chopped garlic, marjoram, chicken broth, and whipping cream to the pot. Simmer for 1 hour, adding more chicken broth until the desired consistency is achieved. Refrigerate, covered, for up to five days or freeze for up to one month.

Beef, Barley, and Vegetable Stew (Gluten-Free)

2 cups pearl barley
4 cloves garlic, chopped
5 cups water
1 teaspoon lemon juice
4 cups beef broth
2 tablespoons olive oil
1 pound beef stew meat
1½ cups frozen peas
3 celery stalks, chopped
2 small bay leaves
3 carrots, chopped

Cook pearl barley in a large pot with 4 cups of the water and 2 cups of the beef broth and simmer for 1 hour. Add the remaining ingredients (except water and broth) and simmer for another 30 minutes. Add more of the water and broth to achieve desired consistency. Serve when cool. Refrigerate, covered, for up to five days or freeze for up to one month.

Rice and Egg Drop Soup (Gluten-Free)

2 cups basmati rice
6 cups water
3 eggs, beaten

Cook the basmati rice in the water for 15 minutes to create a soupy mixture (add more water if needed). Rapidly mix in the beaten eggs and allow the mixture to cool to room temperature. It should firm up as it cools. Serve when cool.

Rice and Beans (Gluten-Free)

    1 cup cooked beans (kidney, navy, or pinto)
    2 cloves garlic, chopped
    2 cups cooked rice (basmati or brown; can be cooked in a meat-based stock or with a bouillon cube
        for extra flavor)
    4 tablespoons olive oil

Sauté the garlic in the olive oil for one minute. Add in the cooked beans and stir to reheat the beans. Add the rice in and mix well to warm the entire meal. Serve when cool. Store in the refrigerator, covered, for up to five days.

Chicken and Rice (Gluten-Free)

    2 cloves garlic, diced
    2 cups boneless chicken pieces
    4 tablespoons olive oil
    1 cup carrot, diced
    2 cups brown rice
    ½ cup celery, diced
    6 cups water or chicken stock
    ¼ cup parsley, chopped

In a large pot, lightly sauté the garlic in the olive oil. Add the uncooked rice and stir thoroughly. Add the water or chicken stock and simmer for 1 hour. Add in the chicken pieces and vegetables and cook for another 20 minutes, adding more water or stock if needed to create the desired consistency. Serve when cool. Refrigerate, covered, for up to five days.

Hungarian Goulash

    2 pounds chuck or round, diced
    ½ cup olive oil
    16-ounce bag of frozen carrots and peas
    2 cups yogurt
    dash paprika
    8 cups whole-wheat macaroni, cooked (replace with
        8 cups of cooked brown rice for gluten-free or
        8 cups cooked white potatoes, cubed, for grain-free)

Place the oil in a skillet and add the diced meat. Sauté the meat in the oil until browned. Add the frozen peas and carrots and mix in until the vegetables are cooked in with the meat. Stir in the yogurt and paprika. Remove from heat and cool before mixing in the pasta.

Hearty Stews

These economical and ecologically prepared stews allow you to store enough to feed several dogs or a large dog for several days. We save all of our healthy leftovers, such as broccoli stems, eggshells, children's leftovers, cauliflower leaves, carrot tops, potato peels, and the like. These "hearty man stews" are fun to make because there is always some innovation in every dish. Once you get the hang of it, you'll find yourself inventing new ways to make a big pot of delicious stew, and your dog will love you all the more for it. For example, one of my clients loves making stews in a slow cooker. He has several chestnut trees and throws fresh chestnuts into his recipes.

When preparing these recipes, please note that eggshells, leftover vegetables, and fresh herbs are welcome in any of these recipes in addition to the listed ingredients. Also note that you should leave the skins on potatoes and carrots if they are organic because the skins are rich in nutrients. With all potatoes and carrots, be sure to wash them well.

Hearty Man Pork Stew (Gluten-Free)

3 pounds pork with bones or 1 pound boneless pork, cubed or diced
5 cloves garlic
2 cups parsnips or carrots
1 tablespoon dried rosemary or 3 tablespoons fresh rosemary
½ cup olive oil
3½ cups brown rice (replace with 3½ cups cubed white or sweet potatoes for grain-free)

Place pork and 3 quarts of water in a 5-quart stockpot and bring to a boil. If using pork with bones, cook for 90 minutes or until the meat is very tender, and then cool and pull the meat off of the bones. If using diced or cubed pork, simmer for 30 minutes. Add the garlic, rosemary, olive oil, vegetables, and brown rice (plus eggshells or any extra vegetables) to the stockpot. Bring to a simmer and cook for 1 hour and 15 minutes. Cool and serve. Divide the rest into meal-sized portions in zipper-sealed bags and refrigerate or freeze.

Tarragon Chicken Hearty Man Stew (Grain-Freee and Gluten-Free)

1 large chicken (or 12 legs or 7 breasts), frozen or fresh
¼ cup olive oil
3 cups carrots, sliced
3 cups potatoes, cubed
4 parsnips, sliced
2 cups broccoli stems, sliced
6 cloves garlic, sliced
teaspoon tarragon

Place chicken in a large pot with 2 quarts of water, bring to a boil, and then reduce to a simmer and cook until the meat is tender. Cool the chicken, remove the meat from the bones, and return the meat to the pot. Add the olive oil, carrots, potatoes, parsnips, garlic, tarragon, and broccoli stems. Return to a boil and then simmer again for 30 minutes. Remove from heat, cool, and serve. Divide the rest into meal-sized portions in zipper-sealed bags and refrigerate or freeze.

Stick Your Neck Out Hearty Man Stew

2 pounds chicken necks
6 medium potatoes
4 large carrots
3 cups quinoa
1 teaspoon sage
3 tablespoons parsley

Place all ingredients into a large pot with 3 quarts of water, bring to a boil, and then reduce to a simmer for 30 minutes. Remove from heat, cool, and serve. Divide the rest into meal-sized portions in zipper-sealed bags and refrigerate or freeze.

Beef and Barley Hearty Man Stew (Gluten-Free)

1½ pounds cubed beef
2 cups barley (replace with 4 cups cubed potatoes for grain-free)
2 cups potatoes, cubed
1 cup carrots, sliced
½ cup celery, sliced
2 cups canned corn
5 cloves garlic, sliced
½ cup olive oil
1 teaspoon turmeric

Fill a large stockpot with 3 quarts of water. Add all ingredients to the pot, bring to a boil, and then reduce to a simmer for 70 minutes. Remove from heat, cool, and serve. Divide the rest into meal-sized portions in zipper-sealed bags and refrigerate or freeze.

Always stir these recipes occasionally while cooking and add more water if needed.

Fruits of the Sea Hearty Man Stew (Gluten-Free)

2 pounds tilapia, cubed
1 flat sheet kombu seaweed
3 tablespoons parsley
5 cloves garlic, sliced
2 cups carrots, sliced
4 cups basmati or jasmine white rice (replace with 4 cups cubed white potatoes for grain-free)

Fill a stockpot with 3 quarts of water. Add all ingredients to the pot, bring to a boil, and then simmer for 30 minutes. Cool, remove sheet of kombu, and serve. Divide the rest into meal-sized portions in zipper-sealed bags and refrigerate or freeze.

Liver and Brown Rice Hearty Man Stew (Gluten-Free)

   2 pounds liver
   4 cups brown rice (replace with 4 cups cubed white potatoes for grain-free)
   2 beets, cubed, with greens
   3 tablespoons fresh parsley (or more, if desired)
   1 teaspoon rosemary
   ⅔ cup olive oil

Place the olive oil in large stockpot, add the liver, and lightly sauté. Add the rest of ingredients plus 3 quarts of water. Bring to a boil and then simmer for 75 minutes. Remove from heat, cool, and serve. Divide the rest into meal-sized portions in zipper-sealed bags and refrigerate or freeze.

Be patient because these large pots of stew take a few hours to cool. In a pinch, you can take one serving out of the pot and ladle it onto a cookie sheet to speed cooling for a dog who just can't wait!

Sweet and Woolly Hearty Man Stew (Grain-Free and Gluten-Free)

   2 pounds lamb, minced
   8 cups sweet potatoes or yams, diced
   2 tablespoons molasses
   2 teaspoons ground cinnamon

In a large stockpot, combine all ingredients with 10 cups of water. Bring to a boil and then simmer for 35–40 minutes or until sweet potatoes/yams are tender. Remove from heat, cool, and serve. Divide the rest into meal-sized portions in zipper-sealed bags and refrigerate or freeze.

Toss and Serve

Your dog is in the mood for some home cooking, and you want to make something special with minimal fuss. Toss and serve meals do not require a lot of effort. If you are in a rush, you can substitute pasta for potatoes.

Fish and Chips (Grain-Free and Gluten-Free)

1 pound frozen breaded fish sticks
8 medium potatoes (white, sweet, or yams)
½ cup olive oil
2 tablespoons parsley, chopped

Preheat oven to 350°F. Slice the potatoes into small wedges and then place the wedges on an oiled cookie sheet and sprinkle with the olive oil and parsley. Bake for 45 minutes. During the potatoes' cooking time, put the fish sticks in the oven according to the recommended time on the package so that they will bake along with the potato wedges and finish at about the same time. Remove from oven, let cool, toss fish sticks and potatoes together, and serve.

Potatoes and Cheese (Grain-Free and Gluten-Free)

2 cups potatoes, diced
1 stalk broccoli stems, chopped
½ cup ricotta cheese
1 tablespoon chopped parsley
½ cup half and half

Boil diced potatoes for 45 minutes and then strain them through a colander. Add the remaining ingredients and mix everything together well. Serve when cool. Refrigerate leftovers, covered, for up to five days.

Yams and Chicken (Grain-Free and Gluten-Free)

4 yams, skinned
3 cups boneless chicken
1 cup grated vegetable of your choice

Preheat oven to 400°F and bake the skinned yams for 60–90 minutes or until thoroughly cooked. Cut the chicken into pieces and cook however you like (except frying). Mash the cooked yams and mix in the cooked chicken pieces and grated vegetables. Serve when cool. Refrigerate leftovers, covered, for up to three days.

Salmon and Potatoes (Grain-Free and Gluten-Free)

3 medium potatoes
1 can low-salt salmon
½ cup grated carrot

Cook potatoes however you desire. Add in the salmon and carrots and mix well. Serve when cool. Refrigerate leftovers, covered, for up to three days.

Venison and Potatoes (Grain-Free and Gluten-Free)

    3 cups potatoes, skin on, diced
    1 cup venison, cubed
    1 cup frozen peas and carrots
    ⅓ cup olive oil
    ½ teaspoon powdered rosemary

Place the diced potatoes in a large pot and fill with just enough unsalted water to cover the potatoes. Bring to a boil and then simmer until the potatoes are soft. Add the cubed venison, rosemary, and olive oil and simmer for another 10 minutes. Add the frozen peas and carrots and simmer for another 10 minutes. Remove from heat, cool, and serve.

Yams and Ginger* (Grain-Free and Gluten-Free)

    2 yams, skinned
    ½ teaspoon ginger, grated fine, or ¼ teaspoon powdered ginger
    1 tablespoon butter

Preheat oven to 400°F and bake the skinned yams for 60–90 minutes or until thoroughly cooked. Mash yams with ginger and add the butter to the warm mixture. Serve when cool. Refrigerate leftovers, covered, for up to five days.

Potato Salad (Grain-Free and Gluten-Free)

    2 cups potatoes, sliced
    3 eggs
    ½ cup mayonnaise

Boil potatoes for 45 minutes. While the potatoes are cooking, boil the eggs for about 20 minutes. Put the potatoes, eggs (shells optional), and mayonnaise in a casserole dish and mix well. Serve when cool. Refrigerate leftovers, covered, for up to five days.

Liver Toss

    2 cups liver, cubed
    ½ cup olive oil
    3 garlic cloves, diced
    3 cups whole-wheat pasta, cooked (replace
        with 3 cups cubed white potato, cooked,
        for grain-free)
    1 tablespoon Italian herb mix

Warm the olive oil in a frying pan and add liver and garlic. Sprinkle on Italian herbs. Cook for about 10 minutes, stirring, until the meat is light pink inside. Mix liver, spice, and oil mixture into the pasta (or potatoes) and toss.

Hypoallergenic Meals

Mackerel and Oatmeal

3 cups steel-cut oats, cooked
12–16-ounce can mackerel
3 tablespoons fresh parsley, chopped, or 2 teaspoons of dried parsley

Place 1 cup of the steel-cut oats in 3½ cups of water. Bring to a quick boil and then simmer on very low heat for 30–40 minutes, checking regularly and adding more water if needed. Put oatmeal in a large bowl, fluff it up, and allow it to cool a bit. Add the canned mackerel, parsley, and rest of oatmeal and mix. Finish cooling and serve.

Tilapia and Potatoes (Grain-Free and Gluten-Free)

1 pound fresh tilapia or other white fish
4 cups white potatoes; skin on, chopped
1 teaspoon dried rosemary
⅓ cup olive oil

Place the potatoes in a large pot with the rosemary, olive oil, and enough unsalted water to just cover the potatoes. Bring to boil and cook until the potatoes are tender. Slice the fish into strips and add it to the potatoes and water. Mix in well and bring to a boil again for another 10–15 minutes or until the fish is cooked through. Remove from heat, cool, and serve.

Quinoa, Cauliflower, and Tasty Turkey

1 cup quinoa
turkey parts (thighs and/or wings)
1 cup cauliflower, chopped
2 tablespoons fresh parsley, chopped
⅓ cup olive oil

Rinse the quinoa with tap water to remove any bitter taste from the outside husks and set aside. Place 4 cups of water in a saucepan and add the turkey pieces. Bring to a boil and then simmer, covered, until the turkey is cooked. Cool. Remove the turkey bones and place the turkey meat back into the water. Add the quinoa, cauliflower pieces, and olive oil. Bring back to a boil and immediately reduce to a simmer with a cover for 30 minutes. Remove from heat and mix in the parsley. Let cool and serve.

Quinoa is a grain with high protein content. It is also a complete protein. This grain was historically grown in the Andes Mountains of South America.

Rice and Salmon (Gluten-Free)

    3 cups basmati rice, cooked
    1 can low-salt salmon

Mix salmon into cooked rice. Serve when cool. Refrigerate leftovers, covered, for up to three days.

Rice and Lamb

    lamb meat, with or without bones
    1 ½ cups brown rice
    1 cup carrots, chopped
    ½ teaspoon dried rosemary
    ⅓ cup olive oil

Cook lamb meat, carrots, and rosemary in 4½ cups of water. Remove lamb from water (remove meat from bones if needed) and let cool. Retain the water. Heat the water that was used for the lamb to a boil and pour the rice into the boiling water. Cover and simmer on low heat for 75 minutes. Let the rice cool and then add in 1 cup of the lamb meat, the carrots, and the olive oil. Mix well.

Potatoes and Cottage Cheese

    4 cups potatoes, skin on, sliced
    1 cup cottage cheese
    1 cup greens (i.e., kale or string beans), chopped
    ⅓ cup olive oil
    1 teaspoon Italian herbs
    1 clove garlic, chopped fine

Cook the sliced potatoes in unsalted boiling water and then strain and let cool. Lightly steam the chopped green vegetables and then strain and let cool. In a large bowl, mix together the potatoes and greens and add the cottage cheese, olive oil, herbs, and garlic. Mix well.

Eggs and Omelets

Dogs do not get hardening and thickening of the arteries as people do. Perhaps this is because, unlike humans, they make their own vitamin C, and vitamin C is a potent antioxidant. Be assured that you cannot overdose your dog on eggs. They are simple to make, and dogs love them.

Eggshells
Placing whole eggs, with the shells, in the blender to beat them will add extra healthy calcium to the meal.

Easy Eggs and Toast

    3 eggs
    3 pieces of whole-grain bread (substitute potato bread or grain-free bread for grain-free)
    1 tablespoon fresh parsley, chopped

Soft-boil eggs in a pan of water. Toast the bread lightly in the toaster. Crumble the bread in the bottom of a bowl. Mash the eggs and shells with a fork and place the mashed eggs on top of the bread. Sprinkle with parsley and serve when cool.

Scrambled Eggs and Cottage Cheese (Grain-Free and Gluten-Free)

    1 tablespoon olive oil
    1 tablespoon butter
    ½ cup cottage cheese
    2 tablespoons parsley, chopped
    8 eggs

Place the butter and oil in a large frying pan on medium heat. When the butter has melted, stir in the cottage cheese and cook until creamy. Beat the eggs, mix in the parsley, and pour the egg/parsley mixture into the pan. As soon as eggs begin to set, stir until firmed up but still moist. Cool and serve.

Scrambled Eggs with Meat and Spinach (Grain-Free and Gluten-Free)

    2 tablespoons olive oil
    ½ cup meat (chicken, steak, turkey, bacon, or ham)
    8 eggs
    1 cup fresh spinach, chopped

Place oil in a large frying pan. Add the meat to the oil and sauté until done (if you are using lunchmeat, wait and add the meat at the same time as the spinach.) Beat the eggs, add them to the pan, and stir them in lightly with the meat. Immediately add the spinach (and lunchmeat) and stir into the eggs quickly. Keep stirring in the pan until the eggs are set. Cool and serve.

Scrambled Eggs and Rosemary Rice (Gluten-Free)

    4 tablespoons olive oil
    4 eggs, beaten
    2 cups cooked brown rice
    ½ teaspoon rosemary

Heat the oil in a 12-inch frying pan. Combine the beaten eggs, rice, and rosemary and pour this mixture into the hot pan. Cook over medium heat until the eggs are set. Cool and serve.

Omelets

Potato, Feta, and Herb Omelet (Grain-Free and Gluten-Free)

    2 tablespoons olive oil
    1 cup potatoes, skin on, cooked (steamed or baked) and diced
    ½ cup crumbled feta cheese (can replace with any kind of of cheese)
    5 eggs, beaten
    ¼ teaspoon sage
    ¼ teaspoon thyme

No Flipping Needed
The cover eliminates the need for flipping the omelet (unless you really want to!).

Heat the oil in a 10–12-inch frying pan. When the oil is warm, add the potatoes, sage, and thyme and stir everything together lightly. Immediately add the beaten eggs to the pan and reduce the heat. Sprinkle the cheese on top and cover the frying pan. Reduce heat a little more. Cook over very low heat for 4–6 minutes or until done. Cool, cut into slices or pieces, and serve.

Eat Your Vegetables Omelet
(Grain-Free and Gluten-Free)

    2 tablespoons olive oil
    1 cup broccoli, finely chopped
    ½ cup kale, finely chopped
    1 clove garlic, diced or chopped
    1 tablespoon parsley
    4 eggs, beaten

Warm the oil in a 10–12-inch frying pan and then add the garlic and lightly sauté it for a few seconds. Add the broccoli, kale, and parsley to the pan and sauté lightly for one minute. Pour the beaten eggs into the pan and over the vegetables. Cover the frying pan and cook over low heat until done, approximately 4–6 minutes. Cool, cut into slices or pieces, and serve.

Mix and Match Meals

You can make these meals *al fresco* or prepare ahead of time and store.
Pick one from Column A and one from Column B and serve.

Column A

2 cups whole grain, no-sugar,
   breakfast cereal
2 cups whole oats, soaked or cooked
2 cups white potatoes, cooked
2 cups sweet potatoes or yams, cooked
2 cups whole-wheat pasta
2 cups rice
2 cups crumbled whole-grain bread
2 cups cooked barley

Column B

1 cup buttermilk
1 cup plain yogurt
1 cup kefir
2 large eggs, scrambled
2 large eggs, hard-boiled and
   mashed with shells on
1 cup cottage cheese
1 cup farmer's cheese
1 cup beef
1 cup chicken
1 cup salmon
1 cup white fish
1 cup canned kidney beans
1 cup frozen fish sticks, cooked

Raw Diets

If you wish to feed a raw-food diet, you want plenty of variety within the diet plan to afford your dog a good balance of vitamins, minerals, and other essential nutrients. While balance is the key to all diets, I like to pay particular attention to the mineral balance in raw diets.

You do not need to trim the fat from raw meat. Cooked animal fat has a negative health value, but raw animal fat is healthy for your dog. You may want to freeze raw meat for fourteen days before defrosting and serving it because freezing effectively eliminates most parasites that raw meat can harbor.

Studies have shown that some raw diets tend to be deficient in calcium, linoleic acid, and iodine. Calcium is a very important mineral that must be added to raw-food diets. Linoleic acid, or omega-6 fatty acid, is found in grains and seeds. Coconut oil, walnut oil, and olive oil contain linoleic acid.

It is important that the calcium added to a raw diet be bioavailable calcium. Meat is high in phosphorus and low in calcium. Calcium must be added to the food to ensure the correct balance of these minerals for bone growth and bone density. Dry, desiccated, ground bone meal is not bioavailable. A few sources of well-utilized calcium are listed in the resources section of this book. Additionally, the eggshell recipes that follow provide two "homegrown" ways of preparing healthy bioavailable calcium.

Seaweed and seaweed products are chock full of iodine. I like to serve cooked grains along with raw meat, and these grains can be cooked with a piece of kombu seaweed in the water to add iodine to the diet. Nori seaweed comes in flat, dry sheets, and my dogs love nori as a snack. Powdered seaweed products are also available.

Easy Eggshell Recipe #1

Wash eggshells with water. Break the shells into small pieces and cover with lemon juice or vinegar. Let the shells sit for a few days, and they will dissolve completely. The remaining liquid is an excellent source of calcium that your dog can easily assimilate.

Easy Eggshell Recipe #2: Lemon Egg by Dr. Ian Shillington

Place whole, washed, uncooked, uncracked *organic* eggs in a clean glass or ceramic bowl. Cover the eggs with fresh organic lemon juice (not concentrated lemon juice). Cover the eggs loosely and place them in the refrigerator. Several times each day, agitate the liquid very gently. As the calcium from the shells leaches into the lemon juice, bubbles will appear around the eggs. Approximately 48 hours later, the bubbling should have stopped, and you can carefully remove the eggs from the bowl. Put the liquid in a covered glass jar and shake the mixture.

Chicken and Barley Raw Diet

   1 cup raw chicken
   2 cups barley, cooked
   1 cup broccoli stems, finely chopped
   1 tablespoon coconut oil or 3 tablespoons olive or walnut oil
   1 teaspoon ground flax seeds
   2 cloves raw garlic, diced
   1 teaspoon eggshell calcium or suggested dose of water-soluble calcium

Mix all ingredients together and serve.

Beef and Oatmeal Raw Diet

   1 cup raw beef, cubed
   2 cups oatmeal, soaked overnight in water
   1 cup carrots, squash, or yams
   3 tablespoons olive oil
   1 tablespoon molasses
   2 pieces nori seaweed, torn into small pieces
   1 teaspoon eggshell calcium or suggested dose of water-soluble calcium

Mix all ingredients together and serve.

Raw-Diet Facts

* The protein and grain sources can vary in raw-food diets.

* Grains, except for oatmeal, must be cooked or sprouted.

* All meals should include olive oil, walnut oil, or coconut oil (coconut oil is a thick consistency, comparable to shortening).

* Cooking the grains with seaweed or adding dried nori seaweed increases the nutritional value of the meal.

* Spices, such as rosemary, garlic, Italian herbs, and the like, are healthy to add to raw food.

* All raw diets must be supplemented with calcium.

Industrious Stocks

Plain water can always be used to cook grains and food in general, but grains cooked in stocks are more flavorful. Cooking with stock will also increase the protein content of the meal. You can prepare stock from scratch when you have time, but you can also use canned beef or chicken stock or put a bouillon cube in plain water. Vegetarians can find meat-free options that impart a nice flavor, and vegetable-based stocks are rich in minerals.

Meat Stock Yields 14 cups

12 cups water
3 pounds beef or lamb (with bones)
8 long parsley sprigs
2 pounds stew beef or lamb
½ teaspoon dried thyme
4 carrots
½ cup vinegar
3 ribs celery
5 garlic cloves

Place the bones into a large pot filled with 12 cups of water. Cut the meat into cubes and place in the pot. Cut the carrots and celery into 1-inch pieces and add to the pot. Peel the garlic cloves and place in the pot. Chop the parsley sprigs and add to the pot along with the thyme, vinegar, and water. Bring stock to a boil, reduce to a simmer, and cook, uncovered, for 1 hour. Remove all of the bones from the stock; you can then strain the stock through a colander and put the vegetable and meat pieces back into the stock if you desire. Refrigerate for up to one week or freeze for up to one month.

Chicken Stock Yields 12 cups

10 cups water
2½ pounds chicken wings or chicken thighs
¼ teaspoon dried thyme
2 carrots, coarsely chopped
1 tablespoon vinegar
3 ribs celery, coarsely chopped
4 garlic cloves
6 sprigs parsley, coarsely chopped

Place the chicken into a large pot filled with 10 cups of water. Add all of the rest of the ingredients to the pot and bring stock to a boil. Reduce to a simmer and cook, uncovered, for 1 hour. Remove all of the bones from the stock; you can then strain the stock through a colander and put the vegetable and meat pieces back into the stock if you desire. Refrigerate for up to one week or freeze for up to one month.

Fish Stock Yields 8 cups

8 cups water
1 pound bones and trimmings from any type of white fish
12 long parsley sprigs, chopped
2 tablespoons fresh lemon juice

Combine all ingredients in a large pot with 8 cups of cold water. Bring to a boil and then reduce to a simmer for 30 minutes. Strain through a colander and remove any fish bones; use the strained stock only. Refrigerate for up to three days or freeze for up to one month.

Fruits

Beauty and Cole's Favorite Frozen Treat

assorted fruits, cut in pieces
yogurt or kefir
hollowed marrow bones, ice cube trays, or
    hollow toys

Mix fruit pieces with yogurt or kefir. Put the mixture into clean hollowed marrow bones, ice cube trays, or hollow toys and place in the freezer until the mixture is solid. When the treats are ready, I call out, "Who wants a treat?" and Beauty and Cole come running. They have become connoisseurs of these favorite frozen treats.

Apples, Couscous, and Cinnamon

    3 apples, peeled, cored, and diced
    2 cups dry couscous
    ½ teaspoon cinnamon
    2 tablespoons butter

Place all ingredients into a large saucepan with 5 cups of water. Bring the mixture to a boil and then simmer for 10 minutes. Cool and serve.

Pears, Honey, and Oatmeal

    3 pears, peeled, cored, and diced
    4 cups oatmeal, cooked
    2 tablespoons honey

Mix pears with warm oatmeal. Place in dishes to serve and allow to cool. Add a dollop of honey to each dish right before serving.

Blueberries and Muesli

    3 cups plain muesli
    1 cup blueberries
    1 cup cottage cheese

Mix all ingredients together and serve.

Snacks and Treats

As far as our canine friends are concerned, we have finally gotten to the heart of the matter. A little nosh here and there is what makes a good day a great day! These treats store well in the fridge and are very welcome surprises.

Baked Yam Chips

6 organic yams or sweet potatoes
1 tablespoon cinnamon
½ cup olive oil

Preheat oven to 350°F. Slice the yams or sweet potatoes into thin slices. Place the slices on oiled cookie trays and drizzle with olive oil. Sprinkle the cinnamon on top. Bake for 35 minutes or until fully cooked and a little crunchy. Cool, serve, and store.

All Dogs Love 'Em Liver Treats

2 pounds calf liver
2 cups oatmeal, uncooked
4 tablespoons whole-wheat flour
4 cloves garlic
3 tablespoons chopped parsley
4 eggs

Preheat oven to 350°F. Place all of the ingredients in a blender and mix until smooth. Place a good amount of olive oil on a 10- by 15-inch cookie tray and spread the mixture onto the tray until it is about ½ inch or so thick. Bake for 30–35 minutes or until mixture is firm. Cool and cut into treat-sized squares. Freeze extras and defrost as needed.

Salmon Fudge

14-ounce can salmon, undrained
1½ cups oat flour
1 tablespoon garlic powder or granulated garlic
2 eggs, lightly beaten
½ cup Parmesan cheese, grated

Preheat oven to 350°F. Mix together all of the ingredients in a bowl or with a food processor. Spread on an oiled or nonstick cookie sheet to the desired thickness. Bake for 20 minutes. Slice with a pizza cutter to the desired size.

Sausage Balls

1 lb sausage, uncooked
4 cups premade, ready-to-cook biscuit mix
½ pound cheddar cheese, grated
2 tablespoons parsley

Preheat oven to 350°F. Work all of the ingredients together and roll into balls. Place on the balls on a lightly greased cookie sheet and bake for 20 minutes. Freeze and defrost as needed.

Easy Bruschetta Treat

4–6 slices whole-wheat bread
2 tablespoons olive oil
1 tablespoon nutritional yeast (optional)

Preheat oven to 250°F. Lightly brush the bread slices with olive oil. If desired, lightly sprinkle the nutritional yeast on top of the oiled bread. Cut the bread into 1-inch strips and place on a baking sheet. Bake for 1 hour. Cool and serve. If you left out the nutritional yeast, you can spread some chopped liver or cream cheese on the cooled treats for additional flavor. Store in the refrigerator for up to five days.

Herb Biscotti Yields 2½ dozen

2 cups whole-wheat flour
¼ teaspoon dried rosemary
7 tablespoon cold unsalted butter
1 teaspoon baking powder
1 teaspoon dried thyme
1 teaspoon dried marjoram
2 large eggs
1 tablespoon water

Preheat oven to 350°F. Place all of the dry ingredients in a large mixing bowl and mix well. Add the softened butter, eggs, and water, using an electric mixer to combine all ingredients. The mixture will hold together in a soft dough. Remove the dough from the mixing bowl and place it on a lightly floured surface. Note: If the dough is sticky and hard to work with, it is too soft. Flatten the dough into a disk, cover it with plastic wrap, and place it in the refrigerator for at least one hour to fix.

Divide the dough into three equal pieces. Work each piece into a 1½-diameter rope of the same length that will fit on your baking sheet. Place two of the biscotti ropes on a parchment-covered baking sheet (only two will fit on a baking sheet because they spread as they bake). Bake for approximately 30 minutes or until golden brown. Remove from oven and allow to cool slightly.

Using a serrated knife, slice the biscotti diagonally into ½-inch-long cookies while the dough is still warm. Reduce the oven temperature to 300°F and place the slices on the baking sheet to bake for another 10–15 minutes. Serve when cool. Store in airtight containers at room temperature for two weeks or freeze for up to two months.

Repeat the process for the third rope or use two baking sheets to bake all three ropes at one time.

Almond Butter Cookies Yields 3 dozen

½ cup butter
1 cup almond butter
⅔ cups brown sugar, firmly packed
½ teaspoon baking soda
1 egg
1½ cups unbleached white flour

Preheat oven to 375°F. Beat the butter and almond butter together until it is soft. Add the sugar and beat until the mixture is light and fluffy. Add the egg and beat the mixture until all of the ingredients are well combined. Add the remaining ingredients, starting with 1 cup of flour and the baking soda. Mix until just combined. Add more flour, but just enough to form a nonsticky dough. Roll the dough into small balls. Place the balls on a buttered cookie sheet and flatten them with a fork. Bake for 10–12 minutes. Serve when cool. Store in airtight containers at room temperature for up to two weeks.

Oatmeal Cookies Yields 3½ dozen

8 ounces unsalted butter
1 teaspoon cinnamon
½ cup firmly packed brown sugar
pinch of nutmeg
3 tablespoons honey
4 cups rolled oats
2 eggs
1½ cups pecans
1½ cups unbleached all-purpose flour

Preheat oven to 375°F. Cream the butter and brown sugar in a large mixing bowl. Beat in the honey and eggs until smooth. Sift the flour, cinnamon, and nutmeg together and stir into the butter mixture. Add the oats and pecans and stir well. Shape the dough into 1-inch balls. Place the balls on a buttered cookie sheet and flatten them with a fork. Bake until light brown, approximately 15 minutes. Serve when cool. Store in an airtight container at room temperature for up to two weeks.

Poultry Delights Yields 2½ dozen

For cookies:
2 cups whole-wheat flour
2 tablespoons olive oil
⅔ cup corn meal
½ cup chicken broth
½ cup sunflower and/or sesame seeds
2 eggs
¼ cup low-fat yogurt

For egg glaze:
1 beaten egg
1 tablespoon milk

Preheat oven to 350°F. In a large mixing bowl, mix together all of the dry ingredients. Combine the eggs with the yogurt in a separate bowl. Next, mix the wet ingredients (egg/yogurt mixture, oil, and broth) with the dry ingredients. The result should be a firm dough. Allow the dough to rest for 20 minutes. Roll out the dough on a lightly floured surface to a thickness of 1/4 inch. Cut out shapes using your favorite cookie cutters. Mix the egg-glaze ingredients together and brush the shapes with the egg glaze. Bake for 30 minutes or until golden brown. Serve when cool. Store in an airtight container at room temperature for about two weeks.

Sesame Ball Treats Yields 6–8 treats

½ cup sesame butter
1¼ cup sesame seeds
2 tablespoons wheat germ

Mix together sesame butter, wheat germ, and ¾ cup of sesame seeds. Form into small round balls. Roll the balls in the remaining sesame seeds. Refrigerate, covered, for up to five days or freeze for up to six weeks.

Carob Chews Yields 2 dozen

½ cup carob powder
1 cup sunflower seeds
¾ cup honey
½ cup rolled oats
1 cup almond, sesame, or peanut butter
½ cup powdered milk

Combine the carob powder, honey, and almond (or sesame or peanut) butter in a large bowl and mix well. Add in the sunflower seeds and rolled oats and mix thoroughly. Form into small balls and roll the balls in the powdered milk. Refrigerate for up to five days or freeze for up to six weeks.

Easy Chicken Necks

several pounds chicken necks
olive oil
garlic powder

Preheat oven to 350°F. Cut the chicken necks into bite-sized pieces appropriate for your dog's size. Put the pieces on oiled cookie sheets and drizzle with olive oil. Sprinkle on the garlic powder. Bake for 25 minutes. Cool, serve, and store.

Hot Dog Delights

several pounds turkey, chicken, or beef hot dogs
olive oil
mixed Italian herbs

Preheat oven to 350°F. Slice the hot dogs into bite-sized pieces. Place the pieces on oiled cookie sheets and drizzle with the olive oil. Sprinkle with the Italian herbs. Bake for 15 minutes. Cool, serve, and store.

Fish Sticks

several pounds frozen fish sticks
olive oil
dried tarragon

Place fish sticks on oiled cookie sheets and sprinkle with the olive oil and tarragon. Bake according to the directions on the package. Cool, serve, and store.

Baked Liver Licks

2 pounds liver
½ cup olive oil
garlic powder
powdered parsley

Preheat oven to 350°F. Dice liver into treat-sized pieces. Place the pieces on well-oiled cookie trays and dust them with the garlic powder and dried parsley. Bake for 25 minutes. Cool, serve, and store.

Simply Biscuits Yields 4 dozen

⅓ cup olive oil
2 teaspoons garlic powder
1¼ cups rye flour
¾ cup water
½ cup skim milk, powdered
1 egg, beaten
2 cups whole-wheat flour

Preheat oven to 350°F. In a large bowl, mix the olive oil and flour together and set aside. In a separate bowl, mix the powdered skim milk and garlic powder in the water until dissolved. Next, mix in the beaten egg. Slowly stir the egg mixture into the flour mixture until well blended. Knead dough on a lightly floured surface for about 5 minutes. The dough should stick together and be easy to work with. Roll the dough to a ¼-inch thickness and cut into desired shapes with cookie cutters. Place biscuits on a greased cookie sheet and bake for 45 minutes. Allow to cool in oven for several hours and then store at room temperature for up to four weeks.

Tartar Fighters Yields 5 dozen

¾ cup skim milk
1 cup all-purpose flour
½ cup stone-ground cornmeal
1½ cups low-salt chicken broth
¼ bulghur wheat
1 cup rolled oats
1½ cups whole-wheat flour
1 egg, beaten

Preheat oven to 350°F. In a large bowl, mix together the dry ingredients. Heat the chicken broth until warm. Add the rolled oats to the chicken broth and allow to stand for 5 minutes. Next, mix in the beaten egg. Slowly add the egg mixture to the dry ingredients while mixing thoroughly. Knead dough on a lightly floured surface for about 5 minutes. The dough should stick together and be easy to work with. Roll dough to a ¼-inch thickness and cut into desired shapes with cookie cutters. Use a cookie sheet lined with foil and bake for 45 minutes. Allow the biscuits to cool in the oven for several hours and then store at room temperature for up to four weeks.

Flea Buster Biscuits Yields 8 dozen

2 cups low-salt beef broth
1 cup cornmeal
1 cup rolled oats
½ cup brewer's yeast
1½ cups all-purpose flour

3 tablespoons garlic powder
2½ cups whole-wheat flour
¼ cup shredded carrot
½ cup olive oil
1 egg, beaten

Preheat oven to 325°F. In a large bowl, combine the dry ingredients. Slowly mix the oil, egg, and beef broth into the dry ingredients until well blended. Knead the dough on a lightly floured surface for 5 minutes. Roll dough out to a ¼-inch thickness and cut into desired shapes with cookie cutters. Bake for 1 hour and 40 minutes on a foil-lined cookie sheet. Allow biscuits to cool in the oven for several hours and then store at room temperature for up to four weeks.

Meat Lover's Biscuit Yields 6 dozen

1 pound lean ground beef
1½ cups rolled oats
2 eggs, beaten
1½ cups water
3 cups whole-wheat flour

Preheat oven to 325°F. Mix together the beef and eggs in a bowl, using your hands if necessary to completely mix. In a separate bowl, mix the flour with the oats. Gradually mix the beef/egg mixture into the flour/oats mixture, again using your hands if needed until mixed thoroughly. Add the water to form a sticky dough. Knead the dough on a lightly floured surface for 3 minutes. Roll the dough out to a ¼-inch thickness and cut into desired shapes with cookie cutters. Bake for 80 minutes on a greased cookie sheet. Allow to cool in the oven for several hours and then store at room temperature for up to four weeks.

Vegetarian Treats Yields 8 dozen

1¼ cup rolled oats
1 egg, beaten
½ cup olive oil
1 cup cornmeal
1¾ cups hot water
1½ cups wheat germ

3 cloves garlic, crushed
2 cups all-purpose flour
½ cup whole-wheat flour
½ cup sunflower seeds. ground
½ cup powdered skim milk

Preheat oven to 325°F. In a large bowl, mix together the rolled oats, olive oil, and hot water and allow to stand for 5 minutes. In a skillet, sauté the garlic in a small amount of olive oil. Add the garlic, powdered milk, and egg to the rolled-oats mixture and blend well. In a separate bowl, mix together the flour, wheat germ, and sunflower seeds. Gradually add the flour mixture until well blended. Knead the dough on a lightly floured surface for 3 minutes. Roll the dough out to a ¼-inch thickness and cut into desired shapes with cookie cutters. Use a foil-lined cookie sheet and bake for 45 minutes. Allow the biscuits to cool in the oven for several hours and then store at room temperature for up to four weeks.

Birthday Treats

I cannot imagine anything more special than celebrating your best friend's birthday with a cake. If you don't know when your dog was born, make up a date and stick to it. It will be just as much fun, and your dog will enjoy this special occasion. Invite friends to celebrate with you! I do, however, suggest that you make a "people" cake along with one of the following recipes. Dogs love these tried-and-true canine-friendly recipes, but I prefer chocolate cake for myself!

Birthday Cake #1: Carrot Cake with Cream-Cheese Icing

Cake:
- 1 ½ cups melted unsalted butter
- 3 teaspoons baking powder
- 1½ cups honey
- 1 teaspoon cinnamon
- 4 eggs
- 2½ cups carrot, finely shredded
- 4 cups whole-wheat flour
- ¾ cup sesame seeds
- ½ teaspoon baking soda

Icing:
- 16 ounces cream cheese, softened
- 8-ounce stick of unsalted butter, softened

Preheat oven to 350°F. In one large bowl, mix together the butter, honey, and eggs. In a separate bowl, sift together the flour, baking powder, baking soda, cinnamon, carrot, and seeds. Gently and slowly mix the dry ingredients into the butter mixture; do not beat.

Generously butter one large pan or two loaf pans and pour cake mixture into the pan(s). Bake for 45 minutes and then remove from oven and allow to cool. Mix together the icing ingredients in a medium-sized bowl. Ice the cooled birthday cake and then refrigerate the cake for up to one week.

Birthday Cake #2: Carob Cake with Peanut Butter Filling

Cake:
   ½ cup unsalted butter, softened
   1 cup honey
   2½ cups whole-wheat flour
   ¼ cup water
   2 teaspoons baking powder
   ⅔ cup milk mixed with 1 teaspoon vinegar
   1 cup sugar-free peanut butter
   1 cup carob powder mixed with ½ cup water
   ½ teaspoon vanilla
   2 eggs

Icing:
   1 cup carob powder
   ¼ cup honey
   1 teaspoon vanilla
   ⅓ cup whole milk

Preheat oven to 350°F. In a large mixing bowl, mix together the butter, honey, eggs, water, milk/vinegar mixture, and vanilla. In a separate bowl, mix together the carob powder/water mixture, flour, and baking powder. Slowly mix the dry ingredients in with the wet ingredients and mix well with a rotary beater. Pour into two well-buttered cake pans and bake for 25 minutes. Allow time to cool. Spread one cup of sugar-free peanut butter on top of one of the cakes and then place the other cake on top of it so that the peanut butter is the middle layer between the two cakes.

To make the carob icing, mix together the carob powder, honey, and vanilla. Slowly add the milk while gently mixing to achieve the desired icing consistency. Cover the cake with plastic wrap and refrigerate after you've iced the cake.

Special-Needs Recipes

This section provides you with recipes designed specifically for dogs with particular medical and emotional problems.

Recovery Broth

This recipe is for a very sick animal who is not eating. The sick dog may be drinking water but is not showing interest in food. Drinking this broth will provide the dog with nourishment. The potato peels are filled with minerals, the carrots are packed with vitamins, and the chicken legs or wings have needed fat and protein. Breaking the bones allows the marrow to be exposed, and this part of the bone offers very special nutrition.

   5 organic potatoes
   2 organic carrots
   6 cups water
   3 chicken legs or wings
   2 cloves garlic, crushed

Peel the potatoes and keep just the peels for this recipe (you can use the potatoes for another meal). Place the potato peels in a large pot. Dice the carrots, leaving the skin on, and add them to the pot. Break the chicken bones, leaving the skin intact, and add the legs or wings to the pot along with the garlic and water. Simmer for 1 hour and then strain through a colander. Be sure to discard all chicken bones. Serve broth when cool. Store broth in the refrigerator for up to one week.

Recipes for Diabetic Dogs

Diabetic Diet #1:

2 cups chicken, cooked
2 cups barley, cooked
chicken broth
1 cup cauliflower, diced
1 cup apples, diced
1 teaspoon powdered cinnamon
½ cup olive oil

Dice or shred cooked chicken when cool. Steam the diced cauliflower and apples with cinnamon in 2 inches of chicken broth. Do not discard broth when done; use it to moisten chicken mixture to a consistency that your dog likes. Mix the chicken, cauliflower, and apples in with the cooked barley. Drizzle with the olive oil and mix in. Toss and let cool before serving.

Diabetic Diet # 2:

2 cups lean beef, cubed
2 tablespoons fresh parsley, chopped
2 cups broccoli, lightly steamed
2 cups barley cooked with ½ teaspoon turmeric
½ cup olive oil

Allow the barley/turmeric mixture to cool. Sauté the beef cubes in some of the olive oil. Just before the meat is done, add the parsley and stir in quickly. Remove from heat. Steam the broccoli lightly and coat with the rest of the olive oil. Mix the beef, barley, and broccoli together and serve.

Diabetic Diet # 3:

2 cups tilapia
3 garlic cloves, chopped
2 cups oatmeal
1 teaspoon cinnamon
1 cup blueberries
1 cup string beans, cut into 1-inch pieces
½ cup olive oil

Sauté the tilapia in the olive oil; add chopped garlic when almost done cooking the fish. Cook the oatmeal with the cinnamon. Lightly steam the string beans. Mix all of these ingredients together and then stir in the blueberries and serve.

Recipe for a Healthy Heart

Heart Diet

3 cups cooked brown or basmati rice or 3 cups boiled white or sweet potatoes, diced
1 cup beef, chicken, or fish
4 tablespoons fresh parsley, chopped
1 can sodium-free asparagus pieces or 1 cup cooked asparagus, chopped
1 tablespoon dandelion greens, chopped (optional)
⅓ cup olive oil
2 garlic cloves

Set the cooked rice or potatoes aside to cool. Finely chop the garlic and let sit for 10 minutes in open air. Warm the olive oil in the skillet and add meat (or fish), parsley, and dandelion greens (optional). Sauté these ingredients together until meat or fish is fully cooked. Cook the asparagus and set aside to cool (if using canned asparagus, retain the juice). Mix all ingredients together and serve.

Recipes for Healthy Kidneys

Biscotti

16-ounce bag dried red kidney beans
4 large eggs
1 cup chopped parsley, including stems,
    chopped
1 garlic clove, peeled
4 cups whole-wheat flour
1 cup salt-free chicken broth, reduced to
    concentrate flavor

Soak the dried kidney beans overnight. Rinse well and drain. Preheat oven to 350°F. Line a large cookie sheet with parchment paper. In a food processor, chop the garlic. Add the eggs, chicken broth, and soaked kidney beans to the food processor and process until well blended but not thoroughly pureed. Mix in the chopped parsley. Put this mixture into a large bowl and stir in the flour a little at a time until it's fully incorporated and the mixture is smooth.

Divide the mixture into two equal portions. Shape each into a 12-inch-long by 3-inch-wide loaf, making the sides and top even and smooth. Place the loaves next to one another on a parchment-lined cookie sheet. Make sure that there are several inches between the two loaves and in between the loaves and the sides of the pan. Bake until the loaves are golden and the tops spring back when poked gently, usually around 30–40 minutes. Remove the loaves from the baking sheet and reduce the oven temperature to 300°F. Cool the loaves until slightly warm but still soft enough to cut into ½-inch biscuits. You will need a sharp knife for this.

Lay the cookies on their sides on two parchment-lined cookie sheets. Begin baking the biscuits for 40 minutes and then flip them over and continue baking for another 30 minutes or until they are crisp. Keep checking to make sure that they are baking slowly and drying out in the baking process. Cool completely and store in a covered container at room temperature for up to two weeks.

Kidney Recipe #1

    2 cups high-fat cottage cheese
    2 eggs, raw or cooked
    3 pieces whole-wheat, whole-grain, sprouted grain bread or oatmeal soaked in chicken broth
    Mixed vegetables, cooked (fresh or frozen)
    Raw kidney, chopped
Mix all of the ingredients together and serve.

Kidney Recipe #2

    1 cup lentils, cooked
    1 large yam or sweet potato, cooked
    1 cup broccoli stems and flowers, chopped
    2 cloves garlic, chopped
    1 cup brown basmati rice, cooked
    2 teaspoons olive oil
Mix all of the ingredients together and serve.

Kidney Recipe #3

    2 large yams, cooked
    ½ cup pineapple, chopped
    1 small banana
    1 teaspoon molasses
    2 hard-boiled eggs, chopped
Mix all of the ingredients together and serve.

Kidney Recipe #4

    2 cups kidney beans, well cooked
    2 cups brown basmati rice, cooked
    2 cloves garlic, diced fine
    ½ cup asparagus, cooked
    1 teaspoon parsley, chopped
    1 tablespoon olive oil
Mix all of the ingredients together and serve.

Kidney Recipe #5

    ½ cup parsnips, diced
    1 cup high-fat cottage cheese
    2 teaspoons parsley, chopped
    2 cups pasta, cooked
Mix all of the ingredients together and serve.

Kidney Recipe #6

½ cup chicken, cooked
1 cup kidney beans or lentils, cooked
3 cloves garlic
3 tablespoons olive oil
1 teaspoon parsley, chopped

2 cups brown basmati rice or pasta, cooked

½ cup broccoli, asparagus, or parsnips, diced

Sauté the garlic in the olive oil. At the end, quickly mix in the parsley. Mix all of the other ingredients together in a separate bowl and then mix in the garlic/parsley mixture and serve.

Recipe for Healthy Weight

Chubby Dog Chow

Morning meal:
¼–1 cup oatmeal
1 teaspoon coconut oil, uncooked
½–1½ cups vegetables, depending on how much your dog needs to be satisfied

Evening meal:
¼–½ cup low-fat cottage cheese, ricotta cheese, or farmer's cheese or ½–2 eggs or ¼–¾ cup lean meat or poultry
¼ –1½ cups high-fiber bran breakfast cereal
Vegetables, as many as your dog wants
1 teaspoon coconut oil, uncooked

Diet Tips
There is a range in the portion sizes; how much you offer your dog depends on his size. Don't forget to also give your dog a high-quality daily multivitamin/multimineral supplement.

Recipe for Nervous Dogs

Calming Diet

This diet is made to relax and calm. Turkey is high in tryptophan while barley and chamomile soothe the nerves.

2 cups turkey, cooked
2 cups barley, cooked with 3 eggshells
2 teaspoons chamomile flowers, made into tea with ½ cup water (or ½ cup strong chamomile tea made with a tea bag)
2 teaspoons parsley
2 cups carrots, cooked
⅓ cup olive oil

Mix all of the ingredients together and serve.

Acknowledgments

This book, from its original conception to its final form, was in the making for many years. It was given its present form after I moved to New Zealand because I finally had time away from my busy practice and made it my first priority to finish the book. More important, this book was created as a gift to all of the wonderful people who brought their pets to me for so many years. Many people and many dogs and cats were so dear to me, and leaving all of them was one of the most difficult things I have ever done. I created this book for them. (No, I haven't forgotten the cats! That's next.) I also created an easy way for my clients to reach me in New Zealand, whether by e-mail or a US toll-free number.

Most important, I thank my family for helping to make *Natural Dog* a reality. My husband, Monte, beamed love and support to me the entire time, and believe you me, one tends to wave people away repeatedly while writing, so he deserves some real recognition. My two sons, Ethan and Damien, helped me with photography and proofreading. I would also like to acknowledge my deceased mother and father, who encouraged me to follow my dreams.

I am indebted as well to another family of mine: my associates and staff at the Animal Healing Center, a place that was a substantial part of my life for so many years. I would like to thank Dr. Sharon Marx, Tina, Tobi, and so many others who supported my work and helped me to fine-tune these holistic modalities to perfection.

Yet more friends contributed mightily: Rosemary Rennicke, who gave me invaluable advice. Nina, Jerry, Dillian, Justie, and Spencer, who are a true extended family. One of my closest friends, a homeopathic MD, Dr. Lucy Nitskansky, meticulously reviewed sections with detailed feedback.

Of course, I am grateful to all those at Kennel Club Books and at i-5 Press who shepherded this project through the publishing process, including Andrew DePrisco, Jarelle Stein, and Amy Deputato. A warm thanks to Kathy Hall, who introduced me to Andrew.

Finally, I must thank my canine and feline patients and their people. People who requested, in cases in which there seemed to be no light at the end of the tunnel, that I try. With this came new successes and the development of better treatment modalities. Joyful successes that would benefit so many other pets destined to come my way. It was and still is exhilarating to create real health. I love being a veterinarian, and the heady bonus of seeing my patients thrive makes it that much better.

Resources

Associations and Organizations

Academy of Veterinary Homeopathy
1283 Lincoln Street
Eugene, OR 97401
(541) 342-7665
theavh.org

The American Botanical Council
PO Box 201660
Austin, TX 78720
(512) 926-4900
www.herbalgram.com

American Holistic Veterinary Medical Association
PO Box 630
Abingdon, MD 21009
(410) 569-0795
www.ahvma.org

American Veterinary Chiropractic Association
623 Main Street
Hillsdale, IL 61257
(3096) 658-2920
www.animalchiropractic.org

Born Free USA
PO Box 32160
Washington, DC 20007
(202) 450-3168
www.bornfreeusa.org

British Homeopathic Association
27A Devonshire Street
London W1N 1RJ England
071-935-2163
www.britishhomeopathic.org

The British Institute of Veterinary Homeopathy
520 Washington Boulevard, #423
Marina Del Rey, CA 90292
(800) 498-6323

The Herb Research Foundation
1007 Pearl Street, #200
Boulder, CO 80302
(303) 449-2265
www.herbs.org

International Association for Veterinary Homeopathy
334 Knollwood Lane
Woodstock, GA 30188
(770) 516-5954
www.iavh.org

International Veterinary Acupuncture Society
1730 South College Avenue, #301
Fort Collins, CO 80525
(970) 266-0666
www.ivas.org

National Center for Homeopathy
801 N. Fairfax, #306
Alexandria, VA 22314
703-548-7790
www.nationalcenterforhomeopathy.org

Recommended Reading

In addition to the listed books and articles, please visit www.doctordeva.com for many informative articles on topics discussed in the book.

Chapter 1

Boone, J. Allen. *Kinship with All Life: Simple, Challenging, Real-Life Experiences Showing How Animals Communicate with Each Other and with the People Who Understand Them.* San Francisco: HarperOne, 1976.

Clothier, Suzanne. *If Bones Would Rain from the Sky: Deepening Our Relationships with Dogs.* New York: Warner Books, 2002.

Curtis, Anita. *Animal Wisdom: Communications with Animals.* Animal Communications, 1996.

Fitzpatrick, Sonya, with Patricia Burkhart Smith. *What the Animals Tell Me: Developing Your Innate Telepathic Skills to Understand and Communicate with Your Pets.* New York: Hyperion, 1998.

Hartmann, Thom. *The Last Hours of Ancient Sunlight: Waking Up to Personal and Global Transformation.* Mythical Books, 1998.

McElroy, Susan Chernak. *Animals as Teachers and Healers: True Stories and Reflections.* New York: Ballantine Books, 1997.

Myers, Arthur. *Communicating with Animals: The Spiritual Connection between People and Animals.* Chicago: Contemporary Books, 1997.

Smith, Penelope. *Animal Talk: Interspecies Telepathic Communication.* Tulsa, OK: Council Oak Books, 2004.

Smith, Penelope. *Animals: Our Return to Wholeness.* Point Reyes Station, CA: Pegasus Publications, 1993.

Chapter 2

Animal Protection Institute of America. "Investigative Report on Pet Food," May 2007. (The Animal Protection Institute of America is now part of Born Free USA; this paper can be found at www.bornfreeusa.org).

Martin, Ann. N. *Food Pets Die For.* Troutdale, OR: New Sage Press, 2008.

National Research Council, Subcommittee on Dog Nutrition. *Nutrient Requirements of Dogs.* Washington, DC: National Academies Press, 1985.

Rowe, John D. *Animal Nutrition.* Keene, KY: Setter Publications, 2007.

Chapter 3

Fahey, William J., and Peter R. Rothschild, MD, PhD. *Free Radicals, Stress and Antioxidant Enzymes: A Guide to Cellular Health.* Honolulu: University Labs Press, 1991.

Chapter 4

Anson, Suzan. *Bone Appetit! Gourmet Cooking for Your Dog.* Chicago: New Chapter Press 1999.

Boyle, Carol. *Natural Food Recipes for Healthy Dogs.* New York: Howell Book House, 1997.

Cusick, William D. *Canine Nutrition: Choosing the Best Food for Your Breed.* Irvine, CA: Doral Publishing, 1997.

Dorosz, Edmund R. *Let's Cook for Our Dog.* Alberta: Our Pets, Inc., 1993.

Laybourn, Carole, *The Original Gourmet Doggie Treat Cook Book.* Paws Publishing, 1995.

McKinnon, Helen L. *It's for the Animals! Natural Care and Resources.* Fairview, NC: Self-published, 1998.

Messonnier, Shawn, DVM. *Natural Supplements for Dogs: Alternative Ways to Promote Health in Your Pet.* Lincolnwood, IL: Keats Publishing, 1998.

Peden, James A. *Vegetarian Cats and Dogs.* Troy, MT: Harbingers of a New Age, 1995

Schultze, Kymythy R. CCN, AHI. *Natural Nutrition for Dogs and Cats: The Ultimate Diet.* Carlsbad, CA: Hay House, 1998.

Weigle, Jaroslav. *A Little Recipe Book for Dogs: Sound Nutrition and Good Homecooking for Your Pet.* New York: Ballantine Books, 1997.

Chapter 5

Anderson, Nina, Howard Peiper, and Alicia McWatters, MS. *Super-Nutrition for Animals! (Birds, Too!) Healthy Advice for Dogs, Cats, and Birds.* Sheffield, MA: Safe Goods, 1996.

Billinghurst, Ian, VVSc (Hons), BScAgr, DipEd. *Give Your Dog a Bone: The Practical Commonsense Way to Feed Dogs for a Healthy Life.* Bathurst, Australia: Self-published, 1993.

———. *Grow Your Pups with Bones: The BARF Program for Breeding Healthy Dogs and Eliminating Skeletal Disease.* Bathurst, Australia: Self-published, 1993.

Messonnier, Shawn, DVM. *Healthy Diet, Healthy Dog: How to Prevent Illness and Maximize a Dog's Health and Energy Through Nutrition.* Lincolnwood, IL: Keats Publishing, 1998.

Pitcairn, Richard, and Susan Hubble Pitcairn. *Dr. Pitcairn's Complete Guide to Natural Health for Dogs and Cats.* Emmaus, PA: Rodale Books, 1995.

Schoeneck, Annelies. *Making Sauerkraut and Pickled Vegetables at Home: The Original Lactic Acid Fermentation Method.* Vancouver: Alive Books, 1995.

Volhard, Wendy, and Kerry Brown. *The Holistic Guide for a Healthy Dog*. New York: Howell Book House, 2000.

Yarnall, Celeste. *Dog Care, Naturally*. Boston: Charles E. Tuttle Co., Inc., 1998.

Chapter 6

Foster, Steven A. and James A. Duke. *Peterson Field Guides: Eastern/Central Medicinal Plants*. Boston: Houghton Mifflin, 1990.

Gladstar, Rosemary. *Herbal Healing for Women*. NewYork: Fireside, 1993.

Keville, Kathi. *The Illustrated Herbal Encyclopedia*. New York: BDD Promotional Book Company, 1991.

Levy, Juliette de Baïracli. *The Complete Herbal Handbooks for the Dog and Cat*. London: Faber and Faber, 1992.

Lust, John. *The Herb Book: The Complete and Authoritative Guide to More than 500 Herbs*. New York: Bantam Books, 1979.

Moore, Michael. *Medicinal Plants of the Pacific West*. Santa Fe, NM: Red Crane Books, 1993.

Mowrey, Daniel B., PhD. *Herbal Tonic Therapies*. New Canaan, CT: Keats Publishing, 1993.

———. *The Scientific Validation of Herbal Medicine*. Lincolnwood, IL: Keats Publishing, 1986.

Reader's Digest. *Magic and Medicine of Plants*. Pleasantville, NY: Reader's Digest, 1990.

Schwartz, Cheryl. *Four Paws, Five Directions: A Guide to Chinese Medicine for Cats and Dogs*. Berkeley, CA: Celestial Arts Publishing, 1996.

Theiss, Barbara and Peter. *The Family Herbal: A Guide to Natural Health Care for Yourself and Your Children from Europe's Leading Herbalists*. Rochester, VT: Healing Arts Press, 1989.

Tierra, Michael. *The Way of Herbs*. New York: Pocket Books, 1998.

Weiss, Rudolph Fritz and Volker Fintelmann. *Herbal Medicine*. New York: Thieme Publishers, 2000.

Treben, Maria. *Health through God's Pharmacy*. Champaign, IL: Balogh Scientific Books, 1994.

Chapter 8

Bach, Edward, MD and F.J. Wheeler, MD. *Bach Flower Remedies*. New York: McGraw-Hill, 1998.

Biddis, K.J. *Homeopathy in Veterinary Practice*. London: Random House, 1987.

Chambreau, Christina. *Homeopathic First Aid for Pets* (video). Davie, FL: Video Remedies, Inc., 1992.

Cummings, Stephen and Dana Ullman. *Everybody's Guide to Homeopathic Medicines*.

Day, Christopher, MA, VetMB, MRCVS, VetFFHom. *The Homeopathic Treatment of Small Animals: Principles and Practice*. London: Random House, 2005.

Dooley, Timothy R. *Homeopathy: Beyond Flat Earth Medicine*. San Diego: Timing Publications, 2002.

Fox, Dr. Michael, MRCVS. *The Healing Touch: The Proven Massage Program for Dogs and Cats*. New York: Newmarket Press, 1990.

Graham, Helen and Gregory Vlamis. *Bach Flower Remedies for Animals*. Forres, Scotland: Findhorn Press, 1999.

Grainger, Janette, and Connie Moore. *Natural Insect Repellents for Pets, People, and Plants*. Austin, TX: Herb Bar, 1991.

Grosjean, Nelly. *Veterinary Aromatherapy*. Saffron Walden, England: C.W. Daniel Company, 2004.

Huisheng, Xie, and Dr. Vanessa Preast. *Traditional Chinese Veterinary Medicine*. Reddick, FL: Chi Institute Press, 2013.

Hunter, Francis. *Homeopathic First Aid for Pets*. London: Thorsons Publishers, 1984.

Janssens, Luc. *Acupuncture Points and Meridians in the Dog*. Chester Springs, PA: International Veterinary Acupuncture Society, 1984.

Kaslof, Leslie J. *The Traditional Flower Remedies of Dr. Edward Bach: A Self-Help Guide*. New Canaan, CT: Keats Publishing, 1988.

Klide, Alan M, and Shiu H. Kung. *Veterinary Acupuncture*. Philadelphia: University of Pennsylvania Press, 2002.

Kowalchick, Clare, and William H. Hylton, eds. *Rodale's Illustrated Encyclopedia of Herbs*. Emmaus, PA: Rodale, 1998.

Levy, Juliette de Baïracli. *Herbal Handbook for Farm and Stable*. London: Faber and Faber, 1992.

Macleod, George, MRCVS, DVSM, VetFFHom. *Dogs: Homeopathic Remedies*. London: Random House UK, 2005.

———. *A Veterinary Materia Medica and Clinical Repertory*. London: Random House UK, 2004.

McKay, Pat. *Natural Immunity: Why You Should Not Vaccinate*. Pasadena: Oscar Publications, 1997.

McTaggart, Lynne. *The Field: The Quest for the Secret Force of the Universe*. New York: HarperCollins, 2008.

Ogden, Donald I., DVM. *Natural Hygienic Care of Pets*. East Sussex, England: Society of Metaphysicians, 1986.

Palika, Liz. *Consumer's Guide to Dog Food: What's in Dog Food, Why It's There, and How to Choose the Best Food for Your Dog*. New York: Howell Book House, 1996.

Puotinen, C. J. *The Encyclopedia of Natural Pet Care*. Lincolnwood, IL: Keats Publishing, 2000.

Raymonde-Hawkins, M., and George Macleod, MRCVS, DVSM, VetFFHom. *The Raystede Handbook of Homoeopathic Remedies for Animals.* Saffron Walden, England: C.W. Daniel Company, 1985.

Scheffer, Mechthild. *Bach Flower Therapy: Theory and Practice.* Rochester, VT: Healing Arts Press, 1986.

Schoen, Allen, DVM. *Love, Miracles and Animal Healing.* New York: Simon and Schuster, 1995.

———. *Veterinary Acupuncture: Ancient Art to Modern Medicine.* St. Louis: Mosby, 2001.

Schoen, Allen, DVM, and Susan Wynn, DVM. *Complementary and Alternative Veterinary Medicine: Principles and Practice.* St. Louis: Mosby, 1998.

Scott, Martin J. and Gael Mariani. *Bach Flower Remedies for Dogs.* Forres, Scotland: Findhorn Press, 1999.

Snow, Amy, and Nancy Zidonis. *The Well-Connected Dog: A Guide to Canine Acupressure.* Larkspur, CO: Tallgrass Publishers, 1999.

Stefanatos, Joanne, DVM. *Bioenergetic Medicine: Homeopathy and Acupuncture for Animals.* Bel Air, MD: American Holistic Veterinary Medical Association, 1997.

Stein, Diane. *Natural Healing for Dogs and Cats.* Santa Cruz, CA: Crossing Press, 1993.

Stein, Petra. *Natural Health Care for Your Dog: Self-Help Using Homeopathy and Bach Flowers.* Hauppauge, NY: Barron's Educational Series, 1997.

Tellington-Jones, Linda, with Sybil Taylor. *The Tellington TTouch: Caring for Animals with Heart and Hands.* New York: Penguin, 2008.

Ullman, Dana, MPH. *Discovering Homeopathy: Medicine for the 21st Century.* Berkeley, CA: North Atlantic Books, 1991.

Vithoulkas, George. *Homeopathy—Medicine of the New Man.* Arco Publishing Company, 1979.

Volhard, Wendy, and Kerry Brown, DVM. *Holistic Guide for a Healthy Dog.* New York: Howell Book House, 2000.

Winter, William G., DVM. *Safe, EffectiveTreatment Plans for the Companion Animal Practitioner.* Lakeville, MN: Galde Press, 1997.

Wulff-Tilford, Mary. *Herbal Remedies for Dogs & Cats: A Pocket Guide to Selection and Use.* Mountain Weed Publishing, 1997.

Yarnall, Celeste. *Natural Dog Care: A Complete Guide to Holistic Health Care for Dogs.* New York: Castle Book, 2000.

Chapter 9

Plechner, Alfred J., and Martin Zucker. *Pet Allergies: Remedies for an Epedemic.* Inglewood, CA: Very Healthy Enterprises, 1985.

Chapter 12

Severino, Elizabeth. *The Animals' Viewpoint on Dying, Death, and Euthanasia.* Turnersville, NJ: The Healing Connection, 2002.

Recommended Products

Dry Dog Foods

Addiction Foods
www.addictionfoods.com
Wild Kangaroo and Apples

Artemis Pet Foods
www.artemiscompany.com
Power Formula

Azmira Holistic Animal Care
www.azmira.com
Classic Formula

Bench & Field Holistic Natural Canine
www.benchandfield.com
Holistic Natural Formula

Blue Buffalo
www.bluebuffalo.com
Chicken

By Nature Organics
By Nature Pet Foods
www.bynaturepetfoods.com
Chicken

California Natural
Natura Pet Products
www.naturapet.com
Chicken Meal and Rice

Canidae
www.canidae.com
All Life Stages Formula

Canine Caviar Holistic
www.caninecaviar.com
Lamb and Pearl Millet

Drs. Foster and Smith
drsfostersmith.com
Lamb

Eagle Pack Holistic Select
Eagle Pet Products, Inc.
www.eaglepack.com
Anchovy, Sardine, and Salmon Meal

Evanger's Dog and Cat Food Company
www.evangersdogfood.com
Pheasant and Brown Rice

Evolve
www.evolvepetfood.com
Maintenance Formula

Firstmate Pet Foods
www.firstmate.com
Ultra Premium Naturally Holistic Formula

Fromm Family Pet Foods
Fromm Four Star Nutritionals
www.frommfamily.com
Chicken à la Veg

Go! Natural
Petcurean Pet Nutrition
www.petcurean.com
Chicken, Fruit, and Vegetable

Hund-N-Flocken
Solid Gold Health Products
www.solidgoldpet.com

LIFE4K9
www.life4k9.com
Oven-Baked Chicken and Barley

Lifespan
Petguard
www.petguard.com

Merrick Pet Care
www.merrickpetcare.com
Cowboy Cookout

MMillennia
Solid Gold Health Products
www.solidgoldpet.com

Natural Balance Organic
Dick Van Patten's Natural Balance
www.naturalbalanceinc.com
Organic Formula

Natural Balance Ultra Premium
Dick Van Patten's Natural Balance
www.naturalbalanceinc.com
Ultra Premium Formula

Newman's Own Organics
newmansownorganics.com
Adult Dog Formula

NutriSource Pet Foods
www.nutrisourcedogfood.com
Adult Formula

Organix
Castor & Pollux Pet Works
www.castorpolluxpet.com
Organix Canine Formula

Petguard
www.petguard.com
Organic Vegetarian Formula

Performatrin Ultra
www.performatrinultra.com
Chicken

PHD Viand
Perfect Health Diet Products
www.phdproducts.com
Canine Growth and Maintenance Viand Formula

Pinnacle
Breeder's Choice Pet Foods
www.breeders-choice.com
Trout and Sweet Potato

Prairie
Nature's Variety
www.naturesvariety.com
New Zealand Venison

Premium Edge
www.premiumedgepetfood.com
Chicken, Rice, and Vegetable

Prime Life Plus
Owen & Mandeville Pet Products
www.ompetproducts.com
Prime Life Plus Formula

Raw Instinct
Nature's Variety
www.naturesvariety.com

Royal Canin Natural Blend
Royal Canin
www.royalcanin.us
Medium Breed Adult Formula

Royal Canin Veterinary Diet
Royal Canin
www.royalcanin.us
Potato and Rabbit

Showbound Naturals
Healthy Pet Foods, Inc.
www.healthypetfoodsinc.com
Chicken and Brown Rice

Timberwolf Organics
Yukon Nutritional Company
www.timberwolforganics.com
Lamb, Barley, and Apples

Ultra Holistic Nutrition
Nutro Products, Inc.
www.ultraholistic.com
Ultra Adult Dry Formula

VéRUS
www.veruspetfoods.com
Advanced Opticoat Diet

Wenaewe
www.wenaewepet.com

Wysong
www.wysong.net
Anergen Formula

Zinpro
Lincoln Biotech
www.lincolnbiotech.com
Skin and Coat Formula

Wet Dog Foods

Addiction Foods
www.addictionfoods.com
Venison and Avocado

Advanced Pet Diets
Breeder's Choice Pet Foods
www.breeders-choice.com
APD Select Choice Chicken and Rice

Artemis Pet Foods
www.artemiscompany.com
Beef

Avo-Derm
Breeder's Choice Pet Foods
www.breeders-choice.com
Original Formula

Azmira Holistic Animal Care
ww.azmira.com
Beef and Chicken

Blue Buffalo
www.bluebuffalo.com
Chicken

By Nature Organics
www.bynaturepetfoods.com
Organic Turkey, Sweet Potato, and Peas

California Natural
Natura Pet Products
www.naturapet.com
Salmon and Sweet Potato

Canidae
www.canidae.com
Chicken, Lamb, and Fish

Canine Caviar Holistic
www.caninecaviar.com

Drs. Foster & Smith
www.drsfostersmith.com
Lamb and Brown Rice

Eagle Pack Holistic Select
Eagle Pet Products, Inc.
www.eaglepack.com
Chicken

Entrée for Dogs
Three Dog Bakery
www.threedog.com
Chicken, Vegetables, and Rice

Evanger's for Dogs
www.evangersdogfood.com
Duck and Sweet Potato Dinner

Evolve
www.evolvepetfood.com
Turkey

Fromm Four Star Nutritionals
Fromm Family Pet Foods
www.frommfamily.com
Beef

Innova
Natura Pet Products
www.naturapet.com
Adult Formula

EVO
Natura Pet Products
www.naturapet.com
95% Beef

Lamaderm
Natural Life Pet Products
www.nlpp.com

Merrick
www.merrickpetcare.com
Thanksgiving Day Dinner

Natural Balance
Dick Van Patten's Natural Balance
www.naturalbalanceinc.com
Beef

Natural Balance Eatables for Dogs
Dick Van Patten's Natural Balance
www.naturalbalanceinc.com
Irish Stew

Natural Life
Natural Life Pet Products
www.nlpp.com
Adult Formula

Neura Meats
Old Mother Hubbard
www.oldmotherhubbard.com
95% Beef

Newman's Own Organics
www.newmansownorganics.com
Chicken

Nutro Natural Choice
Nutro Products. Inc.
www.nutroproducts.com
Chicken, Rice, and Oatmeal

Organix
Castor & Pollux Pet Works
www.castorpolluxpet.com
Adult Formula

Performatrin Ultra
www.performatrinultra.com
Chicken and Wild Rice Stew

Petguard
www.petguard.com
Organic Chicken & Vegetable

Pet Promise
Natural Pet Nutrition
www.petpromiseinc.com
Chicken and Brown Rice

Pinnacle
Breeder's Choice Pet Foods
www.breeders-choice.com
Trout and Sweet Potato

Prairie
Nature's Variety
www.naturesvariety.com
Beef

Precise Plus
Precise Pet Products
www.precisepet.com
Foundation Formula Adult

Sensible Choice
Royal Canin
www.sensiblechoice.com
Turkey and Rice Adult Formula

Showbound Naturals
Healthy Pet Foods, Inc.
www.healthypetfoodsinc.com
Chicken

Solid Gold
Solid Gold Health Products
www.solidgoldhealthpet.com
Turkey, Ocean Fish, Carrots, and Sweet Potatoes

Triumph
www.triumphpet.com
Chicken, Rice, and Vegetable

VéRUS
www.veruspetfoods.com
Chicken and Rice

Weruva
www.weruva.com

Commercial Raw Diets

A Place for Paws
www.aplaceforpaws.com

Aunt Jeni's Home Made
www.auntjeni.com

Bravo!
www.bravorawdiet.com

Evanger's Game Meats
www.evangersdogfood.com

Halshan Premium Raw Food
www.halshan.com

The Honest Kitchen
www.thehonestkitchen.com

Prairie
Nature's Variety
www.naturesvariety.com

Oma's Pride
www.omaspride.com

Pet Orlando
www.petorlando.com

Pets 4 Life
www.pets4life.com

Purely Primitives
Teddy's Freezer
www.teddysfreezer.com

Steve's Real Food for Dogs
www.stevesrealfood.com

Urban Wolf
www.urbanwolf.cc

Cookie-Type Treats

Bellyrubs Dog Treats
Meyer County Farms
www.meyercountyfarms.com

Organic Whole Food Dog Snacks
Brew Brew Brand
www.brewbrewbrand.com

Buddy Biscuits
Cloud Star Corporation
www.cloudstar.com

Charlee Bear Dog Treats
www.charleebear.com

Dudley's Do Right Training Treats
Bark Stix
www.barkstix.com

Grandma Lucy's Dog Treats
www.grandmalucys.com

Healthy Dog Treats
The Hand That Feeds You Healthy
Dog Bakery
www.healthydogbakery.com

Heidi's Homemade Dog Treats
www.heidisbakery.com

Henry & Son's Vegetarian Cookies
www.henryandsons.com

Howlin' Gourmet
Dancing Paws Bakery
www.dancingpaws.com

Lakta's Treats
www.delicioustreats.com

Lick 'n Crunch
Three Dog Bakery
www.threedog.com

Liver Biscotti
Premier Pet Products
www.liverbiscotti.com

Mother Nature Natural Dog Biscuits
Natura Pet Products
www.naturapet.com

Nature Nosh
www.nature-nosh.com

Newman's Own Premium Dog
Treats
Newman's Own Organics
www.newmansownorganics.com

Old Mother Hubbard Dog Biscuits
www.oldmotherhubbard.com

Simon & Huey's Doggoned Tasty
Treats
www.simonandhuey.com

Smooches for Pooches
The Honest Kitchen
www.thehonestkitchen.com

Sojos Good Dog Treats
Sojourner Farms
www.sojos.com

Toy Temptations
Dogchewz NYC
www.dogchewz.com

Wagatha's Biscuits for Dogs
www.wagathas.com

Waggers Dog Treats
Pet Central
www.waggers.com

Wellness Wellbars
www.wellnesspetfood.com

Wet Noses Herbal Dog Treats
www.wet-noses.com

Meat-Based/Jerky-Style Treats

Canine Caviar Wild Alaskan
Salmon
Canine Caviar Pet Foods
www.caninecaviar.com

Dogswell Premium Dog Treats
www.dogswell.com

Dr. Becker's Bites
www.drbeckersbites.com

Dr-Chew Sweet Potato Treats
Landy Corporation
www.dr-chew.com

Etta Says! Meaty Treats
www.ettasays.com

Nothing Else But... Treats
A Place for Paws
www.aplaceforpaws.com

Real Food Toppers
Complete Natural Nutrition
www.realfoodtoppers.com

Rosie's Rewards
Rosebud, Inc.
www.rosiesrewards.com

Waggers Champion Chips
Pet Central
www.waggers.com

Wellness Pure Rewards and Wellness
Wellbites
www.wellnesspetfood.com

Whole Life Pet Treats
www.wholelifepet.com

Ziwipeak Good Dog Treats
www.ziwipeak.com

Zuke's Treats for Dog
www.zukes.com

Herbs and Vitamins

Ambrican Enterprises, Ltd.
541-899-2080

Animal's Apawthecary
Animal Essentials
www.animalessentials.com

Avena Botanicals
www.avenabotanicals.com

Blessed Herbs
www.blessedherbs.com

California School of Herbal Studies
www.cshs.com

Deserving Pets
www.deservingpets.com

East Earth Trade Winds
www.eastearthtrade.com

Eastpark Research, Inc.
www.eastparkresearch.com

Flora Distributors
www.florahealth.com

Frontier Cooperative Herbs
www.frontiercoop.com

Green Terrestrial Herbs
802-375-8087

Herb Pharm
www.herb-pharm.com

Herbs Plus
www.herbs-plus.com

Island Herbs (Ryan Drum)
www.ryandrum.com

Mountain Rose Herbs
www.mountainroseherbs.com

Myristin for Dogs
www.deservingpets.com

Native Essence Herb Company
www.herbmed.com

Omega Nutrition USA, Inc.
www.omeganutrition.com

ProZyme
www.prozyme.com

Richters Herbs
www.richters.com

Sage Mountain Herb Products
www.sagemountain.com

Starwest Botanicals
www.starwest-botanicals.com

Swissette Herb Farm
845-496-7841

Tasha's Herbs for Dogs and Cats
800-315-0142

TransPacific Health Products
800-336-9636

Vitamin Shoppe
www.vitaminshoppe.com

Willner Chemists
www.willner.com

Young Living Essential Oils
www.youngliving.com

Calcium Sources

Natural Calcium
Animal Essentials
www.animalessentials.com

Wysong Call of the Wild
www.wysong.net

Green Blends

All Systems Go! Total Health Aid
Aunt Jeni's
www.auntjeni.com

Organic Green Alternative
Animal Essentials
www.animalessentials.com

Berte's Green Blend
B-Naturals
www.b-naturals.com

SeaMeal
Solid Gold Health Products
solidgoldhealth.com

Homeopathic and Flower Remedies

Anaflora: Flower Essence Therapy
for Animals
www.anaflora.com

Ayush Herbs, Inc.
www.ayush.com

Boericke & Tafel, Inc.
Nature's Way
www.natureswav.com

Boiron-Borneman
www.boironusa.com

Deserving Pets
www.deservingpets.com

Dolisos America, Inc.
702-871-7153

Dr. Goodpet
www.goodpet.com

Flower Essence Services
www.fesflowers.com

Nelsons Natural World
www.nelsonsnaturalworld.com

Standard Homeopathic Company
P.O. Box 61067
Los Angeles, CA 90061
(800) 624-9659

Standard Process, Inc.
www.standardprocess.com

Washington Homeopathic Products
www.homeopathyworks.com

Cancer Remedies

Advanced Medicine and Research
Company
www.polymvasurvivors.comm

Buck Mountain Neoplasene
(must obtain through veterinarian)
www.buckmountainbotanicals.net

Cansema Salve
Alpha Omega Labs
www.alphaomegalabs.com

Coriolus Versicolor
I'm-Yunity for Dogs
www.imyunityfordogs.com

Deserving Pets Preventive
Supplement
www.deservingpets.com

Double Helix Water
www.deservingpets.com

Glutathione
Consult your veterinarian

Immutol
www.immunocorp.com

Polysaccharide Polypeptide (PSP)
Cellunlar Nutrition (CN)
http://agnrg.com

Tocotrieonols (concentrated)
Consult your veterinarian

Veterinary Immune Tabs,
Professional Formula
(must obtain through veterinarian)
Ramaeker's Nutrition
www.ramaekersnutrition.com

Photo Credits

Index

Page numbers in **bold** typeface indicate a recipe.

About the Author

Dr. Deva K. Khalsa, a licensed doctor of veterinary medicine, earned her VMD degree from the University of Pennsylvania. She is a member of the American Veterinary Medical Association, the American Holistic Veterinary Medical Association, and the International Veterinary Acupuncture Society. She has studied homeopathy for more than thirty years, as well as other alternative therapies, and she lectures nationally and internationally on her fresh and successful approach to veterinary medicine. She is the coauthor of *Healing Your Horse: Alternative Therapies* (Howell Book House, 1993). Her work stems from her belief that animals are at their best and happiest only when they are in a healthy and natural state. Dr. Khalsa focuses on empowering people to discover and nurture this natural state in their pets and, in doing so, to connect with and celebrate the true spirit of animals. Visit Dr. Khalsa online at www.doctordeva.com.